Benjamin Franklin

AUTOBIOGRAPHY

OF

BENJAMIN FRANKLIN

EDITED FROM HIS MANUSCRIPT, WITH NOTES
AND AN INTRODUCTION,

BY

JOHN BIGELOW.

GenNext Publication

Published by

GenNext Publication
5, Ansari Road
New Delhi-110002

Distribution Network
gyanbooks.com
India, USA, Canada, UK, Australia, France

ISBN: 978-93-938-6319-5 (HB)

15 impression 2022

***Printed at:* Goyal Offset Printers, Delhi.**

Benjamin Franklin

CONTENTS

PAGE

INTRODUCTORY 9

FRANKLIN'S OUTLINE OF TOPICS 58

THE AUTOBIOGRAPHY OF FRANKLIN 62

APPENDIX 292

I.

It is proper that I state the circumstances which seem to have imposed upon me the duty of adding another to the already numberless editions of Dr. Franklin'sAutobiography. It is well known that Franklin prepared so much of the celebrated Memoirs of his life as was originally in tended for publication, mainly at the solicitation of one of his most cherished friends in France–M. le Veillard,then Mayor of Passy. Towards the close of the year1789 he presented to this gentleman a copy of all this sketch that was then finished. At the Doctor's death, his papers, including the original of the manuscript, passed into the hands of one of his grandsons, William Temple Franklin,* who undertook to prepare an edition of thelife and writings of his grandfather for a publishing house in London.

For the greater convenience of the printer in the preparation of this edition–so goes the tradition in the Le Veillard family–William Temple Franklin exchanged the original autograph with Mrs. Le Veillard, then a widow, for her copy of the Memoirs; and thus the autograph passed out of the Franklin family.

At the death of the widow le Veillard this manuscript has been passed to her daughter; and at her death, in 1834, it became the property of her cousin, M. de Senarmont, whose grandson, M. P. de Senarmont, transferred it to me on the 26th of January, 1867, with several other memorials of Franklin which had descended to him with the manuscript. Among the latter were the famous pastel portrait of Franklin by Duplessis which he presented to M. le Veillard; a number of letters to M. Le Veillard from Dr.Franklin and from his grandsons,

---

* Benjamin Franklin died on the 17th of April, 1790, aged eightyfour years and three months.

William Temple Franklin and Benjamin Franklin Bache; together with a minute outline of the topics of his Memoirs, brought down to the termination of his mission to France.

I availed myself of my earliest leisure to subject the Memoirs to a careful collation with the edition which appeared in London in 1817, and which was the first and only edition that ever purported to have been printed from the manuscript. The results of this collation revealed the curious fact that more than twelve hundred separate and distinct changes had been made in the text, and, what is more remarkable, that the last eight pages of the manuscript, which are second in value to no other eight pages of the work, were omitted entirely.

Many of these changes are mere modernizations of style; such as would measure some of the modifications which English prose had undergone between the days of Goldsmith and Southey. Some, Franklin might have approved of; others he might have tolerated; but it is safe to presume that very many he would have rejected without ceremony.

A few specimens taken from the first chapter will show the general character of these changes.

It is a curious fact that the very first words of the edition of 1817 are interpolations. It commences:

"To William Franklin, Governor of New Jersey."

" Dear Son, &c."

The autograph commences with " Dear Son," naming no person.

Though William Franklin was the Doctor's only son, and in 1771, when this was commenced, was also Governor of New Jersey, it is very unlikely that the Doctor would have given his son any titles in addressing him a communication of this domestic and confidential character. This improbability is increased by the circumstance that at the time this manuscript was revised and copied to be sent to his friend, Le Veillard, William Franklin not only the Governor of New Jersey, but was not living upon terms even of friendly correspondence with his grandfather. The fact that the French version commences with "Mon cher fils," omitting the name and title, leaves no doubt that the titles were added by the editor in the edition of 1817.

A*

(From the Edition of 1817, p. 1)*

Imagining it may be equally agreeable to you to *learn* the circumstances of my life, many of which you are unacquainted with, and expecting the enjoyment of *a few weeks'* uninterrupted leisure, I sit down to write them. Besides, there are some other inducements *that excite me to this undertaking.* From the poverty and obscurity in which I was born, *and in which I passed my earliest years, I have raised myself* to a state of affluence and some degree of *celebrity* in the world. *As constant good fortune has accompanied me even to an advanced period of life, my posterity will perhaps be desirous of learning the means which I employed, and which, thanks to Providence, so well succeeded with me. They may also deem them fit to be imitated, should any of them find themselves in similar circumstances.*

(From the Edition of 1817, *p.* 4.)

My grandfather Thomas, who was born 1598, lived at Ecton till he was too old to *continue* his business, when *he retired* to Banbury in Oxfordshire to the house of his son John with whom my father served an apprenticeship. There my uncle died and lies buried.

(From the Autograph, p. 1.)

Imagining it may be equally agreeable to you to *know* the circumstances of my life, many of which you are *yet* unacquainted with, and expecting *a week's* uninterrupted leisure *in my present country retirement,* I sit down to write them *for you.*

To which I have besides some other inducements. *Having emerged* from the poverty and obscurity in which I was born *and bred* to a state of affluence and some degree of *reputation* in the world, *and having gone so far*

* Whenever I shall have occasion to cite the edition of 1817, reference will be made to the American edition of this work, in six vols., published in Philadelphia in 1818.

through life with a considerable share of felicity, the conducing means I made use of, which, with the blessing of God, so well succeeded, my posterity may like to know, as they may find some of them suitable to their own situations, and therefore fit to be imitated.

*(From the Autograph, p.*1.)

My grandfather Thomas, who was born in 1598, lived at Ecton till he *grew* too old to *follow business longer* when he *went to live with his son John, a dyer, at Banbury in Oxfordshire* with whom my father served an apprenticeship. There my *grandfather* died and lies buried.

(Edition of 1817,*p.* 4.)

My grandfather had four sons who grew up, viz.: Thomas, John, Benjamin and Josiah. *Being at a distance from my papers, I* will give you what account I can of them from memory, and if my papers are not lost in my absence, you will *find among them* many more particulars.

(Omitted)

(From the Edition of 1817, . 10.)

I *suppose* you may like to know *what kind of a man my father was.* He had an excellent constitution, and was of *a* middle stature, well set, and very strong; he could draw prettily, *and* was a little skilled in music; *his voice was sonorous and agreeable* so that when he played on his violin and sung withal, *as he was accustomed to do after the business of the day was over,* it was extremely agreeable to hear. He had some knowledge of mechanics, and on occasion was very handy with other tradesmen's tools but his great excellence was his sound understanding etc.

(Edition of 1817, *p.* 15.)

About this time I met *with* an odd volume of the Spectator. I had never before seen any of them.

(Autograph, p. 2.)

My grandfather had four sons *that* grew up, viz.: Thomas, John, Benjamin and Josiah. I will give you what account I can of them *at this distance from my papers, and if these are not lost in my absence,* you will, *among them, find many* more particulars.

(Autograph, p. 3.)

I was named after this uncle, there being a particular affection between him and my father.

(From the Autograph, p. 7.)

I think you may like to know *something of his person and character.* He had an excellent constitution *of body,* was of middle stature, *but* well set and very strong; he *was ingenious;* could draw prettily, and was skilled a little in music, *and had a clear, pleasing voice,* so that when he played *psalm tunes* on his violin, and sung withal, *as he sometimes did in an evening,* after the business of the day was over, it was extremely agreeable to hear. He had a *mechanical genius too,* and on occasion was very handy *in the use of* other tradesmen's tools but his great excellence *lay in a* sound understanding, etc.

(Autograph, p. 13.)

About this time I met with an odd volume of the Spectator. *It was the third.* I had never before, etc

(From Edition of 1817, *p* 16.)

The time *I allotted for writing* Exercises and for reading was at night or before *work* began in the morning or on Sunday, when I contrived to be in the printing house, *evading* as much as'I could the *constant* attendance *at* public worship, which my father used to exact from me when I was under his care and which I still continued to *consider as a* duty, though I could not afford time to practice it.

(Edition of 1817, *p.* 21.)

He agreed with the captain of a New York sloop *to take me* under *pretence* of my being a young man of his acquaintance that *had an intrigue with a girl of bad character,* whose parents would compel me to marry her; and that I could *neither* appear or come away publicly.

{From the Edition of 1817,*p* 23.)

On approaching the island, we found it was in a place where there could be no landing, there being a great surf on the stony beach, so we dropped anchor and *swung out our cable* towards the shore. Some people came down *to the shore* and hallooed as we did to them, but the wind was so high and the surf so loud that we could not understand each other. There were some small boats near the shore and we made signs and called them to

(From the Autograph, p, 14.)

My time *for these exercises* and for reading was at night *after work,* or before *it* began in the morning or on Sundays, when I contrived to be in the printing house *alone, avoiding* as much as I could the *Common* attendance *on* public worship which my father used to exact from me when I was under his care and which, *indeed,* I still *thought* a duty, though I could not, *as it seemed to me,* afford time to practice it.

(Autograph, p, 22.)

He agreed with the captain of a New York sloop *for my passage,* under the *notion* of my being a young *acquaintance of his* that had *got a naughty girl with child,* whose friends would compel me to marry her, and *therefore* I could *not* appear, or come away publicly.

(From the Autograph, p, 24.)

When we drew near the island we found it was *at* a place where there could be no landing, there being a great surf on the stony beach, so we dropped anchor and swung *around toward the shore.* Some people came down to the *water edge* and hallooed *to* us as we did to them, but the wind *was* so high and the surf so loud, that we could not *hear, so as to* understand each other. There were *canoes* on the shore, and we made signs and hoi- fetch us; but they either did not *comprehend us, or it was* impracticable, so they went off; *night approaching*, we had no remedy *but to have patience* till the wind abated, and in the meantime the boatman and *myself* concluded to sleep if we could; and so we crowded into the *hatches* where we joined the Dutchman, who was still wet, and the spray breaking over the head of our boat, etc.

(From the Edition of 1817, p.29.)

I was not a little surprised, and Keimer stared with astonishment.

(Edition of 1817, *p.* 33.)

But during my absence he had acquired a habit of *drinking of brandy;* and I found by his own account *as well as that of others,* that he had been drunk every day since his arrival at New York, and behaved himself in *a very extravagant manner,*

* * * * * *

The Governor *received* me with great civility, showed me his library, which was *a considerable one,* and we had a good deal of conversation *relative* to books and authors.

* * * * * *

Collins wished to be employed in some counting house, but whether they discovered his *dram drinking* by his breath, or, etc.

(Edition 1817, *p.* 34.)

The violation of my trust respecting Vernon's money was, etc.

loed that they should fetch us, but they either did not *understand* us or *thought it* impracticable, so they went away, and night *coming on,* we had no remedy but to wait till the wind *should* abate; and, in the meantime, the boatman and *I* concluded to sleep if we could; and so crowded into the *scuttle* with the Dutchman who was still wet, and the spray *beating* over the head of *our* boat, etc.

(From the Autograph, p. 34.)

I was not a little surprised, and Keimer stared like a pig poisoned.

(From the Autograph, p. 39.)

But during my absence he had acquired a habit of *sotting with* brandy; and I found by his own account and *what I heard from others,* that he had been drunk every day since his arrival at New York, and behaved *very oddly.*

* * * * * *

The Governor *treated* me with great civility, showed me his library, which was a *very large one,* and we had a good deal of conversation *about* books and authors.

* * * * * *

Collins wished to be employed in some counting house, but whether they discovered his *dramming* by his breath, or, etc.

(*Autograph, p.* 40.)
The *breaking into this money* of Vernon's, was, etc.

(*Edition* 1817, *p.* 47.)
I drank only water, the other workmen, near fifty in number, were great *drinkers* of beer.

(*Edition* 1817, *p.* 55.)
At length, receiving his quarterly allowance of fifteen guineas, instead of discharging his debts he *went* out of town, hid his gown in a furze bush and *walked* to London.

(*Autograph, p.* 53.)
I drank only water, the other workmen, near fifty in number, were great *guzzlers* of beer.

(*Autograph, p.* 62.)
At length, receiving his quarterly allowance of fifteen guineas, instead of discharging his debts he *walked* out of town, hid his gown in a furze bush, and *footed* it to London.

By whom were these changes made in the text of this manuscript?

How came the closing pages to be overlooked?

Why was the publication which purported to be made from the manuscript deferred for twenty-seven years after their author's death?

How happened it that this posthumbus work which may be read in nearly every written language and is one of the half-dozen most widely popular books ever printed, should have filled the book-marts of the world for a quarter of a century without having ever been verified by the original manuscript?

I doubt if it will ever be possible to determine all these questions with absolute certainty; but I propose to lay before the reader such information as I have been able to glean from a variety of sources, both published and unpublished, leaving him to draw from them such conclusions as he thinks the testimony will warrant. The array which I shall make, if it do not settle all these questions, may lead, it is to be hoped, to the production of latent testimony that will.

II

Dr. Franklin informs us, in the very first paragraph of his Memoirs, that he had undertaken to prepare them for the edification of his family. The first eighty-seven pages of the MS., which embrace the first twenty-five years of his life down to his marriage, appear to have been written in 1771, during one of his visits to Twyford, the countryseat of Dr. Shipley, then Bishop of St. Asaph, and without any view to publication.*

The MS. of this part was shown to some of his friends, among others to Mr. Benjamin Vaughan, Mr. Abel James, and to M. Le Veillard, who were all so pleased with, it that they urged him to resume and publish them. He was persuaded to do so, and in 1784, while residing at Passy, then a suburb of Paris, wrote the succeeding pages of the MS. to page 104. The part written in England was followed with this memorandum, written, doubtless, when he revised the Memoirs in 1789:

"MEM.—Thus far was written with the intention expressed in the beginning, and therefore contains several little family anecdotes of no importance to others. What follows was written many years after, and in compliance with the advice contained in these letters, † and accord-ingly intended for the public. The affairs of the Revolution occasioned the interruption."

---

* "Expecting," he says, " a week's uninterrupted leisure in my present country retirement, I sit down to write them for you." The MS. shows that he had originally written it "for your perusal." "Perusal" was afterward stricken out, and " use" written after it. This word was also stricken out, and the phrase left as in the text. The editor of the edition of 1817 strikes out the words "to you" also.

† The letters here referred to are from Messrs. Vaughan and James, and will be found in their proper place.

Another reason for continuing his Memoirs, and giving them to the press, has been assigned by M. Castera, who published a French edition of some of Franklin's works in 1793. He attributes the Autobiography to a desire on the part of Franklin and his French friends to neutralize the pernicious influence of Rousseau's Confessions, which, during the latter part of Franklin's residence in Paris, were the topic of every salon. These friends thought that it would be curious to compare the history of a writer who seemed to have used his brilliant imagination merely to render himself miserable, with that of a philosopher who employed all the resources of an equally gifted intellect to assure his own happiness by contributing to the happiness of others.*

---

* For the whole Preface, see Appendix, No. 1. It is a curious circumstance that the copy of the Memoirs given in this collection of Castera was translated from an English edition, which was itself only a translation from the first French translation, thus removed by three translations from the original. The gossips of Paris used to circulate a story illustrative of Franklin's constitutional propensity to take cheerful views of things. The author of *Correspondence secrite intdite sur Louis XVI., Marie Antoinette, la Cour et la Ville, de* 1777 *b* 1792, edited by M. Lescure, and published by M. Henri Pilon in 1866, writing from Versailles the 6th February, 1777, says: "I fear to speak to you of the Americans. The British Minister represents them as beaten, destroyed, dispersed, annihilated even. Letters from St. Domingo, from our own ports and to M. Franklin, assure us on the contrary that the English are in a bad way; that Howe has been whipped, &c. We wait for confirmation of the news. Meantime I must tell you that Franklin is not the *mtdecin tant pis.* For whenever they speak to him at Paris of any check experienced by the Americans, he cries out, *'tant mieux,'* the English will be caught at last". Vol. i. p. 18.

A comparison of dates will show that M. Castera's theory was purely imaginary.

* * * The self-torturing sophist, wild Rousseau,
The apostle of affliction, * * *

wrote the first part of his Confessions during his residence in England in the years 1766 and 1767. The second was composed in Dauphiny and at Trye in the years 1768 and 1770. It was his intention that they should not be printed until 1800, presuming that by that time all who figured in them would have ceased to live; but the period he had fixed for their publication was anticipated. The first part was printed in 1781, and the second in 1788. It is not likely that Franklin or any of his friends knew anything of them till the first part was published in 1781, and all of Franklin's Memoirs that Castera published or knew anything of had been written ten years before.

The Doctor returned to the United States in the summer of 1785. In the fall of that year he received a note from his friend, Mr. Edward Bancroft, the tenor of which is sufficiently explained in the following extract from the Doctor's reply:

"PHILADELPHIA, *26th November*, 1785.

" DEAR SIR :

" I received your kind letter of September 5th, informing me of the intention Mr. Dilly has of printing a new edition of my writings, and of his desire that I would furnish him with such additions as I may think proper. At present all my papers and manuscripts are so mixed with other things, by the confusions occasioned in sudden and various removals during the late troubles, that I can hardly find anything. But having nearly finished an addition to my house, which will afford me room to put all in order, I hope soon to be able to comply with such a request; but I hope Mr. Dilly will have a good understanding in the affair with Henry & Johnson, who, having risked the former impressions, may suppose they thereby acquired some right in the copy. As to the *Life* proposed to be written, if it be by the same hand who furnished a sketch to Dr. Lettsom, which he sent me, I am afraid it will be found too full of errors for either you or me to correct; and having been persuaded by my friends, Messrs. Vaughan and M. Le Veillard, Mr. James, of this place, and some others, that such a Life written by myself may be useful to the rising generation, I have made some progress in it, and hope to finish it this winter; so I cannot but wish that project of Mr. Dilly's biographer may be laid aside. I am nevertheless thankful to you for your friendly offer of correcting it.******

The Doctor's hopes of completing the Memoirs during the winter of 1785 were not realized, nor did he resume work upon them until three years later.

"As to the little history † I promised you," he writes to his friend, Le Veillard, the 15th April, 1787, "my purpose still continues of completing it, and I hoped to do it this summer, having built an addition to my house, in which I have placed my library,and where I can write without being disturbed by the noise of the children ; but the

---

* Sparks' Works of Franklin, vol. x. p. 240.

† The only letter we have from M. le Veillard bears date, Passy, Oct 9, 1785. He says, in allusion to this subject: "I hope you have been industrious during your passage, and that you have finished your Memoirs, and will send them to me." Sparks' Works of Franklin, vol. x. p. 231.

General Assembly having lately desired my assistance at a great convention to be held in May next for amending the Federal Constitution,
I begin to doubt whether I can make any progress in it till that business is over." *

In the same letter he adds farther on:

"You blame me for writing three pamphlets and neglecting to write the little history: you should consider they were written at sea, out of my own head; the other could not so well be written there for want of the documents that could only be had here."

On the 24th of October, 1788, the Doctor writes to M. Le Veillard as follows:

" I have been much afflicted the last summer with a long continued fit of the gout, which I am not quite clear of, though much better; my other malady is not augmented. I have lately made great progress in the work you so urgently demand, and have come as far as my fiftieth year. Being now free from public business, as my term in the Presidentship is expired, and resolving to engage in no other public employment, I expect to have it finished in about two months, if illness or some unforeseen interruption does not prevent. I do not, therefore, send a part at this time, thinking it better to retain the whole till I can view it all together, and make the proper corrections."†

William Temple Franklin also writes on the 17th of November, 1788:

" Our new government goes on in its way. Many
States have elected their Senators. The people are soon to elect their representatives. It is in March next they should meet.

---

* Le Veillard Collection. For the entire letter, see Appendix, No. 2.

† Ibid. For the entire letter, see Appendix, No. 3.

There is but one voice for the President- General, the illustrious Washington. In respect to the Vice President, opinions are shared between General Knox, Messrs. Hancock, Adams, &c. My grandfather having served the three years as President of this State, Genl. Mifflin has been elected in his place.

My grandfather now calls himself a free man, and I believe it would be difficult to induce him to change his condition. No one could more enjoy his liberty and repose. He is now occupied in writing the continuation of his life, which you have so urgently desired of him. His health improves every day. Farewell, my friend. Recall me to the recollection of all our common friends, and say a thousand tender things to all your family. I write to your son.

"W. T. F."*

In three other letters to M. le Veillard, written during the year 1788, Dr. Franklin alludes to his promise and his reasons for not having hitherto been able to keep it. Under date of February 17, 1788, he writes :

"I should have proceeded in the history you mention, if I could well have avoided accepting the chair of President for this third and last year; to which I was again elected by the *unanimous* voice of the Council and General Assembly in November. If I live to see this year expire, I may enjoy some leisure, which I promise you to employ in the work you do me the honor to urge so earnestly." †

Scarcely two months later, and under date of April 22, he writes again:

" I received but a few days since your favor of Nov. 30, 1787, in which you continue to urge me to finish the Memoirs.

---

* Le Veillard Collection. See Appendix, No. 4.

† Sparks' Works of Franklin, vol. x. p. 336.

My three years of service will expire in October, when a new President must be chosen, and I had the project of retiring then to my grandson's estate, in New Jersey, where I might be free from the interruption of visits, in order to complete that work for your satisfaction ; for in this city my time is so cut to pieces by friends and strangers, that I have sometimes envied the prisoners in Bastille. But considering now the little remnant of life I have left, the accidents that may happen between this and October, and your earnest desire, I have come to the resolution to proceed in that work tomorrow, and continue it daily till finished, which, if my health permits, may be in the course of the ensuing summer. As it goes on I will have a copy made for you, and you may expect to receive a part by the next packet."*

About six weeks after the foregoing, and under date of June 6, he writes again:

" Eight States have now agreed to the proposed new Constitution; there remain five who have not yet discussed it, their appointed times of meeting not having yet arrived. Two are to meet this month ; the rest later. One more agreeing, it will be carried into execution. Probably some will not agree at present, but time may bring them in; so that we have little doubt of its becoming general, perhaps with some corrections. As to your friend's taking a share in the management of it; his age and infirmities render him unfit for the business, as the business would be for him. After the expiration of the term of his Presidentship, which will now be in a few months, he is *determined* to engage no more in public affairs even if required; but his countrymen will be too reasonable to require it. You are not so considerate. You are a hard taskmaster. You insist

---

* Sparks' Works of Franklin, vol. x. p. 345.

on his writing his life, already a long work, and at the same time would have him continually employed in augmenting the subject, while the term shortens in which the work is to be executed."*

The Doctor did resume the Memoirs in 1788, and probably wrote about this time all of the remainder that has hitherto been published in English. It appears, however, from the following passage in a letter to M. Le Veillard, dated September 5, 1789, that he had then abandoned all hope of completing the Memoirs, and was making arrangements to transmit a copy of what was done, to M. Le Veillard and to Mr. Vaughan. Whether he intended one for each or for both is not quite certain:

"I hope you have perfectly recovered of your fall at Madame Helvetius's, and that you now enjoy perfect health; as to mine, I can give you no good account. I have a long time been afflicted with almost constant and grievous pain, to combat which I have been obliged to have recourse to opium, which indeed has afforded me some ease from time to time, but then it has taken away my appetite, and so impeded my digestion that I am become totally emaciated, and little remains of me but a skeleton covered with a skin. In this situation, I have not been able to continue my Memoirs, and now I suppose I shall never finish them. Benjamin has made a copy of what is done for you, which shall be sent by the first safe opportunity."*

Shortly before this letter was written—on the 3rd of June of that year—the Doctor wrote to his friend Vaughan, who, it appears, had been urging him to go on with the Memoirs:

"I received your kind letter of March 4th, and wish I may be able to complete what you so earnestly desire— the Memoirs of my life. But of late I am so interrupted by extreme pain, which obliges me to have recourse to opium, that, between

---

* Sparks' Works of Franklin, vol. x. p. 349.

* Le Veillard Collection, Appendix, No. 5.

the effects of both, I have but little time in which I can write anything. My grandson, however, is copying what is done, which will be sent to you for your opinion by the next vessel; and not merely for your opinion, but for your advice ; for it is a difficult task to speak decently and properly of one's own conduct; and I feel the want of a judicious friend to encourage me in scratching out." †

On the 2d of November he writes again to Mr. Vaughan in the same desponding strain of his health, though still more hopeful of continuing the Memoirs than he appeared when he wrote the letter last cited to M. le Veillard:

" I thank you much for your intimations of the virtues of hemlock ; but I have tried so many things with so little effect that I am quite discouraged, and have no longer any faith in remedies for the stone. The palliating system is what I am now fixed in. Opium gives me ease when I am attacked by pain, and by the use of it I still make life tolerable. Not being able, however, to bear sitting to rite, I now make use of the hand of one of my grandsons, dictating to him from my bed. I wish, indeed, I had tried this method sooner; for so I think I might by this time have finished my Memoirs, in which I have made no progress for these six months past. I have now taken the resolution to endeavor completing them in this way of dictating to an amanuensis. What is already done I now send you, with an earnest request that you and my good friend, Dr. Price, would be so good as to take the trouble of reading it, critically examining it, and giving me your candid opinion whether I had best publish or suppress it; and if the first, then what parts had best be expunged or altered. I shall rely upon your opinions; for I am now grown so old and feeble in mind, as well as body, that I cannot place

† Sparks' Works of Franklin, vol. x. p. 393.

any confidence in my own judgment. In the mean time, I desire and expect that you will not suffer any copy of it, or of any part of it, to be taken for any purpose whatever."*

This was the last allusion to the Memoirs of which I find any trace in the Doctor's correspondence. The only evidence, beyond the promise contained in his letter of the 3rd of June, that he sent a copy to Mr. Vaughan, is a statement made by the Duc de la Rochefoucault in a eulogium which he pronounced before a society in Paris on the 13th of June, 1789. In this discourse he says:

"The most voluminous of his works is the history of his own life, which he commenced for the use of his son, and for the continuation of which we are indebted to the ardent solicitations of Monsieur le Veillard, one of his most intimate friends. It employed his leisure hours during the latter part of his life ; but the bad state of his health and his excruciating pains, which gave him little respite, frequently interrupted his work; and the two copies–one of which was sent by him to London, to Dr. Price and Mr. Vaughan, and the other to Monsieur le Veillard and me–reach no farther than the year 1757. He speaks of himself as he would have done of another person, delineating his thoughts, his actions, and even his errors and faults; and he describes the unfolding of his genius and talents with the simplicity of a great man, who knows how to do justice to himself, and with the testimony of a clear conscience, void of reproach and ' of offence toward God and toward man.'

His Memoirs, gentlemen, will be published as soon as we receive from America the additions he may have made to the manuscript in our possession ; and we then intend to give a complete collection of his works."

The Duke had evidently derived his information in regard to the Memoirs exclusively from the letter last cited to M. le Veillard.

---

* Sparks' Works of Franklin, vol x. p. 397.

The Doctor died in a little less than six months after his letter of the 2nd of November to Mr. Vaughan. By his will, made in the summer of 1788, he bequeathed his books, manuscripts, and papers, after deducting a few special bequests, to his grandson, William Temple Franklin. Among the manuscripts was the original text of these Memoirs.

On the 22nd of May, Wm. Temple wrote M. le Veil- 3 lard, announcing his grandfather's death and the interest he had acquired in the Memoirs, which might be said to have owed their existence to M. le Veillard's pertinacity ; his intention to prepare them for publication, and requesting M. le Veillard to show them to no one unless to the Academician who should be charged to make the eulogy of the deceased, and to permit no one to take a copy of what had been sent him. He adds that he himself has the original. This letter was written in French.*

"PHILADELPHIA, 22 *May,* 1790.

"You have already learned, my dear friend, the loss which you and I, and the world, have experienced, in the death of this good and amiable papa. Although we have long expected it, we were none the less shocked by it when it arrived. He loved you very tenderly, as he did all your family, and I do not doubt you will share my just sorrow. I intended writing you the details of his death by M. de Chaumont, but the duty of arranging his affairs, and especially his papers, prevents my answering your last, as well as the one which your daughter was pleased to write me, accompanying her work. I have been touched with this mark of her condescension and friendship, and I beg you to testify to her my gratitude until I have an opportunity of writing to her, which will certainly be by the first occasion for France. Now, as I am about writing, her goodness will awaken me. This letter will reach you by way of England.

---

* Le Veillard Collection. For the original see Appendix, No. 6.

" I feel it my duty to profit by this occasion to inform you that my grandfather, among other legacies, has left all his papers and manuscripts to me, with permission to turn them to what profit I can. Consequently, I beg you, my dear friend, to show to no one that part of his Life which he sent you some time since, lest some one copy and publish it, which would infinitely prejudice the publication which I propose to make as soon as possible, of his entire Life and of his other works. As I have the original here of the part which you have, it will not be necessary for you to send it to me, but I beg you at all events to put it in an envelope, well sealed, addressed to me, in order that by no accident it may get into other hands.

" If, however, it should be necessary to assist the person who will pronounce his eulogy at the Academy, you may lend it for that purpose, with the stipulation that no copy of it shall be made, and with such other precautions as you deem necessary. The foreign representatives of our Government have not yet been named. It is possible I may be one, which would put me in the way to assist in the publication of my grandfather's works; but even if they think no more of me, it is very probable that I shall conclude to go to Europe, inasmuch as I am persuaded I can derive more advantage from the publication in England or in France than in this country.

"Adieu for the present. In two or three weeks I hope to be able to write to you directly, as well as to my other friends, male and female, in France. Love me, my dear friend. I have more need than ever of your friendship.

"W. T. FRANKLIN."

In the course of a few months after this letter was written, William Temple Franklin arrived in London, where he pretended to be engaged in preparing an edition of the Life and works of his grandfather, which he then expected to have ready in the course of the year. But it was ordained that this pre-eminently American work should be first presented to the world in a foreign tongue. A French translation appeared at Paris in 1791.* It embraced only the first eighty-seven pages of the manuscript. In his preface the editor seems to question the good faith of William Temple's promise to publish the Memoirs entire. As this preface is not readily accessible, and as it constitutes an important link in the history of this manuscript, I need offer no apology for giving it entire:

" I shall not enter into an uninteresting detail relative to the manner in which the original manuscript of these Memoirs, which are written in the English language, came into my possession. They appeared to me to be so interesting that I did not hesitate a single moment to translate them into French.

" The name of Franklin will undoubtedly become a passport to a work of this nature, and the character of truth and simplicity discernible in every page must guarantee its authenticity. I have no manner of occasion to join other testimonies.

" If, however, any critic chooses to disbelieve my assertion, and is desirous to bring the existence of the original manuscript into doubt, I am ready to verify it by means of an immediate impression ; †but as I am not certain of the sale of a work written in a foreign language, I cannot publish it in any other manner than by means of a subscription large enough to indemnify me for the money advanced.

"That part of the *Memoirs* of Franklin in my possession includes no more than the first period of a life, the remainder of which has become illustrious by events of the highest

---

* Memoirs de la vie privée de Benjamin Franklin, Merits par lui meme et addressees a son fils, suivis d'un precis historique de la vie politique, et de plusieurs pieces, relatives, à ce pére de la libertye. A Paris, chez Buisson, Libraire, Rue Hautefeuille, No. 20. 1791.

† " Those who may be desirous of reading the Memoirs of the public life of Franklin in the original are requested to leave their names with Buisson, bookseller, Rue Hautefeuille, No. 20 The work will be sent

importance ; it terminates at the epoch when, after having married, he began to render himself celebrated by plans and establishments of public utility.

"It is very possible that he may have written more of his history; for the portion of it which I now present to the public concludes, according to his own account, with the year 1771.*

"If this be the case, the heirs of that great man will not fail some day to publish it, either in England or in Pennsylvania, and we shall doubtless have a French translation, which will be received by the public with great eagerness; but I am persuaded that his family will not disclose any other than the most brilliant period of his life—that which is connected with the memorable part he acted in the world, both as a philosopher and a statesman. They will never be prevailed upon to narrate the humble details of his early days and the simple but interesting anecdotes of his origin, the obscurity of which, although it enhances the talents and the virtues of this great man, may yet wound their own vanity.

"If my conjecture prove right; if the Memoirs which they are about to publish under the name of Franklin should be mutilated ; if the first part, so essential to readers capable of feeling and judging, should be suppressed, I shall applaud myself for having preserved it; and the world will be obliged to me for having enabled them to follow the early developments of the genius, and the first exertions of the sublime and profound mind of a man who afterward penetrated the mystery of electricity and discovered the secret measures of despotism—who preserved the universe from the ravages of thunder, and his native country from the horrors of tyranny!

---

* to the press as soon as there are 400 subscribers. The price is 48 sols (or cents)."

* This date is erroneous. Dr. Franklin commenced writing his Memoirs in 1771, but in the portion of his Memoirs published in 1791 he " did not bring down the narrative of his life beyond the year 1730.30

" If I am accidentally mistaken, if the life of Franklin should appear entire, the public will still have the advantage of anticipating the interesting part of a history which it has long and impatiently expected.

" The principal object proposed by the American philosopher in writing these Memoirs was, to instruct posterity and amuse his own leisure hours. He has permitted his ideas to flow at the will of his memory and his heart, without ever making any effort to disguise the truth, notwithstanding it is not always very flattering to his selflove–but I here stop; it belongs to Franklin to speak for himself.

" It will be easily perceived that I have preserved as much as possible the ease and simplicity of his style in my translation. I have not even affected to correct the negligence of his language, or to clothe his sentiments with a gaudy dress, for which they have no manner of occasion ; I should have been afraid of bereaving the work of one of its principal ornaments.

"As these Memoirs reach no farther than his marriage,

I have made use of other materials in order to complete so interesting a history, and I have also added a number of anecdotes and remarks relative to this philosophical American.

THE EDITOR."

Querard* attributes this translation to a Dr. Jaques Gibelin, who, it appears, was a naturalist of some repute; had been occasionally in England; had translated from English philosophical writers, Priestly among others, and had made an abridgment of the Phil. Trans. of the Royal Society, &c. How he obtained possession of the English manuscript is a

---

* Querard, La France Littlraire

M. de Senarmont seems to have been under the impression that this translation was made by M. le Veillard. This M. le Veillard himself most distinctly denied in a note which he communicated to the " Journal de Paris," in 1791, No. 83, of which the following is a translation:

"PASSV, near Paris, 21th *March,* 1791.

mystery which will probably never be solved.*

The following letter from William Temple Franklin, in London, to M. Le Veillard, was written in the spring of 1791, but subsequent to the appearance of the French translation. He represents himself as still engaged upon the Life and works of his grandfather, which he pretended would be ready for the press in a few weeks :

"LONDON, 22 *April,* 1791.

"I received last night, my dear friend, your letter of the 12th inst. I am as sensible as you can be of the advantage that would result from my being at present in

---

* "Shortly before his death, Mr. Franklin sent me the Memoirs of his life, written by himself, and I have only deferred the publication of them out of respect for his family, and especially for Wm. Temple Franklin, his grandson, to whom his grandfather has left all his manuscripts. He proposes to make a complete edition, as well in French as in English, in which he will insert my translation. He is now in England, occupied with this work, and is expected in France, in a few days, to complete it.

"Buisson, a bookseller in the Rue Hautefeuille, has published a volume in 8 vo., entitled *Memoires de la Vie Privle de Benjamin Franklin Merits par lui-méme et addressees* d *san fils.* The first 156 pages of this volume contain in effect the commencement of the Memoirs of Dr. Franklin, almost entirely conforming to the manuscript which I possess. I do not know by what means the translator has procured them, but I declare and think it ought to be known that he did not have them from me; that I had no part in the translation; that this fragment, which ends in 1730, is scarcely a third of what I have, which only comes down to 1757, and which consequently does not terminate this work, the remainder of which is in the hands of Mr. W. T. Franklin, who will plan his edition so that the complete Memoirs of Franklin will form one or two volumes, which may be obtained separately.

" LE VEILLARD."Querard, *La France Littlraire.*

Paris, and I can assure you I am equally desirous of it. But business of the last importance, and that interested me personally, has hitherto detained me here; that, however, is now happily completed, and I am at present constantly occupied in the arrangement of my late grandfather's papers, which were left in the greatest disorder; whether I am able to complete this or not, I shall certainly leave London for Paris in the course of a fortnight. But my wish is, if possible, to finish this, and my bargain with the booksellers, before I set off, that I may not be obliged to return hither merely on that account. Were it only the *Life,* it would already have been done ; but I wish a complete edition of his works to appear at the same time, and as I have no assistance, the necessary preparations

---

* The relations of literary comity which must have subsisted between Gibelin and many of Franklin's English friends whose works he had translated, naturally leads to the suspicion that the copy promised Mr. Vaughan, if ever made and sent, may in some way have fallen into Gibelin's hands. If so, Mr. Vaughan must have construed the Doctor's injunction, not to permit "a copy of the MS. to be taken for any purpose whatever," to have been removed by his death. If such was the case, however, why did he not produce an English edition?

In a notice which Cabanis prepared shortly after the news of Dr. Franklin's death reached Paris, the following allusion is made to this edition of the Memoirs:

" Benjamin Franklin, s'est peint luiméme dans des Memoires dont il n'a paru jusq'ici qu'un fragment; mais ce sont ses ennemis ou des pen- sionnaires du cabinet de Saint James qui lont public. Ils y ont joint de plates notes auxquelles la famille aurait dfl repondre plus tot par la publication du reste de 1'ouvrage. En attendant qu'elle remplisse ce devoir, nous allons rassembler ici quelques traits, que nous avons re- cueillis de la bouche méme de Franklin dans une commerce intime de plusieurs annees."—*Ewvres de Cabanis,* vol. v. p. 221.

are very laborious. I am very sorry that any part of the Life should have already appeared in France—however imperfect, which I understand it is. I have endeavored, and I hope effectually, to put a stop to a translation appearing here.

"Adieu, my dear friend; all will, I hope, go well. With my best affections to all your family, I am, as ever and for ever,

" Sincerely yours,
W. T. FRANKLIN." *

William Temple's apprehensions of an English translation were not without foundation.

Strange as it is that the first version of any portion of these Memoirs should have appeared in a foreign tongue, it is yet more remarkable that the first English version should have been, as it was, a translation from the French.

It appeared in London in 1793,* and was not only the only English version in print until 1817, but continues to this day to be republished by some of the largest houses, not only in Europe, but in America, under the impression that it is both genuine and complete. What measures were taken, if any, to prevent the appearance of an English translation have not transpired.

William Temple's expectations of getting to Paris in a few weeks do not seem to have been realized; for, from the following letter it appears that nearly two months had elapsed and he was still in London, but hoped to set out for France before the end of the month. A speculation, from which he had realized £7,000, is assigned as the cause of his delay. He

---

* Le Veillard Collection.

B*

* "The Private Life of the late Benjamin Franklin, LL.D., late Minister Plenipotentiary from the United States of America to France, etc.,

professes to be much distressed at what M. le Veillard had suffered—in what way is not disclosed—from his not arriving in Paris:

"LONDON, 14 *June,* 1791.

"I am much distressed, my dear friend, at what you say you suffer from my not arriving in Paris. I have been wishing to be there as much as you could wish to see me, but I could not possibly think of leaving this, while a business I had undertaken was pending for which

I rec'd a salary and which, being now completed, affords me a profit of *seven thousand pounds sterling !* This, my dear friend, has hitherto kept me here—having only been finally terminated on the nth inst. I am in hopes you will think my excuse for staying till it was done a good one. I have now only some few arrangements to make in consequence of my success, and shall undoubtedly be with you before the conclusion of this month. My respects to your family and all inquiring friends, and believe me unalterably

" Yours,
"W. T. FRANKLIN."*

---

originally written by himself, and now translated from the French. To which are added some account of his public life, a variety of anecdotes concerning him, by MM. Brissot, Condorcet, Rochefoucault, Le Roy, eta, etc., and the Eulogium of M. Fauchet, Constitutional Bishop of the Department of Calvados and a Member of the National Convention. *Eripuitfulmen Corio, mox sceptra tyrannis.*—TURGOT. *A Paris ce grand homme dans notre ancien regime serait resté dans l obscurit; comment employer le fils d'un Chandelier."*—LE ROY.

London: Printed for J. Parsons, No. 31 Pater Noster Row. 1793.

* Le Veillard Collection.

The letter which follows, dated seven months later than the preceding, authorizes the impression that William Temple Franklin had entered into engagements of some sort with M. le Veillard for bringing out his work simultaneously in France and in England. If so, his failure to keep those engagements furnish a natural and obvious explanation of the sufferings of M. le Veillard, referred to in the preceding letter :

"LONDON, 28 *Feb.*, 1792.

"MY DEAR FRIEND:

" I received lately your favor of the 12th inst., and previous to it, the one you mention from M. Feuillet. I am exceedingly sorry that gentleman cannot complete the translation, as I am confident it would have been well done ; however, it shall not retard the publication of such parts as are translated at the time the original appears here, which at present is not determined, but will not be delayed longer than is absolutely necessary for the arrangement of the materials. This might, perhaps, have been done sooner had I been better calculated for the business, or had not my fortune required my attention to other pursuits, by which it has been most materially benefited. Notwithstanding the opinion you entertain–that I have neglected the publication in question for business less important (which, by the way, you cannot possibly be a judge of)–I can assure you I have given it all the attention I could, consistent with the important concerns above alluded to, in which others being interested, required my first and most diligent care; and, however I may have lost something by not publishing sooner, yet it has been amply compensated by those pursuits you judge less important. I am now almost entirely employed in bringing forward the English edition, and shall not leave this till I have put it into such a train as not to require my presence ; but this will take up more time than you are aware of; for however easy it may be to bring forward a *brochure,* it is no small labor to publish a voluminous work ; and that, too, to be formed out of materials that were left in the greatest confusion. A few months will, I hope, satisfy your impatience and the public curiosity. When matters are in good train here, I shall immediately repair to Paris to forward the translation, and you may rely on it that at least the Life shall appear the *same day in Paris* as in London; sooner I see not the necessity for, and it might expose me hereafter to some difficulties, here; as the French edition appearing previous to the English, a translation might be printed here to the prejudice of my *copy.*

" Adieu, my dearest friend; remember me, in the most affectionate manner, to Madame le Veillard, and every part of your family, and believe me, as ever and for ever,

" Sincerely yours,

"W. T. FRANKLIN.

"P. S.—You have heard, I suppose, of the nomination by the President of Mr. Gouverneur Morris to be minister at your Court? It has, however, suffered some demur in the Senate, and has not been yet confirmed.

"I have no doubt, however, but it will. From the well- known sentiments of Mr. M., this appointment will not, I believe, be very agreeable to the National Assembly. Mr. Short goes to Holland, and I am totally neglected. I shall therefore lose no time, but turn my attention to other pursuits." *

No farther correspondence appears to have passed between William Temple Franklin and M. le Veillard, though the latter gentleman was living till 1794. The interruption to this correspondence was probably the result of an estrangement, of which the letters cited furnish some premonitory symptoms.

Whatever may have been the cause of the delay, William Temple's edition did not appear, as has been already stated, until 1817.

---

* Le Veillard Collection.

But, as I have before intimated, this *editio princeps* of 1817 was not printed from the original manuscripts, but from the copy presented to M. le Veillard. The evi dence of this may be found in the omission of the last eight pages, which are only to be found in the autograph, and in the following memorandum inscribed on its flyleaves in French and in English, in the handwriting, I presume, of M. de Senarmont, or of some member of his family. The English version runs as follows :

"THE LIFE OF BENJAMIN FRANKLIN,

"WRITTEN BV HIMSELF.

" *The only Manuscript Entirely of his own Handwriting.*

Dr. Franklin, when Ambassador in France, was very intimate with M. le Veillard, *gentilhomme ordinaire du Roi,* his neighbor, near Paris. He presented his friend with a fine copy of the Memoirs of his own life.

" When William Temple Franklin, Dr. Franklin's grandson, came to Europe in order to publish the works of his illustrious grandfather, he required from Mad. le Veillard (M. le Veillard had perished on the Revolutionary scaffold) the correct and fine copy given by his grandfather, as more convenient for the printer. 'I give it to you, I shall have nothing more of our friend.' 'I will give you, in place of the copy, the original manuscript of my grandfather.'

"In this manner the original and only manuscript came by inheritance into the hands of M. de Senarmont, M. le Veillard's grandnephew."

The precise time when the exchange here referred to was made does not appear, but the following paragraph from Sir Samuel Rom illy's Diary of a Visit to France in 1802, informs us that he was shown the autograph ; that the copy originally furnished to M. le Veillard, and afterward given to William T. Franklin, was made by a copying-press, and that that copy was exchanged for the original previous to Romilly's visit in 1802 :

"Sept 7. Mad. Gautier procured for me the reading of the original manuscript of Dr. Franklin's Life. There are only two copies—this, and one which Dr. Franklin took with a machine for copying letters, and which is in possession of his grandson. Franklin gave the manuscript to M. le Veillard, of Passy, who was guillotined during the Revolution. Upon his death it came into the hands of his daughter or granddaughter, Mad'lle le Veillard, who is the present possessor of it. It appears evidently to be the first draught written by Franklin, for in a great many places the word originally written is erased with a pen, and a word nearly synonymous substituted in its place, not over the other but further on, so as manifestly to show that the correction was made at the time of the original composition. The manuscript contains a great many additions made upon a very wide margin ; but I did not find that a single passage was anywhere struck out. Part of the work, but not quite half of it, has been translated into French, and from French retranslated into English. The Life comes down no lower than to the year 1757"*

The omission of the eight pages which conclude the manuscript, and which constitute one of the most precious chapters of this famous fragment, is susceptible of the following explanation:

William Temple Franklin exchanged the autograph manuscript for the copy sent to M. le Veillard, without being aware that, between the time that copy was made and its author's death, these pages had been added. Presuming they were the same, probably he did not compare them, and thus overlooked one of the most precious chapters of this famous fragment.

---

* Life of Romilly, 3d ed., vol. i. p. 408.

William Temple Franklin's delay in the publication of the Memoirs, twenty-seven years after the death of their author, cannot be so satisfactorily accounted for.

It brought a reproach upon our country for the lack of " literary enterprise and activity," of which it was thought to convict us, and was also attributed, in part, to motives not entirely honorable to the person directly responsible for the delay. The *Edinburgh Review* gave the most solemn expression to the public discontent in a review of the three-volume edition of Franklin's Works and Memoirs, published by Johnson & Longman, of London, in 1806.*

In the first two paragraphs of this article the writer says :

"Nothing, we think, can show more clearly the singular want of literary enterprise or activity in the States of America than that no one has yet been found in that flourishing republic to collect and publish the works of their only philosopher. It is not even very creditable to the literary curiosity of the English public that there should have been no complete edition of the writings of Dr. Franklin till the year 1806; and we should have been altogether unable to account for the imperfect and unsatisfactory manner in which the work has now been per formed, if it had not been for a statement in a prefatory advertisement, which removes all blame from the editor to attach it to a higher quarter. It is there stated that recently, after the death of the author, his grandson, to whom all his papers had been bequeathed, made a voyage to London for the purpose of preparing and disposing of a complete collection of all his published and unpublished writings, with Memoirs of his life brought down by himself to the year 1757, and continued to his death by his descendant. It was settled that the work should be published in three quarto volumes in England, Germany and France, and a negotiation was

* See *Edinburgh Review*, July, 1806.

commenced with the booksellers as to the terms of purchase and publication. At this stage of the business, however, the proposals were suddenly withdrawn, and nothing more has been heard of the work in this its fair and natural market.

" The proprietor, it seems, had found a bidder of a different description in *some emissary of government* whose object was to *withhold* the manuscripts from the world, not to benefit it by their publication; and they thus either passed into other hands, or the person to whom they were bequeathed received a remuneration for suppressing them.

" If this statement be correct, we have no hesitation in saying that no emissary of government was ever employed on a more miserable and unworthy service. It is ludicrous to talk of the danger of disclosing, in 1795, any secrets of State with regard to the war of American Independence ; and as to any anecdotes or observations that might give offence to individuals, we think it should always be remembered that public functionaries are the property of the public; that their character belongs to history and to posterity, and that it is equally absurd and discreditable to think of *suppressing* any part of the evidence by which their merits must be ultimately determined. But the whole of the works that have been suppressed certainly did not relate to republican politics. The history of the author's life, down to 1757, could not well contain any matter of offence, and a variety of general remarks and speculations which he is understood to have left behind him might have been permitted to see the light, though his diplomatic operations had been interdicted. The emissary of government, however, probably took no care of these things: he was resolved to leave no rubs and botches in his work, and, to stifle the dreaded revelation, he thought the best way was to strangle all the innocents in the vicinage."

William Temple's tardy vindication from these imputations is given in the preface to his edition of his grandfather's works.

He there admits that he delayed-their publication, that " they might not be the means of awakening painful recollections or of rekindling the dying embers of animosity."*

Mr. Sparks thinks that William Temple Franklin had motives for delaying the publication of the writings of his grandfather which he did not assign in his preface. He says : †

" There was a rumor that the British ministry interposed, and offered the proprietor of the papers a large remuneration to suppress them, which he accepted. This rumor was so broadly stated in the preface to Johnson's edition as to amount to a positive charge: and it was reiterated with an assurance that would seem at least to imply that it was sustained by the public opinion. To this charge William Temple Franklin replied when, in the year 1817, he published an edition of his grandfather's works from the manuscripts in his possession. In the preface to the first volume he endeavors to explain the reason why he had so long delayed the publication, and he also takes notice of the charge in question. He treats it with indignation and contempt, and appears not to regard it as worthy of being refuted. He was less reserved in conversation. Dr. John W. Francis, of New York, saw him often in London in the year 1816, while he was preparing his grandfather's papers for the press. 'To me,' says Dr. Francis, ' he peremptorily denied all interference of any official authorities whatever with his intended publication, and assigned, as sufficient causes for the non-exe- cution.of the task committed to him, the interruption of communication and the hostilities between the French and the English nations, and the consequent embarrassments he encountered in collecting the scattered materials.' The reason here assigned for delay is not very satisfactory, and there were doubtless others. His father, William

* The whole of this preface is worth perusing. It will be found at length in Appendix 7.

† Sparks' Life of Franklin, vol. vii. Preface.

Franklin, died in 1813. He had been a pensioner on the British government, in consequence of the part he had taken in the Revolution, and it is probable that he may have been averse to the publication of his father's papers during his lifetime. To say the least, the suspicion that papers were finally suppressed for any cause is without proof and highly improbable. A paper mentioned by Mr. Jefferson, as having been shown to him by Dr. Franklin, and supposed to have been suppressed, was undoubtedly the one relating to a negotiation with Lord Howe and others, for a reconciliation between the two countries, just before Dr. Franklin left England for the last time. This was published by his grandson, and is contained in the fifth volume of the present edition."

The conjecture of Mr. Sparks is, no doubt, correct so far as it goes. There can be no question with any person cognizant of the state of feeling which prevailed at the time in England toward the revolted Colonies, that the publication of an elaborate edition of Franklin's works would have been unacceptable to the governing classes; nor can there be much doubt that such a publication would have had a tendency to compromise William Franklin with the government, and put his pension in peril. When it is further considered that William Franklin not only had no sympathy with the republican cause in America, but did all he could to betray it, and thus entitled himself to the pension upon which he lived, it may safely be inferred that he exerted what influence he possessed over his son, not only to defer the publication, but to unsettle his son's faith in the value and stability of the political fabric which their common ancestor had had such an important agency in erecting. And it is also to be borne in mind, that any representations of that nature which the father might make would have fallen upon the son's mind in a state not wholly unprepared to give it hospitality. Both he and his grandfather thought he had been treated ungraciously by our governmant, from which he had been educated to expect some diplomatic appointment. Immediately after his grandfather's death he left the United States under a feeling of disappointment, ifnot of disgust, at their ingratitude, and never returned. He bore with him in his trunk a manuscript property which could be turned to considerable account in two ways—either by printing it or by suppressing it. The course that he finally took was one which enabled him, if he chose, to take the benefit of both modes of procedure. He delayed the publication until it could no longer work any prejudice to him or his, and then found for it, doubtless, at last as propitious a market as he could have hoped for had he published earlier.

Whether he did profit by this delay, and if so, in what way and to what extent, will probably never be known with absolute certainty. Every one's conclusions will be more or less affected by their knowledge of his character, habits and necessities. There is a paragraph in one of his letters already cited, which must henceforth be weighed in deciding this question. He wrote to M. le Veillard from London on the 14th of June, 1791:

"I am much distressed, my dear friend, at what you say you suffer from my not arriving in Paris. I have been wishing to be there as much as you could wish to see me, but I could not possibly think of leaving this while a business I had undertaken was pending, for which I rec'd a salary ; and which, being now completed, affords me a profit of *seven thousand pounds sterling!* This, my dear friend, has hitherto kept me here—having only been finally terminated on the nth inst. I am in hopes you will think my excuse for staying till it was done a good one. I have now only some few arrangements to make in consequence of my success, and shall undoubtedly be with you before the conclusion of this month."

When this was written, Dr. Franklin had been dead but about a year; the writer had been in London barely six months.

He never pretended in his correspondence before to have any other business there than to edit his grandfather's works ; he suddenly engages himself upon a salary; in less than six months finishes his business, and pockets a profit of £ 7000, or say $35,000. While earning this handsome sum he was apparently a free man, constantly writing to M. le Veillard that he was expecting to go in a few days or weeks to Paris, being only detained in London to finish his book. It is not easy to imagine any salaried employment, especially such a profitable one as this seemed to be, which imposed so slight a restraint upon the movements of its beneficiary.

From whatever source this £ 7000 came, and however little or much the acquisition of it had to do with the delay in the publication of his grandfather's works, it is certainly to be regretted that so little is known of the business engagement which was entered into so suddenly, was of such brief duration, and yet yielded such generous profits. Cabanis* tells us, that when William Franklin asked of the Court of St. James the governorship of one of the colonies†—a favor by which he became unfortunately bound to the Loyalist party—Franklin said to him : "Think what this whistle will some day cost you. Why not rather be a carpenter or a ploughman, if the fortune I leave you prove insufficient? The man who works for his living is at least independent. But," added he, in telling us this story, " the young man was infatuated with the ' Excellency.' He was ashamed to resemble his father."

It is not impossible that the grandson, after residing a while in London, succumbed to a similar weakness.

In the very year that the edition of William Temple Franklin made its appearance, a collection of Franklin's correspondence was compiled and published in Paris, in 2 vols., by M. Charles

---

* CEuvres de Cabanis, vol. v. p. 223.

† New Jersey.

Malo.* The Preface of this book was made the vehicle of a ruthless attack upon William Temple Franklin and upon his editorial enterprise, which, coming as it did from a writer of some reputation, measures the marvelous change which must have taken place in the feelings of the French people toward him since he left Paris, to have rendered such an introduction of his grandfather's works acceptable to them. M. Malo accuses him of selecting from, abridging and belittling the works of the Doctor, and concludes with the question :

"Ought we to inherit from one we have assassinated?" †A feeling seems to have prevailed among the French editors of Franklin's writings that he was ashamed of his grandfather's humble origin and early employments.

---

* Correspondence Inedite et Secrete de Docteur B. Franklin, Ministre Plenipotentiaire des Etats-Unis d'Amerique pres la Cour de France depuis l'annee 1753 jusque en 1790 offrant, en trois parties completes et bien distinctes.

1. Les Memoires de sa Vie privée;
2. Les causes premieres de la Revolution d'Amerique;
3. L'Histoire des diverses negotiations entre l'Angleterre, la France et des Etats-Unis, publiee pour la premiere fois en France, avec des notes, additions, &c. Paris, Janet pere, Libraire Editeur, Rue Saint-Jacques, No. 59. MDCCCXVII.

† For a translation of this diatribe, see the Appendix, No. 8. The author of it, M. Charles Malo, was a voluminous writer, something of a poet, and a warm republican. The list of his works alone fills nearly two pages of Querard. It is not strange that one who published so much should make some ludicrous blunders, of which several specimens may be found among the notes with which he endeavored to illumine

III.

The autograph Memoirs fill 220 pages of foolscap, written both sides of the page. A margin of half its width was left on each page for such additions and corrections as the autobiographer might have occasion to make at a future day. Of this margin the Doctor took frequent advantage.

---

the writings of Franklin. In one of his letters Franklin remarks: "They thought a Yankee was a sort of Yahoo." Upon this M. Malo remarks:

" *Yahoo.*–This must be an animal. They pretend it is an opossum ; but I have not found the word 'Yahoo' in any dictionary of natural history."

Again, in a letter to Buffon, Franklin wrote that he had escaped obesity by eating moderately, drinking neither wine nor cider, and in exercising himself daily with dumb-bells. M. Malo instructs his countrymen that "this term dumb-bell expresses among the English the motion a person seated makes in moving back and forth only the upper part of his body."

In one instance M. Malo presumed to act as a censor upon Dr. Franklin himself. In a letter of the Doctor's, he had quoted with a sort of humorous approval the following lines from an old song :

" With a courage undaunted may I face my last day,
And when I am gone may the better sort say,
In the morning when sober, in the evening when mellow :
He isgone, and has not left behind him his fellow;
For he governed his passions."

M. Malo remarks upon this couplet : " I have not translated the third line literally, for it did not seem to me in very good taste to desire to be praised by honest people, who are sober in the morning and drunk in the evening." So he translated the verse as follows :

" Puisse je avec courage voir arriver mon dernier jour; et quand je ne serai plus, puissent les gens vertueux repeter souvent, ' il est mort, et n'a pas laisse son pareil au monde ! Car il avait sur ses passions un pouvoir absolu."

He had such a clear and distinctchirography that all the MS. is legible, though abounding with interlineations and erasures. The last eight pages only, betray what Cicero terms the *vacillantibus litterulis* of age and infirmity, though they also are perfectly legible. They must have been written in the Doctor's eightyfourth year, and in the intervals of those intense pains with which the latter days of his life were tortured.

The MS. came into my possession half bound in red morocco, with a memorandum, which has already been cited, inscribed on fly-leaves in French and in English, in the handwriting, I presume, of M. le Veillard.

As a part of the history of this manuscript, it is proper that I should add the following memorandum, furnished me in French by M. de Senarmont himself :

"*Note on the autograph manuscript of the Memoirs of Benjamin Franklin.*

"The manuscript of the Memoirs of Franklin is a folio of 220 pages, written with a half page margin on paper not of uniform size.

"M. le Veillard, gentleman in ordinary of the king, and Mayor of Passy, was an intimate friend of Dr. Franklin. He had lived in daily intercourse with him at Passy, near Paris, during the Doctor's residence in France, at the epoch of the American War of Independence. At the departure of his friend, he accompanied him to the ship on which Franklin embarked for America, and it was from his own country that the Doctor sent him, as a token of his friendship, the copy of his Memoirs, subsequently exchanged for the original.

"The original manuscript is unique. Mr. William

Temple Franklin, grandson of Benjamin Franklin, received it at the death of his grandfather, who had left him all his writings. When William Temple returned to France to prepare the edition which he published, he requested of Madame le Veillard her copy to print from, because it appeared more convenient for the printer, on account of its neatness. He gave to Mad. le Veillard in exchange the original manuscript entirely written by the hand of Franklin.

" The original was, however, more complete than the copy, which Mr. Temple had not verified. Proof of this may be found in the second volume of the small edition of the Memoirs, in two volumes in i8mo., published by Jules Renouard, at Paris, in 1828. One may there read, at the commencement of a continuation which then appeared for the first time, a note, page 1, where the editor states that this continuation was communicated to them by the Le Veillard family.*

" The simple inspection demonstrates the authenticity of the manuscript, in support of which may be furnished other positive proofs, drawn from the different pieces accompanying it, such as–

" The three letters of Dr. Franklin to M. le Veillard; three letters from Mr. William Temple to the same; and various letters

---

* The note here referred to, translated, reads as follows: "We publish for the first time this piece, which had never been published in English or French. It is translated from the original manuscript which served for the English edition which William Temple Franklin, published in 1818, of the Memoirs of his grandfather. This manuscript belongs to the family of M. le Veillard, an intimate friend of Franklin, and we owe the communication of it to M. de S., one of the members of this honorable family."

The M. de S. here referred to, we presume, was the father of the M. P. de Senarmont from whom I received the Memoirs and the memorandum now under the reader's eye.

from Benjamin Franklin Bache, Sarah Bache, his wife, and from a bookseller who wished to purchase the manuscript of M. le Veillard in 1791.*

" M. le Veillard, who is the author of the French translation of the Memoirs of Franklin,† has preserved the autograph manuscript, with a sentiment corresponding with that which determined his friend to send him the MS. copy.

"After the death of M. le Veillard, who perished on the Revolutionary scaffold in 1794, the MS. went to his daughter. At her death, in 1834, it became the property of her

---

* The bookseller here referred to is Buisson, who published the first edition of the Memoirs, in French, in 1791. His note reads as follows:

SIR :—I learn that you have manuscripts relating to the life of Dr. Franklin. If it is your intention to dispose of them, I offer to become their purchaser.

I have the honor to be, sir,
Your humble and obedient servant,

BUISSON,
Bookseller, Rue Hautefeuille, No. 2.

I want a word of reply, if you please.
PARIS, 26 *June,* 1791.

What reply was made to this application will probably never be known. That the MS. was not sold is certain, for we know it was afterward exchanged for the autograph.

On the other hand, M. le Veillard, in his note to the *Journal du Paris,* quoted above, distinctly says that he not only had nothing to do with the translation, but did not know how the translator had been able to procure the manuscript from which to make it.

† M. de Senarmont is evidently in error in attributing the French translation that was printed in 1791 to M. le Veillard. M. le Veillard made a translation; but it must have been printed subsequently, if at all

cousin, M. de Senarmont, whose grandson delivered it, on the 26th January, 1867, to Mr. John Bigelow, late Minister of the United States at Paris.

" The manuscript is accompanied by a beautiful portrait in pastel by Duplessis. Franklin sat for this portrait during his sojourn at Passy, and presented it himself to M. le Veillard.

" (Signed) L. DE SENARMONT.

"PARIS, 17th *January,* 1867."

In addition to the continuation of the Memoirs which was overlooked by William Temple Franklin, already referred to, I was so fortunate as to find in the Le Veillard collection a skeleton sketch of the topics which Dr. Franklin originally proposed to treat in the Autobiography. It was, doubtless, the first outline of the work. It is written upon a letter sheet, the first three pages in black ink and in the hand of a copyist, while the continution of seven lines on the fourth page, beginning with " Hutchinson's Letters," are in red ink, and in the hand of Franklin himself.

A line is drawn with a pen through the middle of the first page of the manuscript down to the words: " *Library erected—manner of conducting the project—its plan and utility."* As these are the topics which conclude the first part of the Memoirs, terminating at page 87 of the manuscript, the line was probably drawn by Franklin when he had reached that stage of his work, that he might the more easily know with what topic to resume it when he should have occasion to do so.

I give this Outline as an introduction to the Memoirs.

It will be found extremely interesting, first, as showing how systematically Franklin set about the execution of the task of which these Memoirs are the result; and, secondly, for the notions it gives us of the unexecuted portion of his plan.*

---

* The glimpse given in this Outline of Franklin's habits of composition tempts me to refer the reader to an extract from a letter which Dr. Franklin wrote to Mr. Vaughan in 1789, in which, at Mr. Vaughan's

The printed manuscript ends with his departure to England as agent of the Colony of Pennsylvania, to settle the disputes about the proprietary taxes in 1757, while the Outline comes down to the conclusion of his diplomatic career, of course embracing the most interesting portion of his life. No one can glance over the subjects that were to have been treated in the succeeding pages of the Memoirs without experiencing a new pang of regret at their incompleteness. How precious would have been the personal sketches which he promised to leave of many of the distinguished people among whom he spent the latter years of his life; how interesting the impressions which he would have thought worth recording of his first visit to the Continent in 1766, '67 and '69; of the entertainment given him by the French Academy ; of his mode of prosecuting his electrical discoveries; his analysis of his own character; and, above all, his account of his last residence in France, and of his negotiations for the recognition of the Colonies.

Rich and charming as is his correspondence upon many of these subjects, we miss the limpid narrative.
gemmed all over, like a cloudless firmanent at night, with the pertinent anecdote, curious observation and sage reflections which constitute the unspeakable charm of his Memoirs.

But though it was ordained that this Autobiography should take its place among the famous unfinished projects of human genius, it is a great satisfaction to know, as this document permits us to know, what were the experiences of the most momentous period of his life which Dr. Franklin thought most worthy of being rescued from oblivion, even though, like some familiar memorial of a departed friend, they renew the sense of a loss to which time was beginning to bring its consolations.

---

request, he gives him some counsel on the subject of his style. What he says will help the reader to comprehend the uses for which the Outline referred to in the text was prepared. See Appendix, No. 9.

This volume is embellished by a portrait of Franklin, engraved from the pastel by Duplessis in the Le Veillard Collection. Franklin sat for it to Duplessis in 1783, and presented it to his friend, Le Veillard. At the bottom of the old gilt frame, in front, is the following inscription upon the frame :

"BENJAMIN FRANKLIN,

"A 77 ANS,

"Peint par J S^{d} Duplessis,*

" 1783-

"Donné par Franklin lui-meme."

On the back is the following memorandum, placed there, doubtless, by M. le Veillard:

Benjamin Franklin, a77 ans; peint en 1783 par Duplessis; donné par Franklin lui-meme k M. Louis le Veillard, gentilhomme ordinaire de la Reine, son ami et son voisin k Passy.

Joseph Siffred Duplessis, Academicie, né à. Carpentrar, s'est distingud par une belle intelligence, les effets de la lumiére, sur les chairs et accessoires un pinceau large; bien senti et un coloris vrai. Les personnages de distinction dans ses portraits sont posds avec noblesse et dans des altitudes bien choisies. 11 h. peint le portrait de Louis XVI., ceux de M. et Mme. Neckar, et de plusieurs grands de la Cour.—Les trois sidcles de la peinture la France, par Gault de St Germain. 1808.—Swiback 1'eleve le plus distingud de Duplessis, & surpassd son maitre.

It will be observed that, unmindful of the example of previous editors of these Memoirs, I have limited myself strictly to a reproduction of their text, without attempting to continue and complete the narrative of the Autobiographer's life. I have one sufficient excuse, if any is needed, for this course which none of my predecessors could have pleaded. The delightful and comparatively recent work of Mr. Parton has left no place in English literature for another biography of this most illustrious of our countrymen.

I do not know that I can more appropriately conclude this bibliographical summary than by quoting a few passages from the introduction to the Memoirs of Franklin by Professor Edward Laboulaye, which appeared in Paris in 1866.* The translation of the Memoirs and correspondence of Franklin was one of the many ways by which this distinguished jurist contributed, during our late struggle for the preservation of our Federal Union, to keep alive in France that friendship for the United States which Franklin, more than any other one person, had the merit of inspiring, and to which, for the second time, we have been largely beholden for our national existence :

" What constitutes the charm of the Memoirs is not the recital of events, which are of the most ordinary character ; it is the reflections which accompany their recital. Franklin is a born moralist. The first letter he writes to his sister is a sermon on the virtues of a good housekeeper. The penitent is fifteen and the preacher twenty. From this moment to his death Franklin did not change. He is always the man who reasons out his conduct–the sage who, following the ingenious definition of Mr. Bancroft, never said a word too soon nor a word too late. He never said a word too much, nor failed to say the decisive word at the proper moment. In his letters how many moral lessons, given with as much gayety as power! It is not an author one reads; he is a friend to whom one listens. There is Franklin, with his venerable face, his hair floating back, and his eye always shrewd and quick, presenting altogether one of the most amiable figures of the last century. How many prejudices he playfully dissipated ! how he rallied the selfishness of individuals and the artifices of governments, which are but another form of selfishness! Do not ask of him

* Memoires de Benjamin Franklin, ecrits par lui-méme, traduits de l'Anglais et annotes par Edouard Laboulaye, de 1'Institut de France Paris, Libraire de L. Hachette & Cie. 1866.

anything sublime, nor expect from him those bursts which raise you above the passing world. Franklin never quits the earth ; it is not genius in him; it is good sense expressed in its highest power. Do not seek in him a poet, nor even an orator, but a master of practical life–a man to whom the world belongs. Neither imagine you have to do with a vulgar, worldly wisdom. This amiable mocker, who laughs at.

Everything, is not the less kind-hearted, a devoted patriot, and one of the sincerest friends of humanity. His laugh is not that of Voltaire; there is no bitterness in it; it is the benevolent smile of an old man whom life has taught to be indulgent. In noting without vanity what he terms his errata of conduct, Franklin teaches us that no one has a right to judge another severely, and that in the most correct life there is always many a page to correct. It is thus that he humbles himself to us to encourage us. He is a companion who takes us by the hand, and, talking with us familiarly, little by little, makes us blush at our weaknesses, and communicates to us something of his warmth and goodness. Such are the effects wrought by perusing the Memoirs, and still more by the correspondence–most strengthening reading for all ages and conditions. No one ever started from a lower point than the poor apprentice of Boston. No one ever raised himself higher by his own unaided forces than the inventor of the lightningrod. No one has rendered greater service to his country than the diplomatist who signed the treaty of 1783, and assured the independence of the United States. Better than the biographies of Plutarch, this life, so long and so well filled, is a source of perpetual instruction to all men. Every one can there find counsel and example. * * * Franklin has never played a part–neither with Others nor with himself. He says what he thinks; he does what he says. He knows but one road which leads from destitution to fortune. He knows of but one mode to arrive at happiness, or, at least, to contentment; it is by labor, economy, and probity. Such is the receipt he gives to his readers; but this receipt he commenced by trying himself. We can believe in a secret with which he himself succeeded. In our democratic society, where every one seeks to better his condition–a very legitimate purpose–nothing is worth so much as the example and the lessons of a man who, without influence and without fortune, became master after having been a laborer–gave himself the education which he lacked, and, by force of toil, privations and courage, raised himself to the first rank in his country, and conquered the admiration and respect of the human race. To have the talent of Franklin, or to be favored as he was by events, is not given to all; but every one may have the honor of following such a model, even without the hope of reaching it".

I will venture to add that in my judgment there never was a time in the history of our country when the lessons of humility, economy, industry, toleration, charity, and patriotism, which are made so captivating in this Autobiography, could be studied with more profit by the rising generation of Americans than now. They have burdens to bear unknown to their ancestors, and problems of government to solve unknown to history. All the qualities, moral and intellectual, that are requisite for a successful encounter with these portentous responsibilities were singularly united in the character of Franklin, and nothing in our literature is so well calculated to reproduce them as his own deliberate record of the manner in which he laid the foundation at once of his own and of his country's greatness.

All the notes to this volume, not credited to other sources, are from the manuscript, and, of course, in Franklin's handwriting.

The notes signed " B." are by the Editor.

Those signed " W. T. F." are by William Temple Franklin.

Those signed " Sparks," are from Dr. Sparks' precious Collection of the Writings of Franklin.

I have rigorously followed the orthography of the MS.; not that I attach much importance to this comparatively mechanical feature of the work, but because I thought it would be satisfactory to many readers to see with what defects of early education its author had successfully contended in reaching a celebrity as yet attained by none of his countrymen.

It will be observed that Franklin followed no system of orthography very strictly. He would spell *public* with a " k," and *music* without a " k." In some participles and adjectives ending in " ed" he would substitute an apostrophe for the final " e;" in others he would give the final syllable in full. *Though* is almost uniformly spelt" tho', *job* with two "b's," and *surf* with two " f's" —*extreme,* " extream."

A few gross mistakes occur, such as "sope," for "soap," etc.; yet as a general rule his orthography conformed to that of his time. It may be said, with entire justice, that he spelled the king's English very much better than the king himself did.

JOHN BIGELOW.

THE SQUIRRELS, *December* 28, 1867.

{Copie d'un Projtt tres Curieux de Benjamin Franklin– Esquisse de ses Memoires. Les additions a *d' lencrek rouge sont de la main de Franklin.*

MY writing. Mrs. Dogood's letters. Differences arise between my Brother and me (his temper and mine); their cause in general. His Newspaper. The Prosecution he suffered. My Examination. Vote of Assembly. His manner of evading it. Whereby I became free. My attempt to get employ with other Printers. He prevents me. Our frequent pleadings before our Father. The final Breach. My Inducements to quit Boston. Manner of coming to a Resolution. My leaving him and going to New York (return to eating flesh); thence to Pennsylvania. The journey, and its events on the Bay, at Amboy. The road. Meet with Dr. Brown. His character. His great work. At Burlington. The Good Woman. On the River. My Arrival at Philadelphia. First Meal and first Sleep. Money left. Employment Lodging. First acquaintance with my afterward Wife. With J. Ralph. With Keimer. Their characters. Osborne. Watson. The Governor takes notice of me. The Occasion and Manner. His character. Offers to set me up. My return to Boston. Voyage and accidents. Reception. My Father dislikes the proposal. I return to New York and Philadelphia. Governor Burnet J. Collins. The Money for Vernon. The Governor's Deceit Collins not finding employment goes to Barbados much in my debt Ralph and I go to England. Disappointment of Governor's Letters. Colonel French his Friend. Cornwallis's Letters. Cabbin. Denham. Hamilton. Arrival in England. Get

---

* This memorandum, probably in the handwriting of M. le Veillard, immediately precedes the Outline in the MS.

employment Ralph not. He is an expense to me. Adventures in England. Write a Pamphlet and print 100. Schemes. Lyons. Dr. Pemberton. My diligence, and yet poor through Ralph. My Landlady. Her character. Wygate. Wilkes. Cibber. Plays. Books I borrowed. Preachers I heard. Redmayne. At Watts's. Temperance. Ghost. Conduct and Influence among the Men. Persuaded by Mr. Denham to return with him to Philadelphia and be his clerk. Our voyage and arrival. My resolutions in Writing. My Sickness. His Death. Found D. R. married. Go to work again with Keimer. Terms. His ill usage of me. My Resentment Saying of Decow. My Friends at Burlington. Agreement with H.Meredith.to set up in Partnership. Do so. Success with the Assembly. Hamilton's Friendship. Sewell's History. Gazette. Paper money. Webb. Writing Busy Body. Breintnal Godfrey. His Character. Suit against us. Offer of my Friends, Coleman and Grace. Continue the Business, and M. goes to Carolina. Pamphlet on Paper Money. Gazette from Keimer. Junto credit; its plan. Marry. Library erected. Manner of conducting the project. Its plan and utility. Children. Almanac. The use I made of it Great industry. Constant study. Father's Remark and Advice upon Diligence. Carolina Partnership. Learn French and German. Journey to Boston after ten years. Affection of my Brother. His Death, and leaving me his Son. Art of Virtue. Occasion. City Watch amended. Postoflice. Spotswood. Bradford's Behavior. Clerk of Assembly. Lose one of my Sons. Project of subordinate Juntos. Write occasionally in the papers. Success in Business. Fire companies. Engines. Go again to Boston in 1743. See Dr. Spence. Whitefield. My connection with him. His generosity to me. My returns. Church Differences. My part in them. Propose a College. Not then prosecuted. Propose and establish a Philosophical Society. War. Electricity. My first knowledge of it. Partnership with D. Hall, &c. Dispute in Assembly upon Defence. Project for it Plain Truth. Its success. Ten thousand

Men raised and disciplined. Lotteries. Battery built New Castle. My influence in the Council. Colors, Devices, and Mottos. Ladies' Military Watch. Quakers chosen of the Common Council. Put in the commission of the peace. Logan fond of me. His Library. Appointed Postmaster-General. Chosen Assemblyman. Commissioner to treat with Indians at Carlisle and at Easton. Project and establish Academy. Pamphlet on it. Journey to Boston. At Albany. Plan of union of the colonies. Copy of it. Remarks upon it. It fails, and how. Journey to Boston in 1754. Disputes about it in our Assembly. My part in them. New Governor. Disputes with him. His character and sayings to me. Chosen Aiderman. Project of Hospital. My share in it. Its success. Boxes. Made a Commissioner of the Treasury. My commission to defend the frontier counties. Raise Men and build Forts. Militia Law of my drawing. Made Colonel. Parade of my Officers. Offence to Proprietor. Assistance to Boston Ambassadors. Journey with Shirley, &c. Meet with Braddock. Assistance to him. To the Officers of his Army. Furnish him with Forage. His concessions to me and character of me. Success of my Electrical Experiments. Medal sent me. Present Royal Society, and Speech of President.Denny's Arrival and Courtship to me. His character. My service to the Army in the affair of Quarters. Disputes about the Proprietor's Taxes continued. Project for paving the City. I am sent to England. Negotiation there. *Canada delenda est.* My Pamphlet. Its reception and effect. Projects drawn from me concerning the Conquest. Acquaintance made and their services to me–Mrs. S. M. Small, Sir John P., Mr. Wood, Sargent Strahan, and others. Their characters. Doctorate from Edinburgh, St Andrew's. Doctorate from Oxford. Journey to Scotland. Lord Leicester. Mr. Prat De Grey. Jackson. State of Affairs in England. Delays. Eventful Journey into Holland and Flanders. Agency from Maryland. Son's appointment.My Return. Allowance and thanks. Journey to Boston. John Penn, Governor. My conduct toward him. The Paxton Murders. My Pamphlet. Rioters march to Philadelphia. Governor retires to my House. My conduct. Sent out to the Insurgents. Turn them back. Little thanks. Disputes revived. Resolutions against continuing under Proprietary Government. Anothe. Pamphlet Cool thoughts. Sent again to England with Petition Negotiation there. Lord H. His character. Agencies from New Jersey, Georgia, Massachusetts. Journey into Germany, 1766. Civilities received there. Gottingen Observations. Ditto into France in 1767. Ditto in 1769. Entertainment there at the Academy. Introduced to the King and the Mesdames, Mad. Victoria and Mrs. Lamagnon. Duc de Chaulnes, M. Beaumont Le Roy, D'Alibard, Nollet. See Journals. Holland. Reprint my papers and add many. Books presented to me from many authors. My Book translated into French. Lightning Kite. Various Discoveries. My manner of prosecuting that Study. King of Denmark invites me to dinner. Recollect my Father's Proverb. Stamp Act. My opposition to it. Recommendation of J. Hughes. Amendment of it. Examination in Parliament. Reputation it gave me. Caressed by Ministry.

Charles Townsend's Act. Opposition to it. Stoves and chimney-plates. Armonica. Acquaintance with Ambassadors. Russian Intimation. Writing in newspapers. Glasses from Germany. Grant of Land in Nova Scotia. Sicknesses. Letters to America returned hither. The consequences. Insurance Office. My character. Costs me nothing to be civil to inferiors; a good deal to be submissive to superiors, &c. &c. Farce of Perpetual Motion. Writing for Jersey Assembly. Hutchinson's Letters. Temple. Suit in Chancery. Abuse before the Privy Council. Lord Hillsborough's character and conduct. Lord Dartmouth. Negotiation to prevent the War. Return to America. Bishop of St. Asaph. Congress. Assembly. Committee of Safety. Chevaux-de-frise. Sent to Boston, to the Camp. To Canada, to Lord Howe. To France. Treaty, &c.

The Autobiography

Twyford, *at the Bishop of St. Asaph's** 1771

DEAR SON: I have ever had pleasure in obtaining any little anecdotes of my ancestors. You may remember the inquiries I made among the

---

* The country-seat of the Bishop of St. Asaph, Dr. Jonathan Shipley, the " good Bishop," as Dr. Franklin used to style him. Their relations were intimate and confidential. In his pulpit, and in the House of Lords, as well as in society, the Bishop always opposed the harsh measures of the Crown toward the Colonies. Franklin thus refers to one of his friendly sermons in a letter to his son William :

"I have sent to Mr. Galloway one of the Bishop of St. Asaph's sermons before your Society for Propagating the Gospel. I would have sent you one, but you will receive it of course as a member. It contains such liberal and generous sentiments relating to the conduct of government here toward America that Sir John Pringle says it was written in compliment to me. But from the intimacy of friendship in which I live with the author, I know he has expressed nothing but what he thinks and feels; and I honor him the more that through the mere hope of doing good he has hazarded the displeasure of the Court, and of course the prospect of further preferment" *Sparks' Works of Franklin* vol. viii. p. 40

The following extract from a letter written to his wife by the Doctor, just after one of his visits to Twyford in 1771, reveals the kind of consideration in which the Doctor was held in that household:

"I spent three weeks in Hampshire at my friend the Bishop of St Asaph's. The Bishop's lady knows what children and grandchildren I have, and their ages; so, when I was to come away on Monday, remains of my relations when you were with me in England, and the journey I undertook for that pur-pose. Imagining it yet unacquainted with, and expecting the enjoyment of a week's

---

the 12th, in the morning, she insisted on me staying that one day longer, that we might together keep my grandson's birthday. At dinner, among other nice things, we had a floating island, which they always particularly have on the birthdays of any of their own six children, who were all but one at table, where there was also a clergyman's widow, now above one hundred years old. The chief toast of the day was Master Benjamin Bache, which the venerable old lady began in a bumper of Mountain. The Bishop's lady politely added: ' And that he may be as good a man as his grandfather.' I said I hoped he would be *much better.* The Bishop, still more complaisant than his lady, said, We will compound the matter and be contented if he should not prove quite so good. This chit-chat is to yourself only, in return for some of yours about your grandson, and must not be read to Sally, and must not be spoken of to anybody else; for you know how people add and alter silly stories that they hear, and make them appear ten times more silly." *Sparks' Works of Franklin* vol vii. p. 538.

The " good Bishop" died on the 9th of December, 1788. In reply to a note from his gifted daughter, Miss Catharine Louisa Shipley, announcing her father's death, Dr. Franklin wrote:

" PHILADELPHIA, 27 *April,* 1789.

" It is only a few days since the kind letter of my dear young friend, dated December 24th, came to my hand. I had before, in the public papers, met with the afflicting news that letter contained. That excellent man has then left us! His departure is a loss not to his family and friends only, but to his nation and to the world; for he was intent on doing good—-had wisdom to devise the means and talents to promote

uninterrupted leisure in my present country retirement, I sit down may be equally agreeable to* you to know the circumstances of my life, many of which you are to write them for you. To which I have besides some other inducements. Having emerged from the poverty and obscurity in which I was born and bred, to a state of affluence and some degree of reputation in the world, and having gone so far through life with a considerable share of felicity, the conducing means I made use of, which with the blessing of God so

---

them. His ' sermon before the Society for Propagating the Gospel,' and his speech intended to have been spoken (on the bill for altering the Charters of the Colony of Massachusetts Bay), are proofs of his ability as well as of his humanity. Had his counsels in those pieces been attended to by ministers, how much bloodshed might have been prevented, and how much expense and disgrace to the nation avoided !

" Your reflections on the constant calmness and composure attending his death are very sensible. Such instances seem to show that the good sometimes enjoy in dying a foretaste of the happy state they are about to enter.

" According to the course of years, I should have quitted this world long before him. I shall, however, not be long in following. I am now in my eighty-fourth year, and the last year has considerably enfeebled me, so that I hardly expect to remain another. You will then, my dear friend, consider this as probably the last". B.

* After the words " agreeable to" the words " some of" were interlined and afterward effaced. The Doctor probably had it in his mind to address his Memoirs to his children or family, but finally concluded to address them to his son, perhaps to secure a freedom in treating the events of his life which he would not have had were he addressing his daughter. The words " some of" may not have been effaced until after he had determined to allow the Memoirs to be printed, which there is reason to believe he had not originally contemplated. B.

well succeeded, my posterity may like to know, as they may find some of them suitable to their own situations, and therefore fit to be imitated.

That felicity, when I reflected on it, has induced me sometimes to say, that were it offered to my choice, I should have no objection to a repetition of the same life from its beginning, only asking the advantages authors have in a second edition to correct some faults of the first. So I might, besides correcting the faults, change some sinister accidents and events of it for others more favorable. But though this were denied, I should still accept the offer. Since such a repetition is not to be expected, the next thing most like living one's life over again seems to be a recollection of that life, and to make that recollection as durable as possible by putting it down in writing.

Hereby, too, I shall indulge the inclination so natural in old men, to be talking of themselves and their own past actions; and I shall indulge it without being tiresome to others, who, through respect to age, might conceive themselves obliged to give me a hearing, since this may be read or not as any one pleases. And, lastly (I may as well confess it, since my denial of it will be believed by nobody), perhaps I shall a good deal gratify my own *vanity.* Indeed, I scarce ever heard or saw the introductory words, " *Without vanity I may say"*, &c., but some vain thing immediately followed. Most people dislike vanity in others, whatever share they have of it themselves; but I give it fair quarter wherever I meet with it, being persuaded that it is often productive of good to the possessor, and to others that are within his sphere of action; and therefore, in many cases, it would not be altogether absurd if a man were to thank God for his vanity among the other comforts of life.*

---

* Some twenty years before he commenced his Memoirs, Franklin threw his mantle over this not unprofitable weakness which he termed Vanity, in a letter to his friend Jared Elliott :

"PHILADELPHIA, *September 12th,* 1751.

" DEAR SIR :

• • • • • • • •

What you mention concerning the love of praise is indeed very true: it reigns more or less in every heart; though we are generally hypocrites, in that respect, and pretend to disregard praise, and our nice, modest ears are offended, forsooth ! with what one of the ancients calls *the sweetest kind of music.* This hypocrisy is only a sacrifice to the pride of others, or to their envy, both which, I think, ought rather to be mortified. The same sacrifice we make when we forbear to *praise ourselves,* which naturally we are all inclined to; and I suppose it was formerly the fashion, or Virgil, that courtly writer, would not have put a speech into the mouth of his hero, which now-a-days we should esteem so great an indecency:

'Sum pius .Eneas • • •
• • • fund super aethera notus'

One of the Romans, I forget who, justified speaking in his own praise by saying: " Every freeman had a right to speak what he thought of himself, as well as of others." That this is a natural inclination appears in that all children show it, and say freely, I am a good boy; am I not a good girl ? and the like, till they have been frequently chid, and told their trumpeter is dead, and that it is unbecoming to sound their own praise, etc. But

Naturam espellas fared, tamen usque recurret

Being forbid to praise themselves, they learn instead of it to censure And now I speak of thanking God, I desire with all humility to acknowledge that I owe the men-

---

others, which is only a roundabout way of praising themselves; for condemning the conduct of another, in any particular, amounts to as much as saying, *I* am so honest, or wise, or good, or prudent, that *I* could not do or approve *of* such an action. This fondness for ourselves, rather than malevolence to others, I take to be the general source of censure and backbiting; and I wish men had not been taught to dam up natural currents, to the overflowing and damage of their neighbor's grounds. Another advantage, methinks, would arise from freely speaking our good thoughts of ourselves, viz. : if we were wrong in them, somebody or other would readily set us right; but now, while we conceal so carefully our vain, erroneous self-opinions, we may carry them to our grave, for who would offer physic to a man that seems to be in health ? And the privilege of recounting freely our own good actions might be an inducement to the doing of them, that we might be enabled to speak of them without being subject to be justly contradicted or charged with falsehood ; whereas now, as we are not allowed to mention them, and it is an uncertainty whether others will take due notice of them or not, we are perhaps the more indifferent about them; so that, upon the whole, I wish the out-of-fashion practice of praising ourselves would, like other old fashions, come round into fashion again. But this, *I* fear, will not be in our time. So we must even be contented with what little praise we can get from one another. And I will endeavor to make you some amends for the trouble of reading this long scrawl by telling you, that I have the sincerest esteem for you, as an ingenious young man, and a good one, which, together, make the valuable member of society. As *such,* I am with great respect and affection, dear sir,

" Your obliged, humble servant,

"B. FRANKLIN."

Sparks Works of Franklin vol viii. p. 52.

There is, perhaps, no more interesting or profitable standard with which to compare men than the terms in which they speak of themselves. The year that Franklin wrote the last pages of his Memoirs, Gibbon commenced his. It is curious to observe the different styles in which the diplomatist and the scholar enumerate vanity among the leading and legitimate motives in which the two most fascinating and most renowned autobiographies in any language had their origin.

tioned happiness of my past life to His kind providence, which lead me to the means I used and gave

---

"A lively desire of knowing and of recording our ancestors so generally prevails that it must depend on the influence of some common principle in the minds of men. We seem to have lived in the persons of our forefathers ; it is the labor and reward of vanity to extend the term of this ideal longevity. Our imagination is always active to enlarge the narrow circle in which nature has confined us. Fifty or a hundred years may be allotted to an individual; but we step forward beyond death with such hopes as religion and philosophy will suggest; and we fill up the silent vacancy that precedes our birth by associating ourselves to the authors of our existence. Our calmer judgment will rather tend to moderate than to suppress the pride of an ancient and worthy race. The satirist may laugh, the philosopher may preach, but Reason herself will respect the prejudices and habits which have been consecrated by the experience of mankind. Few there are who can sincerely despise in others an advantage of which they are secretly ambitious to partake. The knowledge of our own family from a remote period will be always esteemed as an abstract preeminence, since it can never be promiscuously enjoyed; but the longest series of peasants and mechanics would not afford much gratification to the pride of their descendant. We wish to discover our ancestors, but we wish to discover them possessed of ample fortunes, adorned with honorable titles, and holding an eminent rank in the class of hereditary nobles, which has been maintained for the wisest and most beneficial purposes in almost every climate of the globe and in almost every modification of political society. Wherever the distinction of birth is allowed to form a superior order in the State, education and example should always, and will often, produce among them a dignity of sentiment and propriety of conduct, which is guarded from dishonor by their own and the public esteem. If we read of some illustrious line so ancient that it has no beginning, so worthy that it ought to have no end, we sympathize in its various fortunes; nor can we blame the generous enthusiasm, or even the harmless vanity, of those who are allied to the honors of its name. For my own part, could I draw my pedigree from a general, a statesman, or a celebrated author, I should study their lives with the diligence of filial love. In the investigation of past events, our curiosity is stimulated by the immediate or indirect reference to ourselves; but in the estimate of honor we should learn to value the gifts of nature above those of fortune; to esteem in them success. My belief of this induces me to *hope,* though I must not *presume,* that the same goodness

---

our ancestors the qualities that best promote the interests of society; and to pronounce the descendant *of a* king less truly noble than the offspring of a man of genius, whose writings will instruct or delight the latest posterity. The family of Confucius is in my opinion the most illustrious in the world. After a painful ascent of eight or ten centuries, our barons and princes of Europe are lost in the darkness of the Middle Ages; but in the vast equality of the empire of China the posterity of Confucius have maintained, above two thousand two hundred years, their peaceful honors and perpetual succession. The chief of the family is still revered, by the sovereign and the people, as the lively image of the wisest of mankind. The nobility of the Spencers has been illustrated and enriched by the trophies of Marlborough; but I exhort them to consider the Faery Queen* as the most precious jewel of their coronet. Our immortal Fielding was of the younger branch of the Earls of Denbigh, who draw their origin from the Counts of Denbigh, who draw their origin from the Counts of Hapsburg, the lineal descendants of Enrico, in the seventh century, Duke of Alsace. Far different have been the fortunes of the English and German divisions of the family of Hapsburg: the former, the Knights and Sheriffs of Leicestershire, have slowly risen to the dignity of a peerage; the latter, the Emperors of Germany and Kings of Spain, have threatened the liberty of the Old, and invaded the treasures of the New World. The successors of Charles the Fifth may disdain their brethren of England ; but the romance of Tom Jones, that exquisite picture of human manners, will outlive the palace of the Escurial and the imperial eagle of the house of Austria. That these sentiments are just, or at least natural, I am the more inclined to believe as I am not myself interested in the cause; for I can derive from my ancestors neither glory nor shame. Yet a sincere and simple narrative of my own life may amuse some of my leisure hours ; but it will subject me, and perhaps with justice, to the imputation of vanity. I may judge, however, from the experience both of past and of the present times, that the public are always curious to know the men who have left behind them any image of their minds; the most scanty

Nor less praiseworthy are the ladies three,
The honor of that noble familie,
Of which I meanest boast myself to be.

SPENCER, *Colin Clout,&c.,* v. 538.

will still be exercised toward me, in continuing that happiness, or enabling me to bear a fatal reverse,

---

accounts of such men are compiled with diligence and perused with eagerness; and the student of every class may derive a lesson, or an example, from the lives most similar to his own. My name may hereafter be placed among the thousand articles of a Biographia Britannica; and I must be conscious that no one is so well qualified as myself to describe the series of my thoughts and actions. The authority of my masters, of the grave Thuanus and the philosophic Hume, might be sufficient to justify my design; but it would not be difficult to produce a long list of ancients and modens who, in various forms, have exhibited their own portraits. Such portraits are often the most interesting, and sometimes the only interesting, parts of their writings; and, if they be sincere, we seldom complain of the minuteness or prolixity of these personal memorials. The lives of the younger Pliny, of Petrarch and of Erasmus, are expressed in the epistles which they themselves have given to the world; the essays of Montagne and Sir William Temple bring us home to the houses and bosoms of the authors. We smile without contempt at the headstrong passions of Benvenuto Cellini and the gay follies of Colley Cibber. The Confessions of St. Austin and Rousseau disclose the secrets of the human heart; the Commentaries of the learned Huet have survived his evangelical demonstration ; and the Memoirs of Goldoni are more truly dramatic than his Italian comedies. The heretic and the churchman are strongly marked in the characters and fortunes of Whiston and Bishop Newton; and even the dullness of Michael de Marolles and Anthony Wood acquires some value from the faithful representation of men and manners. That I am equal or superior to some of these, the effects of modesty or affectation cannot force me to dissemble."

Hume, whose account of his own life was written in 1776, the year he died, and five years after Franklin's was begun, commences and concludes his less pretending story with a similar confession. He commences by saying :

" It is difficult for a man to speak long of himself without vanity; therefore I shall be short. It may be thought an instance of vanity that I pretend at all to write my life; but this narrative shall contain little more than the history of my writings, as, indeed, almost all my life has been spent in literary pursuits and occupations. The first success of most of my writings was not such as to be an object of vanity."

which I may experience as others have done; the complexion of my future fortune being known to Him only in whose power it is to bless to us even our afflictions.

The notes one of my uncles (who had the same kind of curiosity in collecting family anecdotes) once put into my hands, furnished me with several particulars relating to our ancestors. From these notes I learned that the family had lived in the same village, Ecton, in Northamptonshire, for three hundred years, and how much longer he knew not (perhaps from the time when the name of Franklin, that be-

---

He concludes as follows:

" I am, or rather was (for that is the style I must now use in speaking of myself, which emboldens me the more to speak my sentiments); I was, I say, a man of mild dispositions, of command of temper, of an open, social and cheerful humor, capable of attachment, but little susceptible of enmity, and of great moderation in all my passions. Even my love of literary fame, my ruling passion, never soured my temper, notwithstanding my frequent disappointments. My company was not unacceptable to the young and careless, as well as to the studious and literary; and as I took a particular pleasure in the company of modest women, I had no reason to be displeased with the reception I met with from them. In a word, though most men anywise eminent have found reason to complain of calumny, I never was touched, or even attacked by her baleful tooth; and though I want only exposed myself to the rage of both civil and religious factions, they seemed to be disarmed in my behalf of their wonted fury. My friends never had occasion to vindicate any one circumstance of my character and conduct; not but that the zealots, we may well suppose, would have been glad to invent and propagate any story to my disadvantage, but they could never find any which they thought would wear the face of probability. I cannot say there is no vanity in making this funeral oration of myself, but I hope it is not a misplaced one; and this is a matter of fact which is easily cleared and ascertained."

fore was the name of an order of people, was assumed by them as a surname when others took surnames all over the kingdom*), on a freehold of about thirty acres, aided by the smith's business, which had continued in the family till his time, the eldest son being always bred to that business; a custom which he and my father followed as to their eldest sons. When I searched the registers at Ecton, I found an account of their births, marriages and burials from the year 1555 only, there being no registers kept in that parish at any time preceding. By that register I perceived that I was the youngest son the youngest son for five generations back. My grand

---

* As a proof that Franklin was anciently the common name of an order or rank in England, see Judge Fortescue's *De Laudibus Legum Anglia,* written about the year 1412, in which is the following passage, to show that good juries might easily be formed in any part of England: " Regio etiam illa, ita respersa refertaque est possessoribus terrarum et agrorum, quod in ea, villula tarn parva reperiri non poterit, in qua non est miles, armiger, vel pater-familias, qualis ibidem Franleri vulgariter nuncupatur, magnis ditatus possessionibus, nec non libere tenentes et alii valecti plurimi, suis patrimoniis sufficientes ad faciendum juratam, in formfi praenotata." Moreover, the same country is so filled and replenished with landed menne, that therein so small a thorpe cannot be found wherein dweleth not a knight, an esquire, or such an householder, as is there commonly called a Franklin, enriched with great possessions; and also other freeholders and many yeomen able for their livelihoodes to make a jury in form aforementioned.—*Old Translation.*
Chaucer, too, calls his country gentleman a Franklin, and, after describing his good housekeeping, thus characterizes him :

"This worthy Franklin has a purse of silk,
Fixed to his girdle, white as morning milk.
Knight of the Shire, first Justice at the Assize,
To help the poor, the doubtful to advise.
In all employments, generous, just, he proved,
Renowned for courtesy, by all beloved."

father Thomas, who was born in 1598, lived at Ecton till he grew too old to follow business longer, when he went to live with his son John, a dyer at Banbury, in Oxfordshire, with whom my father served an apprenticeship. There my grandfather died and lies buried. We saw his gravestone in 1758. His eldest son Thomas lived in the house at Ecton, and left it with the land to his only child, a daughter, who, with her husband, one Fisher, of Wellingborough, sold it to Mr. Isted, now lord of the manor there. My grandfather had four sons that grew up, viz.: Thomas, John, Benjamin and Josiah. I will give you what account I can of them, at this distance from my papers, and if these are not lost in my absence, you will among them find many more particulars.*

---

* The following is a copy of an original letter, which is in the hands of the publisher in Philadelphia; it is a curious relic, and was found among the wreck of Dr. Franklin's papers several years ago:

"*From Josiah to B. Franklin:*

" Loving Son : As to the original of our name, there is various opinions ; some say that it came from a sort of title, of which a book that you bought when here gives a lively account. Some think we are of a French extract, which was formerly called Franks; some of a free line, a line free from that vassalage which was common to subjects in days of old; some from a bird of long red legs. Your uncle Benjamin made inquiry of one skilled in heraldry, who told him there is two coats of armor, one belonging to the Franklins of the North, and one to the Franklins of the West. However, our circumstances have been such as that it hath hardly been worth while to concern ourselves much about these things any farther than to tickle the fancy a little. The first that I can give account of, is my great-grandfather, as it was a custom in those days among young men too many times to goe to seek their for-

Thomas was bred a smith under his father; but, being ingenious, and encouraged in learning (as all

---

tunes, and in his travels he went upon liking to a taylor; but he kept such a stingy house, that he left him and travelled farther, and came to asmith's house, and coming on a fasting day, being in popish times, he did not like there the first day; the next morning the servant was called up at five in the morning, but after a little time came a good toast and good beer, and he found good housekeeping there; he served and learned the trade of a smith. In Queen Mary's days, either his wife, or my grand-mother, by father's side, informed my father that they kept their Bible fastened under the top of a joint-stool, that they might turn up thebook and read in the Bible, that when anybody came to the dore they turned up the stool for fear of the aparitor, for if it was discovered they would be in hazard of their lives. My grandfather was a smith also,and settled in Eton, in Northamptonshire, and he was imprisoned a year and a day on suspicion of his being the author of some poetry that touched the character of some great man. He had only one son and one daughter; my grandfather's name was Thomas, my mother's namewas Jane. My father was bom at Ecton or Eton, Northamptonshire,on the 18th of October, 1698; married to Miss Jane White, niece to Coll. White, of Banbury, and died in the 84th year of his age. There was nine children of us, who were happy in our parents, who took great care by their instructions and pious example to breed us up in a religiousway. My eldest brother had but one child, which was married to one Mr. Fisher, at Wallingborough, in Northamptonshire. The town was lately burnt down, and whether she was a sufferer or not I cannot tell,or whether she be living or not. Her father dyed worth fifteen hundred pounds, but what her circumstances are now I know not. She hath no child. If you by the freedom of your office, makes it more likely to convey a letter to her, it would be acceptable to me. There is also children of brother John and sister Morris, but I hear nothing from them, and they write not to me, so that I know not where to find them. I have been again to about seeing * * * *, but have mist of being informed."We received yours, and are glad to hear poor Jammy is recovered so well. Son John received the letter, but is so busy just now that he cannot write you an answer, but will do the best he can. Now with hearty love to, and prayer for you all, I rest your affectionate father,

"BOSTON, *May* 26,1739."

"JOSIAH FRANKLIN.

W. T. F.

my brothers were) by an Esquire Palmer, then the principal gentleman in that parish, he qualified himself for the business of scrivener; became a considerable man in the county; was a chief mover of all public-spirited undertakings for the county or town of Northampton, and his own village, of which many instances were related of him ; and much taken notice of and patronized by the then Lord Halifax. He died in 1702, January 6, old style, just four years to a day before I was born. The account we received of his life and character from some old people at Ecton, I remember, struck you as something extraordinary, from its similarity to what you knew of mine.

"Had he died on the same day, you said, ''one might have supposed a transmigration."

John was bred a dyer, I believe of woolens. Benjamin was bred a silk dyer, serving an apprenticeship at London. He was an ingenious man. I remember him well, for when I was a boy he came over to my father in Boston, and lived in the house with us some years. He lived to a great age. His grandson, Samuel Franklin, now lives in Boston. He left behind him two quarto volumes, MS., of his own poetry, consisting of little occasional pieces addressed to his friends and relations, of which the following, sent to me, is a specimen.*

---

* Here follows in the margin the words, in brackets, " here insert it," but the poetry is not given. Mr. Sparks informs us (Life of Franklin, p. 6) that these volumes had been preserved, and were in possession of

He had formed a shorthand of his own, which he taught me, but, never practising it, I have now forgot it. I was named after this uncle, there being a particular affection between him and my father.

Mrs. Emmons, of Boston, great-granddaughter of their author. The following are specimens quoted by Mr. Sparks :

" Sent to his namesake, upon a Report of his Inclination to Martial Affairs, July 7th, 1710:

" Believe me, Ben, it is a dangerous trade,
The sword has many marred as well as made;
By it do many fall, not many rise,
Makes many poor, few rich, and fewer wise;
Fills towns with ruin, fields with blood ; beside '
Tis sloth's maintainer, and the shield of pride.
Fair cities, rich to-day in plenty flow,
War fills with want to-morrow, and with woe.
Ruined estates, the nurse of vice, broke limbs and scars,
Are the effects of desolating wars."

" ACROSTIC,

" Sent to Benjamin Franklin in New England, July 15th, 1710 :

" Be to thy parents an obedient son ;
Each day let duty constantly be done;
Never give way to sloth, or lust, or pride,
If free you'd be from thousand ills beside ;
Above all ills be sure avoid the shelf;
Man's danger lies in Satan, sin, and self
in virtue, learning, wisdom, progress make;
Ne'er shrink at suffering for thy Saviour's sake.

" Fraud and all falsehood in thy dealings flee,
Religious always in thy station be;
Adore the Maker of thy inward part,
Now's the accepted time, give him thy heart;
Keep a good conscience, 'tis a constant friend;
Like judge and witness this thy acts attend.
In heart with bended knee, alone, adore
None but the Three in One for evermore."

The following piece was sent when his namesake was seven years old. It would appear that he had received from him some evidence of his juvenile skill in composition :

He was very pious, a great attender of sermons of the best preachers, which he took down in his short-hand, and had with him many volumes of them. He was also much of a politician; too much, perhaps, for his station. There fell lately into my hands, in London, a collection he had made of all the principal pamphlets relating to public affairs, from 1641 to 1717 ; many of the volumes are wanting as appears by the numbering, butt here

" Sent to Benjamin Franklin, 1713 :

" Tis time for me to throw aside my pen,
When hanging sleeves read, write, and rhyme like men.
This forward spring foretells a plenteous crop;
For if the bud bear grain, what will the top ?
If plenty in the verdant blade appear,
What may we not soon hope *for* in the ear?
When flowers are beautiful before they're blown,
What rarities will afterward be shown !
If trees good fruit un'noculated bear,
You may be sure 'twill afterward be rare.
If fruits are sweet before they're time to yellow,
How luscious will they be when they are mellow!
If first year's shoots such noble clusters send,
What laden boughs, Engedi like, may we expect in the end !"

These lines are more prophetic, perhaps, than the writer imagined. *Sparks.*

This uncle Benjamin died in Boston, in 1728, leaving one son, Samuel, the only survivor of ten children. This son had an only child, who died in 1775, leaving four daughters. There are now no male descendants of Dr. Franklin's grandfather living who bear his name. The Doctor's eldest son William left one son, William Temple Franklin, who died without issue, bearing his name. His second son, Francis Folger, died when about four years of age. His very clever daughter Sarah married Richard Bache in 1767. Their descendants are–Benjamin Franklin Bache, who married Margaret Marcoe; William, who married Catharine Wistar; Deborah, who married William J. Duane; Richard, who married a daughter of Alexander J. Dallas; Sarah, who married Thomas Sargeant, together with their children.

still remain eight volumes in folio, and twenty-four in quarto and in octavo. A dealer in old books met with them, and knowing me by my sometimes buying of him, he brought them to me. It seems my uncle must have left them here when he went to America, which was above fifty years since. There are many of his notes in the margins.*

---

* The Doctor refers to this *trouvaille* in one of his letters to Samuel Franklin, as follows:

" LONDON, 12 JULY, 1771.

"LOVING COUSIN : I received your kind letter of May 17th, and rejoice to hear that you and your good family are well. My love to them. With this I send you the print you desire for Mr. Bowen. He does me honor in accepting it. Sally Franklin presents her duty to you and Mrs. Franklin. Yesterday a very odd accident happened, which I must mention to you, as it relates to your grandfather. A person that deals in old books, of whom I sometimes buy, acquainted me that he had a curious collection of pamphlets bound in eight volumes folio, and twenty- four volumes quarto and octavo, which he thought from the subjects I might like to have, and that he would sell them cheap. I desired to see them, and he brought them to me. On examining, I found that they contained all the principal pamphlets and papers on public affairs that had been printed here from the Restoration down to 1715. In one of the blank leaves at the beginning of each volume the collector had written the titles of the pieces contained in it, and the price they cost him. Also notes in the margin of many of the pieces; and the collector, I find, from the handwriting and various other circumstances, was your grandfather, my uncle Benjamin. Wherefore, I the more readily agreed to buy them. I suppose he parted with them when he left England and came to Boston, soon after your father, which was about the year 1716 or 1717, now more than fifty years since. In whose hands they have been all this time I know not. The oddity is, that the bookseller, who could suspect nothing of any relation between me and the collector, should happen to make me the offer of them. My love to your good wife and children.

" Your affectionate cousin,

"B. FRANKLIN."

This obscure family of ours was early in the Reformation, and continued Protestants through the reign of Queen Mary, when they were sometimes in danger of trouble on account of their zeal against popery. They had got an English Bible, and to conceal and secure it, it was fastened open with tapes under and within the cover of a joint-stool. When my great-great-grandfather read it to his family, he turned up the joint-stool upon his knees, turning over the leaves then under the tapes. One of the children stood at the door to give notice if he saw the apparitor coming, who was an officer of the spiritual court. In that case the stool was turned down again upon its feet, when the Bible remained concealed under it as before. This anecdote I had from my uncle Benjamin. The family continued all of the Church of England till about the end of Charles the Second's reign, when some of the ministers that had been outed for non-conformity holding conventicles in Northamptonshire, Benjamin and Josiah adhered to them, and so continued all their lives: the rest of the family remained with the Episcopal Church.

Josiah, my father, married young, and carried his wife with three children into New England, about 1682. The conventicles having been forbidden by law, and frequently disturbed, induced some considerable men of his acquaintance to remove to that country, and he was prevailed with to accompany them thither, where they expected to enjoy their mode of religion with freedom. By the same wife he had four children more born there, and by a second wife ten more, in all seventeen; of which I remember thirteen sitting at one time at his table, who all grew up to be men and women, and married ; I was the youngest son, and the youngest child but two, and was born in Boston, New England.* My mother, the second wife, was Abiah Folger, daughter of Peter Folger, one of the first settlers of New England, of whom honorable mention is made by Cotton Mather, in his church history of that country, entitled Magnalia Christi Americana, as " *a godly, learned Englishman"* if I remember the words rightly. I have heard that he wrote sundry small occasional pieces, but only one of them was printed, which I saw now many years since. It was written in 1675, in the home-spun verse of that time and people, and addressed to those then concerned in the government there. It was in favor of liberty of conscience, and in behalf of the Baptists, Quakers, and other sectaries that had been under persecution,ascribing the Indian wars, and other distresses that had befallen the country, to that persecution, as so many judgments of God to punish so heinous an offense, and exhorting a repeal of those uncharitable laws. The whole appeared to me as written with a good deal of decent plainness and manly freedom. The six concluding lines I remember, though I have forgotten the two first of the stanza; but the purport of them was, that his censures proceeded from goodwill, and, therefore he would be known to be the author.

---

* He was born January 6th, 1706, old style, being Sunday, and the same as January 17th, new style, which his biographers have usually mentioned as the day of his birth. By the records of the Old South Church in Boston,, to which his father and mother belonged, it appears that he was baptized the same day. In the old public Register of Births, still preserved in the Mayor's Office in Boston, his birth is recorded under the date of January 6th, 1706. At this time his father occupied a house in Milk street, opposite to the Old South Church, but he removed shortly afterward to a house at the corner of Hanover and Union streets, where it is believed he resided the remainder of his life, and where the son passed his early years.—*Sparks.*

" Because to be a libeller (says he)
I hate it with heart;
From Sherburne* town, where now I dwell
My name I do put here;
Without offense your real friend,
It is Peter Folgier."†

---

* The poem, if such it may be called, of which these are the closing lines, extends through fourteen pages of a duodecimo pamphlet, entitled "A Looking-Glass for the Times; or the former spirit of New England revived in this generation, by Peter Folger." It is dated at the end, " April 23rd, 1676." The lines, which immediately precede those quoted by Dr. Franklin, and which are necessary to complete the sentiment intended to be conveyed by the author, are the following :

" I am for peace and not for war,
And that's the reason why
I write more plain than some men do,
That use to daub and lie.
But I shall cease, and set my name
To what I here insert,
Because to be a libeler
I hate it with my heart".

† The author's muse speaks even in the title-page, and explains to the reader his design in writing the " Looking-Glass for the Times:

"Let all that read these verses know,
That I intend something to show

My elder brothers were all put apprentices to different trades. I was put to the grammar-school at eight years of age, my father intending to devote me, as the tithe of his sons, to the service of the Church. My early readiness in learning to read (which must have been very early, as I do not remember when I could not read), and the opinion of all his friends, that I should certainly make a good scholar, encouraged him in this purpose of his. My uncle Benjamin, too, approved of it, and proposed to give me all his short-hand volumes of sermons, I suppose as a stock to set up with, if I would learn his character. I continued, however, at the gram- mar-school not quite one year, though in that time I had risen gradually from the middle of the class of that year to be the head of it, and farther was removed into the next class above it, in order to go with that into the third at the end of the year. But my father, in the mean time, from a view of the expense of a college education, which having so large a family he could not well afford, and the mean living many so educated were afterwards able to obtain–reasons that he gave to his friends in my hearing–altered his first intention, took me from the grammar-school, and sent me to a school for writing and arithmetic,

---

About our war, how it hath been, And also what is the chief sin, That God doth so with us contend, And when these wars are like to end, Read then in love; do not despise What here is set before thine eyes."–*Sparks.*

kept by a then famous man, Mr. George Brownell, very successful in his profession generally, and that by mild, encouraging methods. Under him I acquired fair writing pretty soon, but I failed in the arithmetic, and made no progress in it. At ten years old I was taken home to assist my father in his business, which was that of a tallow-chandler and sope-boiler; a business he was not bred to, but had assumed on his arrival in New England, and on finding his dying trade would not maintain his family, being in little request. Accordingly, I was employed in cutting wick for the candles, filling the dipping mold and the molds for cast candles, attending the shop, going of errands, etc.

I disliked the trade, and had a strong inclination for the sea, but my father declared against it; however, living near the water, I was much in and about it, learnt early to swim well, and to manage boats; and when in a boat or canoe with other boys, I was commonly allowed to govern, especially in any case of difficulty; and upon other occasions I was generally a leader among the boys, and sometimes led them into scrapes, of which I will mention one instance, as it shows an early projecting public spirit, tho' not then justly conducted.

There was a salt-marsh that bounded part of the mill-pond, on the edge of which, at high water, we used to stand to fish for minnows. By much trampling, we had made it a mere quagmire. My proposal was to build a wharff there fit for us to stand upon, and I showed my comrades a large heap of stones, which were intended for a new house near the marsh, and which would very well suit our purpose. Accordingly, in the evening, when the workmen were gone, I assembled a number of my play-fellows, and working with them diligently like so many emmets, sometimes two or three to a stone, we brought them all away and built our little wharff. The next morning the workmen were surprised at missing the stones, which were found in our wharff. Inquiry was made after the removers; we were discovered and complained of; several of us were corrected by our fathers; and, though I pleaded the usefulness of the work, mine convinced me that nothing was useful which was not honest.

I think you may like to know something of his person and character. He had an excellent constitution of body, was of middle stature, but well set, and very strong; he was ingenious, could draw prettily, was skilled a little in music, and had a clear pleasing voice, so that when he played psalm tunes on his violin and sung withal, as he sometimes did in an evening after the business of the day was over, it was extremely agreeable to hear. He had a mechanical genius too, and, on occasion, was very handy in the use of other tradesmen's tools; but his great excellence lay in a sound understanding and solid judgment in prudential matters, both in private and publics affairs. In the latter, indeed, he was never employed, the numerous family he had to educate

she suckled all her ten children. I never knew either my father or mother to have any sickness but that of which they dy'd, he at 89, and she at 85 years of age. They lie buried together at Boston, where I some years since placed a marble over their grave, with this inscription :

JOSIAH FRANKLIN,
and
ABIAH his wife,
lie here interred.
They lived lovingly together in wedlock
fifty-five years.
Without an estate, or any gainful employment,

By constant labor and industry,
with God's blessing,
They maintained a large family
comfortably,
and brought up thirteen children
and seven grandchildren
reputably.
From this instance, reader,
Be encouraged to diligence in thy calling,
And distrust not Providence.
He was a pious and prudent man ;
She, a discreet and virtuous woman.
Their youngest son,
In filial regard to their memory,
Places this stone.
J. F. born 1655, died 1744, 89.
A. F. born 1667, died 1752, 85.*

* The marble stone on which this inscription was engraved having become decayed, and the inscription itself defaced by time, a more durable monument has been erected over the graves of the father and mother of Franklin. The suggestion was first made at a meeting of the Building Committee of the Bunker Hill Monument Association in the autumn of 1826, and it met with universal approbation. A committee of managers was organized, and an amount of money adequate Tr

By my rambling digressions I perceive myself to be grown old. I us'd to write more methodically. But one does not dress for private company as for a publick ball. Tis perhaps only negligence.

– To return: I continued thus employed in my to the object was soon contributed by the voluntary subscriptions of a large number of the citizens of Boston. The cornerstone was laid on the 15th of June, 1827, and an address appropriate to the occasion was pronounced by General Henry A. S. Dearborn. The monument is an obelisk of granite, twenty-one feet high, which rests on a square base measuring seven feet on each side and two feet in height. The obelisk is composed of five massive blocks of granite, placed one above another. On one side is the name of Franklin in large bronze letters, and a little below is a tablet of bronze, thirty-two inches long and sixteen wide, sunk into the stone. On this tablet is engraven Dr. Franklin's original inscription, as quoted in the text, and beneath it are the following lines :

THE MARBLE TABLET,
Bearing the above inscription,
Having been dilapidated by the ravages of time,
A number of citizens,
Entertaining the most profound veneration
For the memory of the illustrious
BENJAMIN FRANKLIN,
And desirous of reminding succeeding generations
That he was born in Boston,
A. D. MDCCVI.,
Erected this
Obelisk
Over the grave of his parents,
MDCCCXXVII.

A silver plate was deposited under the cornerstone, with an inscription commemorative of the occasion, a part of which is as follows: " This monument was erected over the remains of the parents of Benjamin Franklin by the citizens of Boston, from respect to the private character and public services of this illustrious patriot and philosopher, and for the many tokens of his affectionate attachment to his native town."—*Sparks.*

father's business for two years, that is, till I was twelve years old; and my brother John, who was bred to that business, having left my father, married, and set up for himself at Rhode Island, there was all appearance that I was destined to supply his place, and become a tallow-chandler. But my dislike to the trade continuing, my father was under apprehensions that if he did not find one for me more agreeable, I should break away and get to sea, as his son Josiah had done, to his great vexation. He therefore sometimes took me to walk with him, and see joiners, bricklayers, turners, braziers, etc., at their work, that he might observe my inclination, and endeavor to fix it on some trade or other on land. It has ever since been a pleasure to me to see good workmen handle their tools; and it has been useful to me, having learnt so much by it as to be able to do little jobs myself in my house when a workman could not readily be got, and to construct little machines for my experiments, while the intention of making the experiment was fresh and warm in my mind. My father at last fixed upon the cutler's trade, and my uncle Benjamin's son Samuel, who was bred to that business in London, being about that time established in Boston, I was sent to be with him some time on liking. But his expectations of a fee with me displeasing my father, I was taken home again.

From a child I was fond of reading, and all the little money that came into my hands was ever laidout in books. Pleased with the Pilgrim's Progress, my first collection was of John Bunyan's works in separate little volumes. I afterward sold them to enable me to buy R. Burton's Historical Collections; they were small chapmen's books, and cheap, 40 or 50 in all. My father's little library consisted chiefly of books in polemic divinity, most of which I read, and have since often regretted that, at a time when I had such a thirst for knowledge, more proper books had not fallen in my way, since it was now resolved I should not be a clergyman. Plutarch's Lives there was in which I read abundantly, and I still think that time spent to great advantage. There was also a book of De Foe's, called an Essay on Projects, and another of Dr. Mather's, called Essays to do Good, which perhaps gave me a turn of thinking that had an influence on some of the principal future events of my life.

This bookish inclination at length determined my father to make me a printer, though he had already one son (James) of that profession. In 1717 my brother James returned from England with a press and letters to set up his business in Boston. I liked it much better than that of my father, but still had a hankering for the sea. To prevent the apprehended effect of such an inclination, my father was impatient to have me bound to my brother. I stood out some time, but at last was persuaded, and signed the indentures when I was yet but twelve years old. I was to serve as an apprentice till I was twenty-one years of age, only I was to be allowed journeyman's wages during the last year. In a little time I made great proficiency in the business, and became a useful hand to my brother. I now had access to better books. An acquaintance with the apprentices of booksellers enabled me sometimes to borrow a small one, which I was careful to return soon and clean. Often I sat up in my room reading the greatest part of the night, when the book was borrowed in the evening and to be returned early in the morning, lest it should be missed or wanted.

And after some time an ingenious tradesman, Mr. Matthew Adams, who had a pretty collection of books, and who frequented our printing-house, took notice of me, invited me to his library, and very kindly lent me such books as I chose to read. I now took a fancy to poetry, and made some little pieces; my brother, thinking it might turn to account, encouraged me, and put me on composing occasional ballads. One was called *The Lighthouse Tragedy*, and contained an account of the drowning of Captain Worthilake, with his two daughters : the other was a sailor's song, on the taking of *Teach* (or Blackbeard) the pirate. They were wretched stuff, in the Grub-street-ballad style; and when they were printed he sent me about the town to sell them. The first sold wonderfully, the event being recent, having made a great noise. This flattered my vanity ; but my father discouraged me by ridiculing my performances, and tellingme verse-makers were generally beggars. So I escaped being a poet, most probably a very bad one; but as prose writing has been of great use to me in the course of my life, and was a principal means of my advancement, I shall tell you how, in such a situation, I acquired what little ability I have in that way.

There was another bookish lad in the town, John Collins by name, with whom I was intimately acquainted. We sometimes disputed, and very fond we were of argument, and very desirous of confuting one another, which disputatious turn, by the way, is apt to become a very bad habit, making people often extremely disagreeable in company by the contradiction that is necessary to bring it into practice; and thence, besides souring and spoiling the conversation, is productive of disgusts and, perhaps enmities where you may have occasion for friendship. I had caught it by reading my father's books of dispute about religion. Persons of good sense, I have since observed, seldom fall into it, except lawyers, university men, and men of all sorts that have been bred at Edinborough.

A question was once, somehow or other, started between Collins and me, of the propriety of educating the female sex in learning, and their abilities for study. He was of opinion that it was improper, and that they were naturally unequal to it. I took the contrary side, perhaps a little for dispute's sake. He was naturally more eloquent, had a ready plenty of words; and sometimes, as I thought, bore me down more by his fluency than by the strength of his reasons. As we parted without settling the point, and were not to see one another again for some time, I sat down to put my arguments in writing, which I copied fair and sent to him. He answered, and I replied. Three or four letters of a side had passed, when my father happened to find my papers and read them. Without entering into the discussion, he took occasion to talk to me about the manner of my writing; observed that, though I had the advantage of my antagonist in correct spelling and pointing (which I ow'd to the printing-house), I fell far short in elegance of expression, in method and in perspicuity, of which he convinced me by several instances. I saw the justice of his remarks, and thence grew more attentive to the manner in writing, and determined to endeavor at improvement.

About this time I met with an odd volume of the *Spectator*. It was the third. I had never before seen any of them. I bought it, read it over and over, and was much delighted with it. I thought the writing excellent, and wished, if possible, to imitate it. With this view I took some of the papers, and, making short hints of the sentiment in each sentence, laid them by a few days, and then, without looking at the book, try'd to complete at the papers again, by expressing each hinted sentiment at length, and as fully as it had been expressed before, in any suitable words that should come to hand. Then I compared my *Spectator* with the original, discovered some of my faults, and corrected them. But I found I wanted a stock of words, or a readiness in recollecting and using them, which I thought I should have acquired before that time if I had gone on making verses; since the continual occasion for words of the same import, but of different length, to suit the measure, or of different sound for the rhyme, would have laid me under a constant necessity of searching for variety, and also have tended to fix that variety in my mind, and make me master of it. Therefore I took some of the tales and turned them into verse; and, after a time, when I had pretty well forgotten the prose, turned them back again. I also sometimes jumbled my collections of hints into confusion, and after some weeks endeavored to reduce them into the best order, before I began to form the full sentences and compleat the paper. This was to teach me method in the arrangement of thoughts. By comparing my work afterwards with the original, I discovered many faults and amended them ; but I sometimes had the pleasure of fancying that, in certain particulars of small import, I had been lucky enough to improve the method or the language, and this encouraged me to think I might possiblty in time come to be a tolerable English writer, of which I was extreamly ambitious. My time for these exercises and for reading was at night, after work or before it began in the morning, or on Sundays, when I contrived to be in the printinghouse alone, evading as much as I could the common attendance on public worship which my father used to exact of me when I was under his care, and which indeed I still thought a duty, though I could not, as it seemed to me, afford time to practise it.

When about 16 years of age I happened to meet with a book, written by one Tryon, recommending a vegetable diet. I determined to go into it. My brother, being yet unmarried, did not keep house, but boarded himself and his apprentices in another family. My refusing to eat flesh occasioned an inconveniency, and I was frequently chid for my singularity. I made myself acquainted with Tryon's manner of preparing some of his dishes, such as boiling potatoes or rice, making hasty pudding, and a few others, and then proposed to my brother, that if he would give me, weekly, half the money he paid for my board, I would board myself. He instantly agreed to it, and I presently found that I could save half what he paid me. This was an additional fund for buying books. But I had another advantage in it. My brother and the rest going from the printing-house to their meals, I remained there alone, and, despatching presently my light repast, which often was no more than a bisket or a slice of bread, a handful of raisins or a tart from the pastry-cook's, and a glass of water, had the rest of the time till their return for study, in which I made the greater progress, from that greater clearness of head and quicker apprehension which usually attend temperance in eating and drinking.

And now it was that, being on some occasion made asham'd of my ignorance in figures, which I had twice failed in learning when at school, I took Cocker's book of Arithmetick, and went through the whole by myself with great ease. I also read Seller's and Shermy's books of Navigation, and became acquainted with the little geometry they contain; but never proceeded far in that science. And I read about this time Locke *on Human Understandings* and the *Art of Thinkings* by Messrs, du Port Royal.*

---

* Cabanis, in the notice which he prepared of Franklin shortly after the philosopher's death, says, in reference to his reading at this time : "We have it also from him that about this time, for the first, he read a very bad translation of the Provincial Letters. He was ravished by them. He read them over many times. They were one of the French books he most esteemed."—*Euvres Complets,* vol. v., p. 228.

The discrepancy between these two statements provokes the remark that at the time Franklin wrote this portion of the Memoirs he did not know Cabanis. It is probable that he read and was much impressed by both works, and at different epochs of his life and with different persons dwelt sometimes upon the importance of one and sometimes of the other to his intellectual training.

Speaking of the three particular books which may have remotely contributed to form the historian of the Roman Empire, Gibbon says:

" From the Provincial Letters of Pascal, which almost every year I have perused with new pleasure, I learned to manage the weapon of grave and temperate irony even on subjects of ecclesiastical solemnity."—*Miscellaneous Works of Gibbon,* in 5 vols., vol. i. p. 96.

Reasoning *post hoc propter hoc,* Franklin might have made the same confession with equal propriety. Not Gibbon himself was a master of a more refined and decorous irony. I will venture to give an illustration of his skill in the management of this most dangerous weapon

While I was intent on improving my language, I met with an English grammar (I think it was Greenwood's), at the end of which there were two little sketches of the arts of rhetoric and logic, the latter finishing with a specimen of a dispute in the Socratic method; and soon after I procur'd Xenophon's Memorable Things of Socrates, wherein there are many instances of the same method. I was charm'd with it, adopted it, dropt my abrupt contradiction and positive argumentation, and put on the humble inquirer and doubter. And being then, from reading Shaftesbury and Coliins, become a real doubter in many points of our religious doctrine, I found this method safest for myself and very embarassing to those against whom I used it; therefore I took a delight in it, practis'd it continually, and grew very artful and expert in drawing people, even of superior knowledge, into concessions, the consequences

---

here, only because it has never been in print. It appears in a letter written by the Doctor shortly after his final return from Europe, to his friend Le Ray de Chaumont, one of whose houses at Passy he occupied during his entire residence near the Court of France. I am indebted to his grandson, M. le Ray de Chaumont, who still lives in Paris in the enjoyment of a green old age, for a copy of the original. In this letter, referring to a claim sent in by his maitre d'hotel, for bills already once paid, the Doctor says :

"As to Tinck, the maitre d'hotel, he was fairly paid in money for every just demand he could make against us, and we have his receipts in full. But there are knaves in the world whom no writing can bind, and when you think you have finished with them, they come with demands after demands, *sans fin.* He was continually saying of himself, *Je suis honnete homme, je suis honnete homme.* But I always suspected he was mistaken ; and so it proves."

of which they did not foresee, entangling them in difficulties out of which they could not extricate themselves, and so obtaining victories that neither myself nor my cause always deserved. I continu'd this method some few years, but gradually left it, retaining only the habit of expressing myself in terms of modest diffidence; never using, when I advanced any thing that may possibly be disputed, the words *certainly, undoubtedly*, or any others that give the air of positiveness to an opinion; but rather say, I conceive or apprehend a thing to be so and so ; it appears to me, or *I should think it so or so,* for such and such reasons; or *I imagine it to be so;* or *it is so, if I am not mistaken.* This habit, I believe, has been of great advantage to me when I have had occasion to inculcate my opinions, and persuade men into measures that I have been from time to time engag'd in promoting; and, as the chief ends of conversation are to *inform* or to be *informed,* to '*please* or to *persuade,* I wish well-meaning, sensible men would not lessen their power of doing good by a positive, assuming manner, that seldom fails to disgust, tends to create opposition, and to defeat every one of those purposes for which speech was given to us, to wit, giving or receiving information or pleasure. For, if you would inform, a positive and dogmatical manner in advancing your sentiments may provoke contradiction and prevent a candid attention. If you wish information and improvement from the knowledge of others, and yet at the same time express yourself as firmly fix'd in your present opinions, modest, sensible men, who do not love disputation, will probably leave you undisturbed in the possession of your error. And by such a manner, you can seldom hope to recommend yourself in *pleasing* your hearers, or to persuade those whose concurrence you desire. Pope says, judiciously:

"Men should be taught as if you taught them not,
And things unknown propos'd as things forgot;"

farther recommending to us

"To speak, tho' sure, with seeming diffidence."

And he might have coupled with this line that which he has coupled with another, I think, less properly,

"For want of modesty is want of sense."

If you ask, Why less properly? I must repeat the lines,

"Immodest words admit of no defense,
For want of modesty is want of sense."

Now, is not *want of sense* (where a man is so unfortunate as to want it) some apology for his *want of modesty?* and would not the lines stand more justly thus?

"Immodest words admit *but* this defense,
That want of modesty is want of sense."

This, however, I should submit to better judgments.

My brother had, in 1720 or 1721, begun to print a newspaper. It was the second that appeared in America, and was called the New England Courant.
The only one before it was the Boston News-Letter. I remember his being dissuaded by some of his friends from the undertaking, as not likely to succeed, one newspaper being in their judgment, enough for America.* At this time (1771) there are not less than five-and-twenty. He went on, however, with the undertaking, and after having worked in composing the types and printing off the sheets, I was employed to carry the papers thro' the streets to the customers.

He had some ingenious men among his friends, who amus'd themselves by writing little pieces for this paper, which gain'd it credit and made it more in demand, and these gentlemen often visited us. Hearing their conversations, and their accounts of the approbation their papers were received with, I was excited to try my hand among them ; but, being still a boy, and suspecting that my brother would object to printing anything of mine in his paper if he knew it to be mine, I contrived to disguise my hand, and, writing an anonymous paper, I put it in at night under the door of the printing-house. It was found in the morning, and communicated to his writing friends when they call'd in as usual. They read it, commented on it in my hearing, and I had the exquisite pleasure of finding it met with their approbation, and that, in their different guesses at the author, none were named but men of some character among us for learning and ingenuity. I suppose now that I was rather lucky in my judges, and that perhaps they were not really so very good ones as I then esteem'd them.

Encourag'd, however, by this, I wrote and convey'd in the same way to the press several more papers which were equally approv'd; and I kept my secret till my small fund of sense for such performances was pretty well exhausted, and then I discovered it, when I began to be considered a little more by my brother's acquaintance, and in a manner that did not quite please him, as he thought, probably with reason, that it tended to make me too vain. And, perhaps, this might be one occasion of the differences that we began to have about this time.

---

* "This was written from recollection, and it is not surprising that, after the lapse of fifty years, the author's memory should have failed him in regard to a fact of small importance. The " New England Courant" was the fourth newspaper that appeared in America. The first number of the Boston News-Letter was published April 24th, 1704. This was the first newspaper in America. The Boston Gazette commenced December 21st, 1719; the American Weekly Mercury, at Philadelphia, December 22nd, 1719 ; the New England Courant, August 21st, 1721. Dr. Franklin's error of memory probably originated in the circumstance of his brother having been the printer of the Boston Gazette when it was first established. This was the second newspaper published in America."—*Sparks.*

Though a brother, he considered himself as my master, and me as hisapprentice, and, accordingly, expected the same services from me as he would from another, while I thought he demean'd me too much in some he requir'd of me, who from a brother expected more indulgence. Our disputes were often brought before our father, and I fancy I was either generally in the right, or else a better pleader, because the judgment was generally in my favor. But my brother was passionate, and had often beaten me, which I took extreamly amiss; and, thinking my apprenticeship very tedious, I was continually wishing for some opportunity of shortening it, which at length offered in a manner unexpected.*

One of the pieces in our newspaper on some political point, which I have now forgotten, gave offense to the Assembly. He was taken up, censur'd, and imprison'd for a month, by the speaker's warrant, I suppose, because he would not discover his author. I too was taken up and examin'd before the council; but, tho' I did not give them any satisfaction, they content'd themselves with admonishing me, and dismissed me, considering me, perhaps, as an apprentice, who was bound to keep his master's secrets.

During my brother's confinement, which I resented a good deal, notwithstanding our private differences, I had the management of the paper; and I made bold to give our rulers some rubs in it, which my brother took very kindly, while others began to consider me in an unfavorable light, as a young genius that had a turn for libelling and satyr. My brother's discharge was accompany'd with an

---

* I fancy his harsh and tyrannical treatment of me might be a means of impressing me with that aversion to arbitrary power that has stuck to me through my whole life.

order of the House (a very odd one), that " *James Franklin should no longer print the paper called the New England Courant"*.

There was a consultation held in our printinghouse among his friends, what he should do in this case. Some proposed to evade the order by changing the name of the paper; but my brother, seeing inconveniences in that, it was finally concluded on as a better way, to let it be printed for the future under the name of BENJAMIN FRANKLIN ; and to avoid the censure of the Assembly, that might fall on him as still printing it by his apprentice, the contrivance was that my old indenture should be return'd to me, with a full discharge on the back of it, to be shown on occasion, but to secure to him the benefit of my service, I was to sign new indentures for the remainder of the term, which were to be kept private. A very flimsy scheme it was; however, it was immediately executed, and the paper went on accordingly, under my name for several months.

At length, a fresh difference arising between my brother and me, I took upon me to assert my freedom, presuming that he would not venture to produce the new indentures. It was not fair in me to take this advantage, and this I therefore reckon one of the first errata of my life; but the unfairness of it weighed little with me, when under the impressions of resentment for the blows his passion too often urged him to bestow upon me, though he was otherwise not an ill-natur'd man: perhaps I was too saucy and provoking.

When he found I would leave him, he took care to prevent my getting employment in any other printing-house of the town, by going round and speaking to every master, who accordingly refus'd to give me work. I then thought of going to New York, as the nearest place where there was a printer; and I was rather inclin'd to leave Boston when. I reflected that I had already made myself a little obnoxious to the governing party, and, from the arbitrary proceedings of the Assembly in my brother's case, it was likely I might, if I stay'd, soon bring myself into scrapes ; and farther, that my indiscrete disputations about religion began to make me pointed at with horror by good people as an infidel or atheist. I determin'd on the point, but my father now siding with my brother, I was sensible that, if I attempted to go openly, means would be used to prevent me. My friend Collins, therefore, undertook to manage a little for me. He agreed with the captain of a New York sloop for my passage, under the notion of my being a young acquaintance of his, that had got a naughty girl with child, whose friends would compel me to marry her, and therefore I could not appear or come away publicly. So I sold some of my books to raise a little money, was taken on board privately, and as we had a fair wind, in three days I found myself in New York, near 300 miles from home, a boy of but 17,* without the least recommendation to, or knowledge of any person in the place, and with very little money in my pocket.

My inclinations for the sea were by this time worne out, or I might now have gratify'd them. But, having a trade, and supposing myself a pretty good workman, I offer'd my service to the printer in the place, old Mr. William Bradford, who had been the first printer in Pennsylvania, but removed from thence upon the quarrel of George Keith. He could give me no employment, having little to do, and help enough already; but says he, "My son at Philadelphia has lately lost his principal hand, Aquila Rose, by death ; if you go thither, I believe he may employ you." Philadelphia was a hundred miles further; I set out, however, in a boat for Amboy, leaving my chest and things to follow me round by sea.

In crossing the bay, we met with a squall that tore our rotten sails to pieces, prevented our getting into the Kill, and

---

* This was in October, 1723.—B.

drove us upon Long Island. In our way, a drunken Dutchman, who was a passenger too, fell overboard; when he was sinking, I reached through the water to his shock pate, and drew him up, so that we got him in again. His ducking sobered him a little, and he went to sleep, taking first out of his pocket a book, which he desir'd I would dry for him. It proved to be my old favorite author, Bunyan's Pilgrim's Progress, in Dutch, finely printed on good paper, with copper cuts, a dress better than I had ever seen it wear in its own language. I have since found that it has been translated into most of the languages of Europe, and suppose it has been more generally read than any other book, except perhaps the Bible. Honest John was the first that I know of who mix'd narration and dialogue ; a method of writing very engaging to the reader, who in the most interesting parts finds himself, as it were, brought into the company and present at the discourse. De Foe in his Cruso, his Moll Flanders, Religious Courtship, Family Instructor, and other pieces, has imitated it with success ; and Richardson has done the same in his Pamela, etc.

When we drew near the island, we found it was at a place where there could be no landing, there being a great surff on the stony beach. So we dropt anchor, and swung round towards the shore. Some people came down to the water edge and hallow'd to us, as we did to them; but the wind was so high, and the surff so loud, that we could not hear so as to understand each other. There were canoes on the shore, and we made signs, and hallow'd that they should fetch us; but they either did not understand us, or thought it impracticable, so they went away, and night coming on, we had no remedy but to wait till the wind should abate; and, in the mean time, the boatman and I concluded to sleep, if we could; and so crowded into the scuttle, with the Dutchman, who was still wet, and the spray beating over the head of our boat, leak'd thro' to us, so that we were soon almost as wet as he. In this manner we lay all night, with very little rest; but, the wind abating the next day, we made a shift to reach Amboy before night, having been thirty hours on the water, without victuals, or any drink but a bottle of filthy rum, the water we sail'd on being salt.

In the evening I found myself very feverish, and went in to bed; but, having read somewhere that cold water drank plentifully was good for a fever, I follow'd the prescription, sweat plentifully most of the night, my fever left me, and in the morning, crossing the ferry, I proceeded on my journey on foot, having fifty miles to Burlington, where I was told I should find boats that would carry me the rest of the way to Philadelphia.

It rained very hard all the day; I was thoroughly soak'd, and by noon a good deal tired; so I stopt at a poor inn, where I staid all night, beginning now to wish that I had never left home. I cut so miserable a figure, too, that I found, by the questions ask'd me, I was suspected to be some runaway servant, and in danger of being taken up on that suspicion. However, I proceeded the next day, and got in the evening to an inn, within eight or ten miles of Burlington, kept by one Dr. Brown. He entered into conversation with me while I took some refreshment, and, finding I had read a little, became very sociable and friendly. Our acquaintance continu'd as long as he liv'd. He had been, I imagine, an itinerant doctor, for there was no town in England, or country in Europe, of which he could not give a very particular account. He had some letters, and was ingenious, but much of an unbeliever, and wickedly undertook, some years after, to travestie the Bible in doggrel verse, as Cotton had done Virgil. By this means he set many of the facts in a very ridiculous light, and might have hurt weak minds if his work had been published ; but it never was.

At his house I lay that night, and the next morning reach'd Burlington, but had the mortification to find that the regular boats were gone a little before my coming, and no other expected to go before Tuesday, this being Saturday ; wherefore I returned to an old woman in the town, of whom I had bought gingerbread to eat on the water, and ask'd her advice.

She invited me to lodge at her house till a passage by water should offer; and being tired with my foot travelling, I accepted the invitation. She understanding I was a printer, would have had me stay at that town and follow my business, being ignorant of the stock necessary to begin with. She was very hospitable, gave me a dinner of ox-cheek with great good will, accepting only of a pot of ale in return ; and I thought myself fixed till Tuesday should come. However, walking in the evening by the side of the river, a boat came by, which I found was going towardsPhiladelphia, with several people in her. They took me in, and, as there was no wind, we row'd all the way; and about midnight, not having yet seen the city, some of the company were confident we must have passed it, and would row no farther; the others knew not where we were ; so we put toward the shore, got into a creek, landed near an old fence, with the rails of which we made a fire, the night being cold, in October, and there we remained till daylight. Then one of the company knew the place to be Cooper's Creek, a little above Philadelphia, which we saw as soon as we got out of the creek, and arriv'd there about eight or nine o'clock on the Sunday morning, and landed at the Market-street wharf.

I have been the more particular in this description of my journey, and shall be so of my first entry into that city, that you may in your mind compare such unlikely beginnings with the figure I have since made there. I was in my working dress, my best cloaths being to come round by sea. I was dirty from my journey; my pockets were stuff'd out with shirts and stockings, and I knew no soul nor where to look for lodging. I was fatigued with travelling, rowing and want of rest, I was very hungry; and my whole stock of cash consisted of a Dutch dollar, and about a shilling in copper. The latter I gave the people of the boat for my passage, who at first refus'd it, on account of my rowing; but I insisted on their taking it. A man being sometimes more generous when he has but a little money than when he has plenty, perhaps thro' fear of being thought to have but little.

Then I walked up the street, gazing about till near the market-house I met a boy with bread. I had made many a meal on bread, and, inquiring where he got it, I went immediately to the baker's he directed me to, in Second-street, and ask'd for bisket, intending such as we had in Boston; but they, it seems, were not made in Philadelphia. Then I asked for a three-penny loaf, and was told they had none such. So not considering or knowing the difference of money, and the greater cheapness nor the names of his bread, I bad him give me threepenny worth of any sort. He gave me, accordingly, three great puffy rolls. I was surpriz'd at the quantity, but took it, and, having no room in my pockets, walk'd off with a roll under each arm, and eating the other. Thus I went up Market-street as far as Fourth-street, passing by the door of Mr. Read, my future wife's father; when she, standing at the door, saw me, and thought I made, as I certainly did, a most awkward, ridiculous appearance. Then I turned and went down Chesnut-street and part of Walnut-street, eating my roll all the way, and, coming round, found myself again at Marketstreet wharf, near the boat I came in, to which I went for a draught of the river water; and, being filled with one of my rolls, gave the other two to a woman and her child that came down the river in the boat with us, and were waiting to go farther.

Thus refreshed, I walked again up the street, which by this time had many clean-dressed people in it, who were all walking the same way. I joined them, and thereby was led into the great meetinghouse of the Quakers near the market. I sat down among them, and, after looking round awhile and hearing nothing said, being very drowsy thro' labor and want of rest the preceding night, I fell fast asleep, and continu'd so till the meeting broke up, when one was kind enough to rouse me. This was, therefore, the first house I was in, or slept in, in Philadelphia.

Walking down again toward the river, and, looking in the faces of people, I met a young Quaker man, whose countenance I lik'd, and, accosting him, requested he would tell me where a stranger could get lodging. We were then near the sign of the Three Mariners. "Here," says he, "is one place that entertains strangers, but it is not a reputable house; if thee wilt walk with me, I' ll show thee a better. He brought me to the Crooked Billet in Water-street. Here I got a dinner; and, while I was eating it, several sly questions were asked me, as it seemed to be suspected from my youth and appearance, that I might be some runaway.

After dinner, my sleepiness return'd, and being shown to a bed, I lay down without undressing, and slept till six in the evening, was call'd to supper, went to bed again very early, and slept soundly till next morning. Then I made myself as tidy as I could, and went to Andrew Bradford the printer's. I found in the shop the old man his father, whom I had seen at New York, and who, travelling on horseback, had got to Philadelphia before me. He introduc'd me to his son, who receiv'd me civilly, gave me a breakfast, but told me he did not at present want a hand, being lately suppli'd with one; but there was another printer in town, lately set up, one Keimer, who, perhaps, might employ me; if not, I should be welcome to lodge at his house, and he would give me a little work to do now and then till fuller business should offer.

The old gentleman said he would go with me to the new printer; and when we found him, " Neighbor," says Bradford, " I have brought to see you a young man of your business; perhaps you may want such a one." He ask'd me a few questions, put a composing stick in my hand to see how I

work'd, and then said he would employ me soon, though he had just then nothing for me to do; and, taking old Bradford, whom he had never seen before, to be one of the town's people that had a good will for him, enter'd into a conversation on his present undertaking and prospects; while Bradford, not discovering that he was the other printer's father, on Keimer's saying he expected soon to get the greatest part of the business into his own hands,
drew him on by artful questions, and starting little doubts, to explain all his views, what interest he reli'd on, and in what manner he intended to proceed. I, who stood by and heard all, saw immediately that one of them was a crafty old sophister, and the other a mere novice. Bradford left me with Keimer, who was greatly surpris'd when I told him who the old man was.

Keimer's printing-house, I found, consisted of an old shatter'd press, and one small, worn-out font of English, which he was then using himself, composing an Elegy on Aquila Rose, before mentioned, an ingenious young man, of excellent character, much respected in the town, clerk of the Assembly, and a pretty poet. Keimer made verses too, but very indifferently. He could not be said to write them, for his manner was to compose them in the types directly out of his head. So there being no copy, but one pair of cases, and the Elegy likely to require all the letter, no one could help him. I endeavor'd to put his press (which he had not yet us'd, and of which he understood nothing) into order fit to be work'd with; and, promising to come and print off his Elegy as soon as he should have got it ready, I return'd to Bradford's, who gave me a little job to do for the present, and there I lodged and dieted. A few days after, Keimer sent for me to print off the Elegy. And now he had got another pair of cases, and a pamphlet to reprint, on which he set me to work.

These two printers I found poorly qualified for their business. Bradford had not been bred to it, and was very illiterate; and Keimer, tho' something of a scholar, was a mere compositor, knowing nothing of presswork. He had been one of the French prophets, and could act their enthusiastic agitations.* At this time he did not profess any particular religion, but something of all on occasion ; was very ignorant of the world, and had, as I afterward found, a good deal of the knave in his composition. He did not like my lodging at Bradford's while I work'd with him. He had a house, indeed, but without furniture, so he could not lodge me; but he got me a lodging at Mr. Read's, before mentioned, who was the owner of his house; and, my chest and clothes being come by this time, I made rather a more respectable appearance in the eyes of Miss Read than I had done when she first happen'd to see me eating my roll in the street.

I began now to have some acquaintance among the young people of the town, that were lovers of reading, with whom I spent my evenings very pleasantly ; and gaining money by my industry and frugality, I lived very agreeably, forgetting Boston as much as I could, and not desiring that any there should know where I resided, except my friend Collins, who was in my secret, and kept it when I wrote to him. At length, an incident happened that sentme back again much sooner than I had intended. I had a brother-in-law, Robert Holmes, master of a sloop that traded between Boston and Delaware. He being at Newcastle, forty miles below Philadelphia, heard there of me,and wrote me a letter mentioning the concern of my friends in Boston at my abrupt departure, assuring me of their good will to me, and that every thing would be accommodated to my mind if I would return, to which he exhorted me very earnestly.

---

* M. Laboulaye presumes Keimer was one of the Camisards or Protestants of the Cevennes, so persecuted by Louis XIV.—B.

I wrote an answer to his letter, thank'd him for his advice, but stated my reasons for quitting Boston fully and in such a light as to convince him I was not so wrong as he had apprehended.

Sir William Keith, governor of the province, was then at Newcastle, and Captain Holmes, happening to be in company with him when my letter came to hand, spoke to him of me, and show'd him the letter. The governor read it, and seem'd surpris'd when he was told my age. He said I appear'd a young man of promising parts, and therefore should be encouraged; the printers at Philadelphia were wretched ones; and, if I would set up there, he made no doubt I should succeed; for his part, he would procure me the public business, and do me every other service in his power. This my brother in-law afterwards told me in Boston, but I knew as yet nothing of it; when, one day, Keimer and I being at work together near the window, we saw the governor and another gentleman (which proved to be Colonel French, of Newcastle), finely dress'd, come directly across the street to our house, and heard them at the door.

Keimer ran down immediately, thinking it a visit to him; but the governor inquir'd for me, came up, and with a condescension and politeness I had been quite unus'd to, made me many compliments, desired to be acquainted with me, blam'd me kindly for not having made myself known to him when I first came to the place, and would have me away with him to the tavern, where he was going with Colonel French to taste, as he said, some excellent Madeira. I was not a little surprised, and Keimer star'd like a pig poison'd. I went, however, with the governor and Colonel French to a tavern, at the corner of Third-street, and over the Madeira he propos'd my setting up my business, laid before me the probabilities of success, and both he and Colonel French assur'd me I should have their interest and influence in procuring the public business of both governments. On my doubting whether my father would assist me in it, Sir William said he would give me a letter to him, in which he would state the advantages, and he did not doubt of prevailing with him. So it was concluded I should return to Boston in the first vessel, with the governor's letter recommending me to my father. In the mean time the intention was to be kept a secret, and I went on working with Keimer as usual, the governor sending for me now and then to dine with him, a very great honor I thought it, and conversing with me in the most affable, familiar, and friendly manner imaginable.

About the end of April, 1724, a little vessel offer'd for Boston. I took leave of Keimer as going to see my friends. The governor gave me an ample letter, saying many flattering things of me to my father, and strongly recommending the project of my setting up at Philadelphia as a thing that must make my fortune. We struck on a shoal in going down the bay, and sprung a leak; we had a blustering time at sea, and were oblig'd to pump almost continually, at which I took my turn. We arriv'd safe, however, at Boston in about a fortnight. I had been absent seven months, and my friends had heard nothing of me; for my br. Holmes was not yet return'd, and had not written about me. My unexpected appearance surpriz'd the family; all were, however, very glad to see me, and made me welcome, except my brother. I went to see him at his printing-house. I was better dress'd than ever while in his service, having a genteel new suit from head to foot, a watch, and my pockets lin'd with near five pounds sterling in silver. He receiv'd me not very frankly, look'd me all over, and turn'd to his work again.

The journeymen were inquisitive where I had been, what sort of a country it was, and how I lik'd it. I prais'd it much, and the happy life I led in it, expressing strongly my intention of returning to it; and, one of them asking what kind of money we had there, I produc'd a handful of silver, and spread it before them, which was a kind of raree-show they had not been us'd to, paper being the money of Boston. Then I took an opportunity of letting them see my watch; and, lastly (my brother still grum and sullen), I gave them a piece of eight to drink, and took my leave. This visit of mine offended him extreamly ; for, when my mother some time after spoke to him of a reconciliation, and of her wishes to see us on good terms together, and that we might live for the future as brothers, he said I had insulted him in such a manner before his people that he could never forget or forgive it. In this, however, he was mistaken.

My father received the governor's letter with some apparent surprise, but said little of it to me for some days, when Capt. Holmes returning he show'd it to him, ask'd him if he knew Keith, and what kind of man he was; adding his opinion that he must be of small discretion to think of setting a boy up in business who wanted yet three years of being at man's estate. Holmes said what he could in favor of the project, but my father was clear in the impropriety of it, and at last gave a flat denial to it. Then he wrote a civil letter to Sir William, thanking him for the patronage he had so kindly offered me, but declining to assist me as yet in setting up, I being, in his opinion, too young to be trusted with the management of a business so important, and for which the preparation must be so expensive.

My friend and companion Collins, who was a clerk in the post-office, pleas'd with the account I gave him of my new country, determined to go thither also; and, while I waited for my father's determination, he set out before me by land to Rhode Island, leaving his books, which were a pretty collection of mathematicks and natural philosophy, to come with mine and me to New York, where he propos'd to wait for me.

My father, tho' he did not approve Sir William's proposition, was yet pleas'd that I had been able to obtain so advantageous a character from a person of such note where I had resided, and that I had been so industrious and careful as to equip myself so handsomely in so short a time; therefore, seeing no prospect of an accommodation between my brother and me, he gave his consent to my returning again to Philadelphia, advis'd me to behave respectfully to the people there, endeavor to obtain the general esteem, and avoid lampooning and libeling, to which he thought I had too much inclination ; telling me, that by steady industry and a prudent parsimony I might save enough by the time I was one- and-twenty to set me up; and that, if I came near the matter, he would help me out with the rest. This was all I could obtain, except some small gifts as tokens of his and my mother's love, when I embark'd again for New York, now with their approbation and their blessing.

The sloop putting in at Newport, Rhode Island, I visited my brother John, who had been married and settled there some years. He received me very affectionately, for he always lov'd me. A friend of his, one Vernon, having some money due to him in Pensilvania, about thirty-five pounds currency, desired I would receive it for him, and keep it till I had his directions what to remit it in. Accordingly, he gave me an order. This afterwards occasion'd me a good deal of uneasiness.

At Newport we took in a number of passengers for New York, among which were two young women, companions, and a grave, sensible, matronlike Quaker woman, with her attendants. I had shown an obliging readiness to do her some little services, which impress'd her I suppose with a degree of good will toward me; therefore, when she saw a daily growing familiarity between me and the two young women, which they appear'd to encourage, she took me aside, and said, "Young man, I am concern'd for thee, as thou has no friend with thee, and seems not to know much of the world, or of the snares youth is expos'd to; depend upon it, those are very bad women; I can see it in all their actions; and if thee art not upon thy guard, they will draw thee into some danger; they are strangers to thee, and I advise thee, in a friendly concern for thy welfare, to have no acquaintance with them." As I seem'd at first not to think so ill of them as she did, she mentioned some things she had observ'd and heard that had escap'd my notice, but now convinc'd me she was right. I thank'd her for her kind advice, and promis'd to follow it. When we arriv'd at New York, they told me where they liv'd, and invited me to come and see them; but I avoided it, and it was well I did; for the next day the captain miss'd a silver spoon and some other things, that had been taken out of his cabbin, and, knowing that these were a couple of strumpets, he got a warrant to search their lodgings, found the stolen goods, and had the thieves punish'd. So, tho' we had escap'd a sunken rock, which we scrap'd upon in the passage, I thought this escape of rather more importance to me.

At New York I found my friend Collins, who had arriv'd there some time before me. We had been intimate from children, and had read the same books together; but he had the advantage of more time for reading and studying, and a wonderful genius for mathematical learning, in which he far outstript me. While I liv'd in Boston, most of my hours of leisure for conversation were spent with him, and he continu'd a sober as well as an industrious lad; was much respected for his learning by several of the clergy and other gentlemen, and seemed to promise making a good figure in life. But, during my absence, he had acquir'd a habit of sotting with brandy; and I found by his own account, and what I heard from others, that he had been drunk every day since his arrival at New York, and behav'd very oddly. He had gam'd, too, and lost his money, so that I was oblig'd to discharge his lodgings, and defray his expenses to and at Philadelphia, which prov'd extremely inconvenient to me.

The then governor of New York, Burnet (son of Bishop Burnet),* hearing from the captain that a young man,

---

* Governor Burnet was appointed governor of the Colony of New York and New Jersey on the 19th of April, 1720. He entered upon the duties of his office in September following. He was a man of scholarly tastes, fond of accumulating books, with a turn for theological speculation, which he indulged in making a commentary upon the three periods contained in the twelfth chapter of Daniel. The governor married a daughter of Cornelius Van Horne, of New York, who died soon. He was transferred to the governorship of Boston in July, 1728. His administration there, however, was not of long duration. He fell ill from exposure on a fishing excursion, and died on the 7th of September, 1729.

one of his passengers, had a great many books, desir'd he would bring me to see him. I waited upon him accordingly, and should have taken Collins with me but that he was not sober. The gov'r treated me with great civility, show'd me his library, which was a very large one, and we had a good deal of conversation about books and authors. This was the second governor who had done me the honor to take notice of me; which, to a poor boy like me, was very pleasing.

We proceeded to Philadelphia. I received on the way Vernon's money, without which we could hardly have finish'd our journey. Collins wished to be employ'd in some counting-

---

The governor's interest in theology did not commend him especially to the authprities at home.

The Bishop of London complained that clergymen already provided with his license to preach in the colonies were subject to a new examination, conducted in a somewhat unusual manner by the governor.

"Your method (wrote Richard West, the governor's brother-in-law, Solicitor-General to the Board of Trade) is to prescribe him a text, to give him a Bible for his companion, and then lock him into a room by himself, and if he does not in some stated time produce a sermon to your satisfaction, you peremptorily refuse to grant him your instrument (permission to preach). The consequence is, the man must starve. * * * I have seen a great many complaints against governors, but then nobody was surprised, because I could always give some pecuniary reason for what they had done. You surely are the first who ever brought himself into difficulties by an inordinate *care of souls;* and I am sure that makes no part of your commission."

For the best account of this worthy man, see Whitehead's *Contribution* to East Jersey History,* pp. 156-168.—B.

house; but, whether they discover'd his dramming by his breath, or by his behaviour, tho' he had some recommendations, he met with no success in any application, and continu'd lodging and boarding at the same house with me, and at my expense. Knowing I had that money of Vernon's, he was continually borrowing of me, still promising repayment as soon as he should be in business. At length he had got so much of it that I was distress'd to think what I should do in case of being call'd on to remit it.

His drinking continu'd, about which we sometimes quarrel'd for, when a little intoxicated, he was very fractious. Once, in a boat on the Delaware with some other young men, he refused to row in his turn. "I will be row'd home," says he. "We will not row you," says I. "You must, or stay all night on the water," says he, "just as you please." The others said, "Let us row; what signifies it?" But, my mind being soured with his other conduct, I continu'd to refuse. So he swore he would make me row, or throw me overboard; and coming along, stepping on the thwarts, toward me, when he came up and struck at me, I clapped my hand under his crutch, and, rising, pitched him head-foremost into the river. I knew he was a good swimmer, and so was under little concern about him; but before he could get round to lay hold of the boat, we had with a few strokes pull'd her out of his reach; and ever when he drew near the boat, we ask'd if he would row, striking a few strokes to slide her away from him. He was ready to die with vexation, and obstinately would not promise to row. However, seeing him at last beginning to tire, we lifted him in and brought him home dripping wet in the evening. We hardly exchang'd a civil word afterwards, and a West India captain who had a commission to procure a tutor for the sons of a gentleman at Barbadoes, happening to meet with him, agreed to carry him thither. He left me then, promising to remit me the first money he should receive in order to discharge the debt; but I never heard of him after.

The breaking into this money of Vernon's was one of the first great errata of my life; and this affair show'd that my father was not much out in his judgment when he suppos'd me too young to manage business of importance. But Sir William, on reading his letter, said he was too prudent. There was great difference in persons; and discretion did not always accompany years, nor was youth always without it. "And since he will not set you up," says he, " I will do it myself. Give me an inventory of the things necessary to be had from England, and I will send for them. You shall repay me when you are able; I am resolv'd to have a good printer here, and I am sure you must succeed." This was spoken with such an appearance of cordiality, that I had not the least doubt of his meaning what he said. I had hitherto kept the proposition of my setting up, a secret in Philadelphia, and I still kept it. Had it been known that I depended on the governor, probably some friend, that knew him better, would have advis'd me not to rely on him, as I afterwards heard it as his known character to be liberal of promises which he never meant to keep. Yet, unsolicited as he was by me, how could I think his generous offers insincere? I believ'd him one of the best men in the world.

I presented him an inventory of a little printing- house, amounting by my computation to about one hundred pounds sterling. He lik'd it, but ask'd me if my being on the spot in England to choose the types, and see that every thing was good of the kind, might not be of some advantage. " Then," says he, "when there, you may make acquaintances, and establish correspondences in the bookselling and stationery way." I agreed that this might be advantageous. "Then," says he "get yourself ready to go with Annis: "which was the annual ship, and the only one at that time usually passing between London and Philadelphia. But it would be some months before Annis sail'd, so I continu'd working with Keimer, fretting about the money Collins had got from me, and in daily apprehensions of being call'd upon by Vernon, which, however, did not happen for some years after.

I believe I have omitted mentioning that, in my first voyage from Boston, being becalm'd off Block Island, our people set about catching cod, and hauled up a great many. Hitherto I had stuck to my resolution of not eating animal food, and on this occasion I consider'd, with my master Tryon, the taking every fish as a kind of unprovoked murder, since none of them had, or ever could do us any injury that might justify the slaughter. All this seemed very reasonable. But I had formerly been a great lover of fish, and, when this came hot out of the frying-pan, it smelt admirably well. I balanc'd some time between principle and inclination, till I recollected that, when the fish were opened, I saw smaller fish taken out of their stomachs; then thought I, "If you eat one another, I don't see why we mayn't eat you." So I din'd upon cod very heartily and continued to eat with other people, returning only now and then occasionally to a vegetable diet. So convenient a thing it is to be a *reasonable creature,* since it enables one to find or make a reason for every thing one has a mind to do.

Keimer and I liv'd on a pretty good familiar footing, and agreed tolerably well, for he suspected nothing of my setting up. He retained a great deal of his old enthusiasms and lov'd argumentation. We therefore had many disputations. I used to work him so with my Socratic method, and had trepann'd him so often by questions apparently so distant from any point we had in hand, and yet by degrees lead to the point, and brought him into difficulties and contradictions, that at last he grew ridiculously cautious, and would hardly answer me the most common question, without asking first, " *What do you intend to infer from that?"* However, it gave him so high an opinion of my abilities in the confuting way, that he seriously proposed my being his colleague in a project he had of setting up a new sect. He was to preach the doctrines, and I was to confound all opponents. When he came to explain with me upon the doctrines, I found several conundrums which I objected to, unless I might have my way a little too, and introduce some of mine.

Keimer wore his beard at full length, because somewhere in the Mosaic law it is said, " *Thou shalt not mar the corners of thy beard*". He likewise kept the Seventh day, Sabbath; and these two points were essentials with him. I dislik'd both; but agreed to admit them upon condition of his adopting the doctrine of using no animal food. " I doubt," said he, "my constitution will not bear that." I assur'd him it would, and that he would be the better for it. He was usually a great glutton, and I promised myself some diversion in half starving him. He agreed to try the practice, if I would keep him company. I did so, and we held it for three months. We had our victuals dress'd, and brought to us regularly by a woman in the neighborhood, who had from me a list of forty dishes, to be prepar'd for us at different times, in all which there was neither fish, flesh, nor fowl, and the whim suited me the better at this time from the cheapness of it, not costing us above eighteen pence sterling each per week. I have since kept several Lents most strictly, leaving the common diet for that, and that for the common, abruptly, without the least inconvenience, so that I think there is little in the advice of making those changes by easy gradations. I went on pleasantly, but poor Keimer suffered grievously, tired of the project, long'd for the flesh-pots of Egypt, and order'd a roast pig. He invited me and two women friends to dine with him; but, it being brought too soon upon table, he could not resist the temptation, and ate the whole before we came.

I had made some courtship during this time to Miss Read. I had a great respect and affection for her, and had some reason to believe she had the same for me; but, as I was about to take a long voyage, and we were both very young, only a little above eighteen, it was thought most prudent by her mother to prevent our going too far at present, as a marriage, if it was to take place, would be more convenient after my return, when I should be, as I expected, set up in my business. Perhaps, too, she thought my expectations not so well founded as I imagined them to be.

My chief acquaintances at this time were Charles Osborne, Joseph Watson, and James Ralph, all lovers of reading. The two first were clerks to an eminent scrivener or conveyancer in the town, Charles Brogden; the other was clerk to a merchant. Watson was a pious, sensible young man of great integrity; the others rather more lax in their principles of religion, particularly Ralph, who, as well as Collins had been unsettled by me, for which they both made me suffer. Osborne was sensible, candid, frank; sincere and affectionate to his friends; but, in literary matters, too fond of criticising. Ralph was ingenious, genteel in his manners, and extremely eloquent; I think I never knew a prettier talker. Both of them great admirers of poetry, and began to try their hands in little pieces. Many pleasant walks we four had together on Sundays into the woods, near Schuylkill, where we read to one another, and conferr'd on what we read.

Ralph was inclin'd to pursue the study of poetry, not doubting but he might become eminent in it, and make his fortune by it, alleging that the best poets must, when they first began to write, make as many faults as he did. Osborne dissuaded him, assur'd him he had no genius for poetry, and advis'd him to think of nothing beyond the business he was bred to; that, in the mercantile way, tho' he had no stock, he might, by his diligence and punctuality, recommend himself to employment as a factor, and in time acquire wherewith to trade on his own account. I approv'd the amusing one's self with poetry now and then, so far as to improve one's language, but no farther.

On this it was propos'd that we should each of us, at our next meeting, produce a piece of our own composing, in order to improve our mutual observations, criticisms, and corrections. As language and expression were what we had in view, we excluded all considerations of invention by agreeing that the task should be a version of the eighteenth Psalm, which describes the descent of a Deity. When the time of our meeting drew nigh, Ralph called on me first, and let me know his piece was ready. I told him I had been busy, and, having little inclination, had done nothing. He then show'd me his piece for my opinion, and I much approv'd it, as it appear'd to me to have great merit. "Now," says he, "Osborne never will allow the least merit in any thing of mine, but makes 1000 criticisms out of mere envy. He is not so jealous of you; I wish, therefore, you would take this piece, and produce it as yours; I will pretend not to have had time, and so produce nothing. We shall then see what he will say to it." It was agreed, and I immediately transcrib'd it, that it might appear in my own hand.

We met; Watson's performance was read; there were some beauties in it, but many defects. Osborne's was read ; it was much better; Ralph did it justice; remarked some faults, but applauded the beauties. He himself had nothing to produce. I was backward ; seemed desirous of being excused ; had not had sufficient time to correct, etc.; but no excuse could be admitted; produce I must. It was read and repeated; Watson and Osborne gave up the contest, and join'd in applauding it. Ralph only made some criticisms, and propos'd some amendments; but I defended my text. Osborne was against Ralph, and told him he was no better a critic than poet, so he dropt the argument. As they two went home together, Osborne expressed himself still more strongly in favor of what he thought my production; having restrain'd himself before, as he said, lest I should think it flattery. "But who would have imagin'd," said he, "that Franklin had been capable of such a performance; such painting, such force, such fire ! He has even improv'd the original. In his common conversation he seems to have no choice of words; he hesitates and blunders ; and yet, good God ! how he writes !" When we next met, Ralph discovered the trick we had played on him, and Osborne was a little laught at.

This transaction fixed Ralph in his resolution of becoming a poet. I did all I could to dissuade him from it, but he continued scribbling verses till *Pope* cured him.*He became, however, a pretty good prose writer. More of him hereafter. But, as I may not have occasion again to mention the other two,

---

* In one of the later editions of the Dunciad occur the following lines:

" Silence, ye wolves ! while Ralph to Cynthia howls,
And makes Night hideous–answer him, ye owls."

Book iii. line 165.

To this the poet adds the following note :

"James Ralph, a name inserted after the first editions, not known till he write a swearing-piece called Sawney, very abusive of Dr. Swift, Mr. Gay and myself. These lines allude to a thing of his entitled *Night,* a poem. This low writer attended his own works with panegyrics in the journals, and once in particular praised himself highly above Mr. Addison, in wretched remarks upon that author's account of English poets, printed in a London journal, September, 1728. He was wholly illiterate and knew no language, not even French. Being advised to read the rules of dramatic poetry before he began a play, he smiled and replied, ' Shakespeare write without rules.' He ended at last in the common sink of all such writers, a political newspaper, to which he was recommended by his friend Arnal, and received a small pittance for pay; and being detected in writing on both sides on one and the same day, he publicly justified the morality of his conduct".

In the first book of the Dunciad, line 215, there is another allusion to Ralph:

"And see ! the very Gazetteers give o'er,
Ev'n Ralph repents, and Henley writes no more."

To this the poet appends the following note :

I shall just remark here, that Watson died in my arms a few years after, much lamented, being the best of our set. Osborne went to the West Indies, where he became an eminent lawyer and made money, but died young. He and I had made a serious agreement, that the one who happen'd first to die should, if possible, make a friendly visit to the other, and acquaint him how he found things in that separate state. But he never fulfill'd his promise.

" *Gazetteers.*—A band of ministerial writers hired at the price mentioned in the note on book II ver. 316, who, on the very day their patron quitted his post, laid down their paper and declared they would never more meddle in politics."

In the note here referred to Pope says :

" The Daily Gazetteer was a title given very properly to certain papers, each of which lasted but a day. Into this as a common sink was received all the trash which had been before dispersed in several journals and circulated at the public expense of the nation. The authors were the same obscure men; though sometimes relieved by occasional essays from statesmen, courtiers, bishops, deans and doctors. The meaner sort were rewarded with money; others with places or benefices, from a hundred to a thousand a year. It appears from the *Report of the Secret Committee,* for inquiring into the conduct of R. Earl of O., 'that no less than *fifty thousand seventy-seven pounds eighteen shillings* were paid to authors and printers of newspapers, such as Free Britons, Daily Courants, Corn-Cutters, Journals, Gazetteers and other political papers, between February 10, 1731, and February 10, 1741' which shows the benevolence of one minister to have expended for the current dullness of ten years in Britain double the sum which gained Louis XIV, so much honor in annual pensions to learned men all over Europe. In which and in a much longer time not a pension at court nor preferment in the Church or universities of any consideration was bestowed on any man distinguished for his learning, separately from partymerit or pamphlet-writing."

" It is worth a reflection, that of all the panegyrics bestowed by these writers on this great minister, not one is at this day extant or remembered; nor even so much credit done to his personal character by all they have written as by one short occasional compliment of our author:

" Seen him I have ; but in his happier hour Of social pleasure, ill exchanged for power; Seen him uncumbered by the venal tribe, *Smile* without *art* and *win* without a bribe."—B.

The governor, seeming to like my company, had me frequently to his house, and his setting me up was always mention'd as a fixed thing. I was to take with me letters recommendatory to a number of his friends, besides the letter of credit to furnish me with the necessary money for purchasing the press and types, paper, etc. For these letters I was appointed to call at different times, when they were to be ready; but a future time was still named. Thus he went on till the ship, whose departure too had been several times postponed, was on the point of sailing. Then, when I call'd to take my leave and receive the letters, his secretary, Dr. Bard, came out to me and said the governor was extremely busy in writing, but would be down at Newcastle before the ship, and there the letters would be delivered to me.

Ralph, though married, and having one child, had determined to accompany me in this voyage. It was thought he intended to establish a correspondence, and obtain goods to sell on commission; but I found afterwards, that, thro' some discontent with his wife's relations, he purposed to leave her on their hands, and never return again. Having taken leave of my friends, and interchang'd some promises with Miss Read, I left Philadelphia in the ship, which anchor'd at Newcastle. The governor was there ; but when I went to his lodging, the secretary came to me from him with the civillest message in the world, that he could not then see me, being engaged in business of the utmost importance, but should send the letters to me on board, wish'd me heartily a good voyage and a speedy return, etc. I returned on board a little puzzled, but still not doubting.

Mr. Andrew Hamilton, a famous lawyer of Philadelphia, had taken passage in the same ship for himself and son, and with Mr. Denham, a Quaker merchant, and Messrs. Onion and Russel, masters of an iron work in Maryland, had engag'd the great cabin; so that Ralph and I were forced to take up with a berth in the steerage, and none on board knowing us, were considered as ordinary persons. But Mr. Hamilton and his son (it was James, since governor) return'd from Newcastle to Philadelphia, the father being recall'd by a great fee to plead for a seized ship; and, just before we sail'd, Colonel French coming on board, and showing me great respect, I was more taken notice of, and, with my friend Ralph, invited by the other gentlemen to come into the cabin, there being now room. Accordingly, we remov'd thither.

Understanding that Colonel French had brought on board the governor's despatches, I ask'd the captain for those letters that were to be under my care. He said all were put into the bag together and he could not then come at them ; but, before we landed in England, I should have an opportunity of picking them out; so I was satisfied for the present, and we proceeded on our voyage. We had a sociable company in the cabin, and lived uncommonly well, having the addition of all Mr. Hamilton's stores, who had laid in plentifully. In this passage Mr. Denham contracted a friendship for me that continued during his life. The voyage was otherwise not a pleasant one, as we had a great deal of bad weather.

When we came into the Channel, the captain kept his word with me, and gave me an opportunity of examining the bag for the governor's letters. I found none* upon which my name was put as under my care. I picked out six or seven, that, by the handwriting, I thought might be the promised letters, especially as one of them was directed to Basket, the king's printer, and another to some stationer. We arriv'd in London the 24th of December, 1724. I waited upon the stationer, who came first in my way, delivering the letter as from Governor Keith. " I don't know such a person," says he ; but, opening the letter, " O! this is from Riddles- den. I have lately found him to be a complete rascal, and I will have nothing to do with him, nor receive any letters from him." So, putting the letter into my hand, he turn'd on his heel and left me to serve some customer. I was surprised to find these were not the governor's letters; and, after recollecting and comparing circumstances, I began to doubt his sincerity. I found my friend Denham, and opened the whole affair to him.

He let me into Keith's character; told me there was not the least probability that he had written any letters for me; that no one, who knew him, had the smallest dependence on him ; and he laught at the notion of the governor's giving me a letter of credit, having, as he said, no credit to give. On my expressing some concern about what I should do, he advised me to endeavor getting some employment in the way of my business. "Among the printers here," said he, " you will improve yourself, and when you return to America, you will set up to greater advantage."

We both of us happen'd to know as well as the stationer, that Riddlesden, the attorney, was a very knave. He had half ruin'd Miss Read's father by persuading him to be bound for him. By this letter it appear'd there was a secret scheme on foot to the prejudice of Hamilton (suppos'd to be then coming over with us) ; and that Keith was concerned in it with Riddlesden. Denham, who was a friend of Hamilton, thought he ought to be acquainted with it; so, when he arriv'd in England, which was soon after, partly from resentment and ill-will to Keith and Riddlesden, and partly from goodwill to him, I waited on him, and gave him the letter. He thank'd me cordially, the information being of importance to him; and from that time he became my friend, greatly to my advantage afterwards on many occasions.

But what shall we think of a governor's playing such pitiful tricks, and imposing so grossly on a poor ignorant boy ! It was a habit he had acquired. He wish'd to pleased everybody; and, having little to give, he gave expectations. He was otherwise an ingenious, sensible man, a pretty good writer, and a good governor for the people, tho' not for his constituents, the proprietaries, whose instructions he sometimes disregarded.

---

* Evidently intended for " some."–B.

Several of our best laws were of his planning and passed during his administration.

Ralph and I were inseparable companions. We took lodgings together in Little Britain at three shillings and sixpence a week–as much as we could then afford. He found some relations, but they were poor, and unable to assist him. He now let me know his intentions of remaining in London, and that he never meant to return to Philadelphia. He had brought no money with him, the whole he could muster having been expended in paying his passage. I had fifteen pistoles; so he borrowed occasionally of me to subsist, while he was looking out for business. He first endeavored to get into the playhouse, believing himself qualify'd for an actor; but Wilkes,* to whom he apply'd, advis'd him candidly not to think of that employment, as it was impossible he should succeed in it. Then he propos'd to Roberts, a publisher in Paternoster Row, to write for him a weekly paper like the Spectator, on certain conditions, which Roberts did not approve. Then he endeavored to get employment as a hackney writer, to copy for the stationers and lawyers about the Temple, but could find no vacancy.

I immediately got into work at Palmer's, then a famous printing-house in Bartholomew Close, and here I continu'd near a year. I was pretty diligent, but spent with Ralph a good deal of my earnings in going to plays and other places of amusement. We had together consumed all my pistoles, and now just rubbed on from hand to mouth. He seem'd quite to forget his wife and child, and I, by degrees, my engagements with Miss Read, to whom I never wrote more than one letter, and that was to let her know I was not likely soon to return. This was another of the great errata of my life, which I should wish to correct if I were to live it over again. In fact, by our expenses, I was constantly kept unable to pay my passage.

---

* A comedian.–B.

At Palmer's I was employed in composing for the second edition of Wollaston's " Religion of Nature." Some of his reasonings not appearing to me well founded, I wrote a little metaphysical piece in which I made remarks on them. It was entitled " A Dissertation on Liberty and Necessity, Pleasure and Pain." I inscribed it to my friend Ralph; I printed a small number. It occasion'd my being more consider'd by Mr. Palmer as a young man of some ingenuity, tho' he seriously expostulated with me upon the principles of my pamphlet, which to him appear'd abominable. My printing this pamphlet was another erratum.* While I lodg'd in Little Britain, I made an acquaintance with one Wilcox, a bookseller, whose shop was at the next door. He had an immense collection of secondhand books. Circulating libraries were not then in use; but we agreed that, on certain reasonable terms, which I have now forgotten, I might take, read, and return any of his books. This I esteem'd a great advantage, and I made as much use of it as I could.

My pamphlet by some means falling into the hands of one Lyons, a surgeon, author of a book entitled "The Infallibility of Human Judgment," it occasioned an acquaintance between us. He took great notice of me, called on me often to converse on those subjects, carried me to the Homs, a pale alehouse in Lane, Cheapside, and introduced me to Dr. Mandeville, author of the " Fable of the Bees," who had a club there, of which he was the soul, being a most facetious, entertaining companion. Lyons, too, introduced me to Dr. Pemberton, at Batson's Coffee-house, who promis'd to give me an opportunity, some time or other, of seeing Sir Isaac Newton, of which I was extreamely desirous; but this never happened.

I had brought over a few curiosities, among which

---

* No copy of this tract is now known to be in existence. See Franklin to Vaughan, *Sparks' Works of Franklin*, vol. viii. p. 405.–B.

the principal was a purse made of the asbestos which purifies by fire. Sir Hans Sloane heard of it, came to see me, and invited me to his house in Bloomsbury Square, where he show'd me all his curiosities, and persuaded me to let him add that to the number, for which he paid me handsomely.*

In our house there lodg'd a young woman, a milliner, who, I think, had a shop in the Cloisters. She had been genteelly bred, was sensible and lively, and of most pleasing conversation. Ralph read plays to her in the evenings, they grew intimate, she took another lodging, and he followed her. They liv'd together some time ; but, he being still out of business, and her income was not sufficient to maintain them with her child, he took a resolution of going from London, to try for a country school, which he thought himself well qualified to undertake, as he wrote an excellent hand, and was

---

* The following letter to Sir Hans Sloane is published in the Sparks' Collection of Correspondence, *Works of Franklin*, vol. vii. p. I. Franklin was then 19 years of age:

" London, 2 *June*, 1725.

" Sir : Having lately been in the northern parts of America, I have brought from thence a purse made of the *Asbetos*, a piece of the stone, and a piece of the wood, the pithy part of which is of the same nature, and called by the inhabitants Salamander Cotton. As you are noted to be a lover of curiosities, I have informed you of these ; and if you have any inclination to purchase or see them, let me know your pleasure by a line for me at the Golden Fan, Little Britain, and I will wait upon you with them. I am, sir, your most humble servant,

B. Franklin.

" P. S. I expect to be out of town in two or three days, and therefore beg an immediate answer."–B.

a master of arithmetic and accounts. This, however, he deemed a business below him, and confident of future better fortune, when he should be unwilling to have it known that he once was so meanly employed, he changed his name, and did me the honor to assume mine; for I soon after had a letter from him, acquainting me that he was settled in a small village (in Berkshire, I think it was, where he taught reading and writing to ten or a dozen boys, at sixpence each per week), recommending Mrs.T to my care, and desiring me to write to him, directing for Mr. Franklin, schoolmaster, at such a place.

He continued to write frequently, sending me large specimens of an epic poem which he was then composing, and desiring my remarks and corrections. These I gave him from time to time, but endeavor'd rather to discourage his proceeding. One of Young's Satires was then just published. I copy'd and sent him a great part of it, which set in a strong light the folly of pursuing the Muses with any hope of advancement by them.* All was invain; sheets of the poem continued to come by every post. In the mean time, Mrs. T having on his account lost her friends and business,

---

* " Th' abandoned manners of our writing train
May tempt mankind to think religion vain;
But in their fate, their habit, and their mien,
That gods there are is evidently seen :
Heav'n stands absolv'd by vengeance on their pen,
And marks the murderers of fame from men:
Through meagre jaws they draw their venal breath
As ghastly as their brothers in Macbeth :
Their feet thro' faithless leather meets the dirt,
And oftener changed their principles than shirt:
The transient vestments of these frugal men
Hasten to paper for our mirth again:

was often in distresses, and us'd to send for me, and borrow what I could spare to help her out of them. I grew fond of her company, and, being at that time under no religious restraint, and presuming upon

---

Too soon (O merry, melancholy fate!)
They beg in rhyme, and warble thro' a grate;
The man lampooned, forgets it at the sight;
The friend thro' pity gives, the foe through spite;
And though full conscious of his injur'd purse,
Lintot relents, nor Cecil can wish them worse.

"An author, 'tis a venerable name !
How few deserve it and what numbers claim.
Unbless'd with sense, above the peers refin'd,
Who shall stand up, dictators to mankind ?
Nay, who dare shine, if not in virtue's cause?
That sole proprietor of just applause.

"Ye restless men ! who pant for letter'd praise,
With whom would you consult to gain the bays?
With those great authors whose fam'd works you read?
Tis well; go, then, consult the laurel'd shade,
What answer will the laurel'd shade return ?
Hear it and tremble, he commands you burn
The noblest works, his envy'd genius writ,
That boasts of naught more excellent than wit.
If this be true, as 'tis a truth most dread,
Woe to the page which has not that to plead !
Fontaine and Chaucer, dying, wish'd unwrote
The sprightliest efforts of their wanton thought:
Sidney and Waller, brightest sons of fame,

Condemn'd the charm of ages to the flame.
"Thus ends your courted fame—does lucre then,
The sacred thirst of gold, betray your pen ?
In prose 'tis blamabie, in verse 'tis worse,
Provokes the Muse, extorts Apollo's curse;
His sacred influence never should be sold; '
Tis arrant simony to sing for gold;
'Tis immortality should fire your mind,
Scorn a less paymaster than all mankind."

YOUNG, vol. iii. *Epist.* ii., p. 70.—B.

my importance to her, I attempted familiarities (another erratum) which she repuls'd with a proper resentment, and acquainted him with my behaviour. This made a breach between us; and, when he returned again to London, he let me know he thought I had cancell'd all the obligations he had been under to me. So I found I was never to expect his repaying me what I lent to him, or advanc'd for him. This, however, was not then of much consequence, as he was totally unable; and in the loss of his friendship I found myself relieved from a burthen. I now began to think of getting a little money beforehand, and, expecting better work, I left Palmer's to work at Watts's, near Lincoln's Inn Fields, a still greater printing-house. Here I continued all the rest of my stay in London.

At my first admission into this printing-house I took to working at press, imagining I felt a want of the bodily exercise I had been us'd to in America, where presswork is mix'd with composing. I drank only water; the other workmen, near fifty in number, were great guzzlers of beer. On occasion, I carried up to the down stairs a large form of types in each hand, when others carried but one in both hands. They wondered to see, from this and several instances, that the *Water-American,* as they called me, was *stronger* than themselves, who drank *strong* beer ! We had an alehouse boy who attended always in the house to supply the workmen. My companion at the press drank every day a pint before breakfast, a pint at breakfast with his bread and cheese, a pint between breakfast and dinner, a pint at dinner, a pint in the evening about six o'clock, and another when he had done his day's work. I thought it a detestable custom; but it was necessary, he suppos'd to drink *strong* beer, that he might be *strong* to labor. I endeavored to convince him that the bodily strength afforded by beer could only be in proportion to the grain or flour of the barley dissolved in the water of which it was made; that there was more flour in a pennyworth of bread; and therefore, if he would eat that with a pint of water, it would give him more strength than a quart of beer. He drank on, however, and had four or five shillings to pay out of his wages every Saturday night for that muddling liquor; an expense I was free from. And thus these poor devils keep themselves always under.

Watts, after some weeks, desiring to have me in the composing-room, I left the pressmen; a new bien venu or sum for drink, being five shillings, was demanded of me by the compositors. I thought it an imposition, as I had paid below; the master thought so too, and forbad my paying it. I stood out two or three weeks, was accordingly considered as an excommunicate, and had so many little pieces of private mischief done me, by mixing my sorts, transposing my pages, breaking my matter, etc., etc., if I were ever so little out of the room, and all ascribed to the chappel ghost, which they said ever haunted those not regularly admitted, that, notwithstanding the master's protection, I found myself oblig'd to comply and pay the money, convinc'd of the folly of being on ill terms with those one is to live with continually.

I was now on a fair footing with them, and soon acquir'd considerable influence. I propos'd some reasonable alterations in their chappel* laws, and carried them against all opposition. From my example, a great part of them left their muddling breakfast of beer, and bread, and cheese, finding they could with me be suppyl'd from a neighboring house with a large porringer of hot water-gruel, sprinkled with pepper, crumb'd with bread, and a bit of butter in it, for the price of a pint of beer, viz., three half-pence.

---

* "A printing-house is always called a chappel by the workmen, the origin of which appears to have been, that printing was first carried on in England in an antient chapel converted into a printing-house, and the title has been preserved by tradition. The bien venu among the printers answers to the terms entrance and footing among mechanics; thus a journeyman, on entering a printing-house, was accustomed to pay one or more gallons of beer for the good of the chappel : this custom was falling into disuse thirty years ago; it is very properly rejected entirely in the United States."—W. T. F.

This was a more comfortable as well as cheaper breakfast, and kept their heads clearer. Those who continued sotting with beer all day, were often, by not paying, out of credit at the alehouse, and us'd to make interest with me to get beer; their *light,* as they phrased it, *being out.* I watch'd the pay-table on Saturday night, and collected what Istood engag'd for them, having to pay sometimes near thirty shillings a week on their accounts. This, and my being esteem'd a pretty good *riggite,* that is, a jocular verbal satirist, supported my consequence in the society. My constant attendance (I never making a St. Monday) recommended me to the master; and my uncommon quickness at composing occasioned my being put upon all work of dispatch, which was generally better paid. So I went on now very agreeably.

My lodging in Little Britain being too remote, I found another in Duke-street, opposite to the Romish Chappel. It was two pair of stairs backwards, at an Italian warehouse. A widow lady kept the house; she had a daughter, and a maid servant, and a journeyman who attended the warehouse, but lodg'd abroad. After sending to inquire my character at the house where I last lodg'd, she agreed to take me in at the same rate, 3s. 6d. per week; cheaper, as she said, from the protection she expected in having a man lodge in the house. She was a widow, an elderly woman; had been bred a Protestant, being a clergyman's daughter, but was converted to the Catholic religion by her husband, whose memory she much revered; had lived much among people of distinction, and knew a thousand anecdotes of them as far back as the times of Charles the Second. She was lame in her knees with the gout, and, therefore, seldom stirred out of her room, so sometimes wanted company; and hers was so highly amusing to me, that I was sure to spend an evening with her whenever she desired it. Our supper was only half an anchovy each, on a very little strip of bread and butter, and half a pint of ale between us;

but the entertainment was in her conversation. My always keeping good hours, and giving little trouble in the family, made her unwilling to part with me; so that, when I talk'd of a lodging I had heard of, nearer my business, for two shillings a week, which, intent as I now was on saving money, made some difference, she bid me not think of it, for she would abate me two shillings a week for the future; so I remained with her at one shilling and sixpence as long as I stayed in London.

In a garret of her house there lived a maiden lady of seventy, in the most retired manner, of whom my landlady gave me this account: that she was a Roman Catholic, had been sent abroad when young, and lodg'd in a nunnery with an intent of becoming a nun; but, the country not agreeing with her, she returned to England, where, there being no nunnery, she had vow'd to lead the life of a nun, as near as might be done in those circumstances. Accordingly, she had given all her estate to charitable uses, reserving only twelve pounds a year to live on, and out of this sum she still gave a great deal in charity, living herself on water-gruel only, and using no fire but to boil it. She had lived many years in that garret, being permitted to remain there gratis by successive Catholic tenants of the house below, as they deemed it a blessing to have her there. A priest visited her to confess her everyday. "I have ask'd her," says my landlady, " how she, as she liv'd, could possiby find so much employment for a confessor?" "Oh," said she, "it is impossible to avoid *vain thoughts,"* I was permitted once to visit her. She was chearful and polite, and convers'd pleasantly. The room was clean, but had no other furniture than a matras, a table with a crucifix and book, a stool which she gave me to sit on, and a picture over the chimney of Saint Veronica displaying her handkerchief, with the miraculous figure of Christ's bleeding face on it, which she explained to me with great seriousness. She look'd pale, but was never sick; and I give it as another instance on how small an income, life and health may be supported.

At Watts's printing-house I contracted an acquaintance with an ingenious young man, one Wygate, who, having wealthy relations, had been better educated than most printers ; was a tolerable Latinist, spoke French, and lov'd reading. I taught him and a friend of his to swim at twice going into the river, and they soon became good swimmers. They introduc'd me to some gentlemen from the country, who went to Chelsea by water to see the College and Don Saltero's curiosities. In our return, at the request of the company, whose curiosity Wygate had excited, I stripped and leaped into the river, and swam from near Chelsea to Blackfryar's, performing on the way many feats of activity, both upon and under water, that surpris'd and pleas'd those to whom they were novelties.

I had from a child been ever delighted with this exercise, had studied and practis'd all Thevenot's motions and positions, added some of my own, aiming at the graceful and easy as well as the useful. All these I took this occasion of exhibiting to the company, and was much flatter'd by their admiration ; and Wygate, who was desirous of becoming a master, grew more and more attach'd to me on that account, as well as from the similarity of our studies. He at length proposed to me travelling all over Europe together, supporting ourselves everywhere by working at our business. I was once inclined to it; but, mentioning it to my good friend Mr. Denham, with whom I often spent an hour when I had leisure, he dissuaded me from it, advising me to think only of returning to Pennsilvania, which he was now about to do.

I must record one trait of this good man's character. He had formerly been in business at Bristol, but failed in debt to a number of people, compounded and went to America. There, by a close application to business as a merchant, he acquir'd

a plentiful fortune in a few years. Returning to England in the ship with me, he invited his old creditors to an entertainment, at which he thank'd them for the easy composition they had favored him with, and,
when they expected nothing but the treat, every man at the first remove found under his plate an order on a banker for the full amount of the unpaid remainder, with interest.

He now told me he was about to return to Philadelphia, and should carry over a great quantity of goods in order to open a store there. He propos'd to take me over as his clerk, to keep his books, in which he would instruct me, copy his letters, and attend the store. He added, that, as soon as I should be acquainted with mercantile business, he would promote me by sending me with a cargo of flour and bread, etc., to the West Indies, and procure me commissions from others which would be profitable ; and, if I manag'd well, would establish me handsomely. The thing pleas'd me; for I was grown tired of London, remembered with pleasure the happy months I had spent in Pennsylvania, and wish'd again to see it; therefore I immediately agreed on the terms of fifty pounds a year, Pennsylvania money; less, indeed, than my present gettings as a compositor, but affording a better prospect.

I now took leave of printing, as I thought, for ever, and was daily employ'd in my new business, going about with Mr. Denham among the tradesmen to purchase various articles, and seeing them pack'd up, doing errands, calling upon workmen to dispatch, etc.; and, when all was on board, I had a few days' leisure. On one of these days, I was, to my surprise, sent for by a great man I knew only by name, a Sir William Wyndham, and I waited upon him. He had heard by some means or other of my swimming from Chelsea to Blackfriar's, and of my teaching to Wygate and another young man to swim in a few hours. He had two sons, about to set out on their travels; he wish'd to have them first taught swimming, and proposed to gratify me handsomely if I would teach them. They were not yet come to town, and my stay was uncertain, so I could not undertake it; but, from this incident, I thought it likely that, if I were to remain in England and open a swimming-school, I might get a good deal of money; and it struck me so strongly, that, had the overture been sooner made me, probably I should not so soon have returned to America. After many years, you and I had something of more importance to do with one of these sons of Sir William Wyndham, become Earl of Egremont, which I shall mention in its place.

Thus I spent about eighteen months in London; most part of the time I work'd hard at my business, and spent a little upon myself except in seeing plays and in books. My friend Ralph had kept me poor; he owed me about twenty-seven pounds, which I was now never likely to receive; a great sum out of my small earnings! I lov'd him, notwithstanding, for he had many amiable qualities. I had no means to improv'd my fortune; but I had picked up some very ingenious acquaintance, whose conversation was of great advantage to me; and I had read considerably.

We sail'd from Gravesend on the 23rd of July, 1726. For the incidents of the voyage, I refer you to my Journal, where you will find them all minutely related. Perhaps the most important part of that journal is the *plan** to be found in it, which I formed at sea, for regulating my future conduct in life. It is the more remarkable, as being formed when I was so young, and yet being pretty faithfully adhered to quite thro' to old age.

We landed in Philadelphia on the 11th of October, where I found sundry alterations. Keith was no longer governor, being superseded by Major Gordon. I met him walking the streets as a common citizen. He seem'd a little asham'd at seeing me,

---

* The " plan" referred to as the most " important part of the Journal," is not found in the manuscript Journal which was left among Franklin's papers. The copy of the Journal that was found was made at Reading in 1787 ; the original is probably lost. See *Sparks' Memoir of Franklin* , Appendix II.–B.

but pass'd without saying any thing. I should have been as much asham'd at seeing Miss Read, who had no friends, despairing with reason of my return after the receipt of my letter, persuaded her to marry another, one Rogers, a potter, which was done in my absence. With him, however, she was never happy, and soon parted from him, refusing to cohabit with him or bear his name, it being now said that he had another wife. He was a worthless fellow. tho' an excellent workman, which was the temptation to her friends. He got into debt, ran away in 1727 or 1728, went to the West Indies, and died there. Keimer had got a better house, a shop well supply'd with stationery, plenty of new types, a number of hands, tho' none good, and seem'd to have a great deal of business.

Mr. Denham took a store in Water-street, where we open'd our goods; I attended the business diligently, studied accounts, and grew, in a little time, expert at selling. We lodg'd and boarded together; he counsell'd me as a father, having a sincere regard for me. I respected and lov'd him, and we might have gone on together very happy; but, in the beginning of February, 1726/27, when I had just pass'd my twenty-first year, we both were taken ill. My distemper was a pleurisy, which very nearly carried me off. I suffered a good deal, gave up the point in my own mind, and was rather disappointed when I found myself recovering, regretting, in some degree, that I must now, some time or other, have all that disagreeable work to do over again. I forget what his distemper was; it held him a long time, and at length carried him off. He left me a small legacy in a nuncupative will, as a token of his kindness for me, and he left me once more to the wide world ; now the store was taken into the care of his executors, and my employment under him ended.

My brother-in-law, Holmes, being now at Philadelphia, advised my return to my business; and Keimer tempted me, with an offer of large wages by the year, to come and take the management of his printing-house, that he might better attend his stationer's shop. I had heard a bad character of him in London from his wife and her friends, and was not fond of having any more to do with him. I tri'd for farther employment as a merchant's clerk; but, not readily meeting with any, I clos'd again with Keimer. I found in his house these hands: Hugh Meredith, a Welsh Pensilvanian, thirty years of age, bred to country work; honest, sensible, had a great deal of solid observation, was something of a reader, but given to drink. Stephen Potts, a young countryman of full age, bred to the same, of uncommon natural parts, and great wit and humor, but a little idle. These he had agreed with at extre me low wages per week, to be rais'd a shilling every three months, as they would deserve by improving in their business; and the expectation of these high wages, to come on hereafter, was what he had drawn them in with. Meredith was to work at press, Potts at book-binding, which he, by agreement, was to teach them, though he knew neither one nor tother. John a wild Irish man, brought up to no business, whose service, for four years, Keimer had purchased from the captain of a ship; he, too, was to be made a pressman. George Webb, an Oxford scholar, whose time for four years he had likewise bought, intending him for a compositor, of whom more presently; and David Harry, a country boy, whom he had taken apprentice.

I soon perceiv'd that the intention of engaging me at wages so much higher than he had been us'd to give, was, to have these raw, cheap hands form'd thro' me ; and, as soon as I had instructed them, then they being all articled to him, he should be able to do without me. I went on, however, very cheerfully, put his printing-house in order, which had been in great confusion, and brought his hands by degrees to mind their business and to do it better.

It was an odd thing to find an Oxford scholar in the situation of a bought servant. He was not more than eighteen years of age, and gave me this account of himself; that he was born in Gloucester, educated at a grammar-school there, had been distinguish'd among the scholars for some apparent superiority in performing his part, when they exhibited plays; belong'd to the Witty Club there, and had written some pieces in prose and verse, which were printed in the Gloucester newspapers; hence he was sent to Oxford ; where he continued about a year, but not well satisfi'd, wishing of all things to see London, and become a player. At length, receiving his quarterly allowance of fifteen guineas, instead of discharging his debts he walk'd out of town, hid his gown in a furze bush, and footed it to London, where having no friend to advise him, he fell into bad company, soon spent his guineas, found no means of being introduc'd among the players, grew necessitous, pawn'd his cloaths, and wanted bread. Walking the street very hungry, and not knowing what to do with himself, a crimp's bill was put into his hand, offering immediate entertainment and encouragement to such as would bind themselves to serve in America. He went directly, sign'd the indentures, was put into the ship, and came over, never writing a line to acquaint his friends what was become of him. He was lively, witty, good-natur'd and a pleasant companion, but idle, thoughtless, and imprudent to the last degree.

John, the Irishman, soon ran away; with the rest I began to live very agreeably, for they all respected me the more, as they found Keimer incapable of instructing them, and that from me they learned something daily. We never worked on Saturday, that being Keimer's Sabbath, so I had two days for reading. My acquaintance with ingenious people in the town increased. Keimer himself treated me with great civility and apparent regard, and nothing now made me uneasy but my debt to Vernon, which I was yet unable to pay, being hitherto but a poor economist. He, however, kindly made no demand of it.

Our printing-house often wanted sorts, and there was no letter-founder in America; I had seen type cast at James's in London, but without much attention to the manner; however, I now contrived a mould, made use of the letters we had as puncheons, struck the matrices in lead, and thus supply'd in a pretty tolerable way all deficiencies. I also engrav'd several things on occasion ; I made the ink; I was warehouseman, and everything, and, in short, quite a factotum.

But, however serviceable I might be, I found that my services became every day of less importance, on the other hands improv'd in the business ; and, when Keimer paid my second quarter's wages, he let me know that he felt them too heavy, and thought I should make an abatement. He grew by degrees less civil, put on more of the master, frequently found fault, was captious, and seem'd ready for an outbreaking. I went on, nevertheless, with a good deal of patience, thinking that his encumber'd circumstances were partly the cause. At length, a trifle snapt our connections; for a great noise happening near the court-house, I put my head out of the window to see what was the matter. Keimer, being in the street, look'd up and saw me, call'd out to me in a loud voice and angry tone to mind my business, adding some reproachful words, that nettled me the more for their publicity, all the neighbors who were looking out on the same occasion, being witnesses how I was treated. He came up immediately into the printing-house, continu'd the quarrel, high words pass'd on both sides he gave me the quarter's warning we had stipulated, expressing a wish that he had not been oblig'd to so long a warning. I told him his wish was unnecessary, for I would leave him that instant; and so, taking my hat, walk'd out of doors, desiring Meredith, whom I saw below, to take care of some things I left, and bring them to my lodgings.

Meredith came accordingly in the evening, when we talked my affair over. He had conceiv'd a great regard for me, and was very unwilling that I should leave the house while he remain'd in it. He dissuaded me from returning to my native country, which I began to think of ; he reminded me that Keimer was in debt for all he possess'd; that his creditors began to be uneasy; that he kept his shop miserably, sold often without profit for ready money, and often trusted without keeping accounts ; that he must therefore fail, which would make a vacancy I might profit of. I objected my want of money. He then let me know that his father had a high opinion of me, and, from some discourse that had pass'd between them, he was sure would advance money to set us up, if I would enter into partnership with him. "My time," says he, "will be out with Keimer in the spring; by that time we may have our press and types in from London. I am sensible; I am no workman; if you like it, your skill in the business shall be set against the stock I furnish, and we will share the profits equally."

The proposal was agreeable, and I consented; his father was in town and approv'd of it; the more as he saw I had great influence with his son, had prevail'd on him to abstain long from dram-drinking, and he hop'd might break him of that wretched habit entirely, when we came to be so closely connected. I gave an inventory to the father, who carry'd it to a merchant; the things were sent for, the secret was to be kept till they should arrive, and in the mean time I was to get work, if I could, at the other printing-house. But I found no vacancy there, and so remain'd idle for a few days, when Keimer, on a prospect of being employ'd to print some paper money in New Jersey, which would require cuts and various types that I only could supply, and apprehending Bradford might engage me and get the job from him, sent me a very civil message, that old friends should not part for a few words, the effect of sudden passion, and wishing me to return. Meredith persuaded me to comply, as it would give more opportunity for his improvement under my daily instructions; so I return'd, and we went on more smoothly than for some time before. The New Jersey job was obtain'd, I contriv'd a copperplate press for it, the first that had been seen in the country; I cut several ornaments and checks for the bills. We went together to Burlington, where I executed the whole to satisfaction ; and he received so large a sum for the work as to be enabled thereby to keep his head much longer above water.

At Burlington I made an acquaintance with many principal people of the province. Several of them had been appointed by the Assembly a committee to attend the press, and take care that no more bills were printed than the law directed. They were therefore, by turns, constantly with us, and generally he who attended, brought with him a friend or two for company. My mind having been much more improv'd by reading than Keimer's, I suppose it was for that reason my conversation seem'd to be more valu'd. They had me to their houses, introduced me to their friends, and show'd me much civility; while he, tho' the master, was a little neglected. In truth, he was an odd fish; ignorant of common life, fond of rudely opposing receiv'd opinions, slovenly to extream dirtiness, enthusiastic in some points of religion, and a little knavish withal.

We continu'd there near three months; and by that time I could reckon among my acquired friends, Judge Allen, Samuel Bustill, the secretary of the Province, Isaac Pearson, Joseph Cooper, and several of the Smiths, members of Assembly, and Isaac Decow, the surveyor-general. The latter was a shrewd, sagacious old man, who told me that he began for himself, when young, by wheeling clay for the brickmakers, learned to write after he was of age, carri'd the chain for surveyors, who taught him surveying, and he had now by his industry, acquir'd a good estate; and says he, "I foresee that you will soon work this man out of his business, and make a fortune in it at Philadelphia." He had not then the least intimation of my intention to set up there or anywhere. These friends were afterwards of great use to me, as I occasionally was to some of them. They all continued their regard for me as long as they lived.

Before I enter upon my public appearance in business, it may be well to let you know the then state of my mind with regard to my principles and morals, that you may see how far those influenc'd the future events of my life. My parents had early given me religious impressions, and brought me through my childhood piously in the Dissenting way. But I was scarce fifteen, when, after doubting by turns of several points, as I found them disputed in the different books I read, I began to doubt of Revelation itself. Some books against Deism fell into my hands; they were said to be the substance of sermons preached at Boyle's Lectures. It happened that they wrought an effect on me quite contrary to what was intended by them; for the arguments of the Deists, which were quoted to be refuted, appeared to me much stronger than the refutations; in short, I soon became a thorough Deist. My arguments perverted some others, particularly Collins and Ralph; but, each of them having afterwards wrong'd me greatly without the least compunction, and recollecting Keith's conduct towards me (who was another freethinker), and my own towards Vernpn and Miss Read, which at times gave me great trouble, I began to suspect that this doctrine, tho' it might be true, was not very useful. My London pamphlet,* which had for its motto these lines of Dryden :

---

* Printed in 1725.

Dr. Franklin in a part of a letter to Mr. B. Vaughan, dated Nov. 9, 1779, gives a further account of this pamphlet, in these words :

" It was addressed to Mr. J. R., i.e. James Ralph, then a youth of

> " Whatever is, is right. Though purblind man Sees but a part o' the chain, the nearest link: His eyes not carrying to the equal beam, That poises all above

and from the attributes of God, his infinite wisdom, goodness and power, concluded that nothing could possibly be wrong in the world, and that vice and virtue were empty distinctions, no such things existing, appear'd now not so clever aperformance as I once thought it; and I doubted whether

---

about my age, and my intimate friend; afterwards a political writer and historian. The purport of it was to prove the doctrine of fate, from the supposed attributes of God; in some such manner as this: that in erecting and governing the world, as he was infinitely wise, he knew what would be best; infinitely good, he must be disposed, and infinitely powerful, he must be able to execute it: consequently all is right. There were only an hundred copies printed, of which I gave a few to friends, and afterwards disliking the piece, as conceiving it might have an ill tendency, I burnt the rest, except one copy, the margin of which was filled with manuscript notes by Syms, author of the Infallibility of Human Judgment, who was at that time another of my acquaintance in London. I was not nineteen years of age when it was written. In 1730, I wrote a piece on the other side of the question, which began with laying for its foundation this fact: 'That almost all men in all ages and countries, have at times made use of prayer.' Thence I reasoned, that if all things are ordained, prayer must among the rest be ordained. But as prayer can produce no change in things that are ordained, praying must then be useless and an absurdity. God would therefore not ordain praying if everything else was ordained. But praying exists, therefore all things are not ordained, etc. This pamphlet was never printed, and the manuscript has been long lost. The great uncertainty I found in metaphysical reasonings disgusted me, and I quitted that kind of reading and study for others more satisfactory."—B.

some error had not insinuated itself unperceiv'd into my argument, so as to infect all that follow'd, as is common in metaphysical reasonings.

I grew convinc'd that *truth, sincerity* and *integrity* in dealings between man and man were of the utmost importance to the felicity of life; and I form'd written resolutions, which still remain in my journal book, to practice them ever while I lived. Revelation had indeed no weight with me, as such ; but I entertain'd an opinion that, though certain actions might not be bad *because* they were forbidden by it, or good *because* it commanded them, yet probably those actions might be forbidden *because* they were bad for us, or commanded *because* they were beneficial to us, in their own natures, all the circumstances of things considered. And this persuasion, with the kind hand of Providence, or some guardian angel, or accidental favorable circumstances and situations, or all together, preserved me, thro' this dangerous time of youth, and the hazardous situations I was sometimes in among strangers, remote from the eye and advice of my father, without any willful gross immorality or injustice, that might have been expected from my want of religion.* I say willful, because instances I have mentioned had something of *necessity* in them, from my youth, inexperience, and the knavery of others. I had therefore a tolerable character to begin the world with; I valued it properly and determin'd to preserve it. We had not been long return'd to Philadelphia before the new types arriv'd from London. We settled with Keimer, and left him by his consent before he heard of it. We found a house to hire near the market, and took it. To lessen the rent,

---

* The words, " Some foolish intrigues with low women excepted, which from the expense were rather more prejudicial to me than to them," effaced on the revision, and the sentence which follows in the text written in the margin.—B.

which was then but twenty-four pounds a year, tho' I have since known it to let for seventy, we took in Thomas Godfrey, a glazier, and his family, who were to pay a considerable part of it to us, and we to board with them. We had scarce opened our letters and put our press in order, before George House, an acquaintance of mine, brought a countryman to us, whom he had met in the street inquiring for a printer. All our cash was now expended in the variety of particulars we had been obliged to procure, and this countryman's five shillings, being our first-fruits, and coming so seasonably, gave me more pleasure than any crown I have since earned; and the gratitude I felt toward House has made me often more ready than perhaps I should otherwise have been to assist young beginners.

There are croakers in every country, always boding its ruin. Such a one then lived in Philadelphia ; a person of note, an elderly man, with a wise look and a very grave manner of speaking; his name was Samuel Mickle. This gentleman, a stranger to me, stopted one day at my door, and asked me if I was the young man who had lately opened a new printing-house. Being answered in the affirmative, he said he was sorry for me, because it was an expensive undertaking, and the expense would be lost; for Philadelphia was a sinking place, the people already half bankrupts, or near being so; all appearances to the contrary, such as new buildings and the rise of rents, being to his certain knowledge fallacious; for they were, in fact, among the things that would soon ruin us. And he gave me such a detail of misfortunes now existing, or that were soon to exist, that he left me half melancholy. Had I known him before I engaged in this business, probably I never should have done it. This man continued to live in this decaying place, and to declaim in the same strain, refusing for many years to buy a house there, because all was going to destruction; and at last I had the pleasure of seeing him give five times as much for one as he might have bought it for when he first began his croaking.

I should have mentioned before, that, in the autumn of the preceding year, I had form'd most of my ingenious acquaintance into a club of mutual improvement, which we called the JUNTO ; we met on Friday evenings. The rules that I drew up required that every member, in his turn, should produce one or more queries on any point of Morals, Politics or Natural Philosophy to be discuss'd by the company; and once in three months produce and read an essay of his own writing, on any subject he pleased. Our debates were to be under the direction of a president, and to be conducted in the sincere spirit of inquiry after truth, without fondness for dispute, or desire of victory; and to prevent warmth, all expressions of positiveness in opinions, or direct contradiction, were after some time made contraband, and prohibited under small pecuniary penalties.

The first members were Joseph Breintnal, a copyer of deeds for the scriveners, a good-natur'd, friendly, middle-ag'd man, a great lover of poetry, reading all he could meet with, and writing some that was tolerable; very ingenious in many little Nicknack-eries, and of sensible conversation.

Thomas Godfrey, a self-taught mathematician, great in his way, and afterward inventor of what is now called Hadley's Quadrant. But he knew little out of his way, and was not a pleasing companion ; as, like most great mathematicians I have met with, he expected universal precision in every thing said, or was for ever denying or distinguishing upon trifles, to the disturbance of all conversation. He soon left us.

Nicholas Scull, a surveyor, afterward surveyorgeneral, who lov'd books, and sometimes made a few verses.

William Parsons, bred a shoemaker, but, loving reading, had acquir'd a considerable share of mathematics, which he first studied with a view to astrology, that he afterwards laught at it. He also became surveyor-general.

William Maugridge, a joiner, a most exquisite mechanic, and a solid. sensible man.

Hugh Meredith, Stephen Potts and George Webb I have characteriz'd before.

Robert Grace, a young gentleman of some fortune, generous, lively and witty ; a lover of punning and of his friends.

And William Coleman, then a merchant's clerk, about my age, who had the coolest, clearest head, the best heart, and the exactest morals of almost any man I ever met with. He became afterwards a merchant of great note, and one of our provincial judges. Our friendship continued without interruption to his death, upward of forty years; and the club continued almost as long, and was the best school of philosophy, morality, and politics that then existed in the province; for our queries, which were read the week preceding their discussion, put us upon reading with attention upon the several subjects, that we

---

* In a careful and interesting paper read before the American Philosophical Society by Dr. Patterson, one of its Vice-Presidents, on the 25th of May, 1843, in commemoration of its Centennial Anniversary, will be found much new and important information about the Junto. As this paper is not generally accessible, my readers will excuse me for quoting somewhat freely from its pages. Dr. Patterson says:

" The Junto was, properly speaking, a debating society. At first it met at a tavern; but subsequently at the house of one of the members, Robert Grace, whom Franklin characterizes as ' a gentleman of some fortune, generous, lively, and witty, a lover of punning and of his friends, I am happy to say that Robert Grace is not without his successors in our present society.

might speak more to the purpose; and here, too, we acquired better habits of conversation, every thing being studied in our rules which might prevent our disgusting each other. From hence the long continuance of the club, which shall have frequent occasion to speak further of hereafter.*

" One of the rules of the Club was that the institution should be kept a secret; the intention being, as Franklin states, to avoid applications of improper persons for admittance. The number of members at any one time was limited to twelve, but vacancies were filled as they occurred, and the names of twenty-three members are preserved.

"On admission into the Club, a course was followed which is too remarkable in itself, and in its bearing upon a difficult question in the history of this Society, not to be here introduced. It is thus presented in Franklin's papers:

"Any person to be qualified–to stand up, and lay his hand upon his breast, and be asked these questions, viz.:

" '1st Have you any particular disrespect to any present member ? Answer : I have not

" ' 2nd Do you sincerely declare that you love mankind in general, of what profession or religion soever ? Ans. I do.

" ' 3rd Do you think any person ought to be harmed in his body, name, or goods, for mere speculative opinions, or his external way of worship? Ans. No.

" ' 4th Do you love truth for truth's sake, and will you endeavor impartially to find and receive it yourself, and communicate it to others ? Ans. Yes.

" No minutes of the proceedings of the original Junto are preserved, but Franklin mentions in his Autobiography several questions of great interest which were discussed at it, and several pieces read before it and afterwards published in his newspaper.

But my giving this account of it here is to show something of the interest I had, every one of these

---

" It was at one time proposed to increase the number of members; but to this Franklin was opposed, and instead of it he made ' a proposal that every member separately should form a subordinate club, with the same rules respecting queries, etc., and without informing them of the connection with the Junto.' This project was approved, and every member undertook to form a club; but they did not all succeed. Five or six only were completed, which were called by different names, as the Vine, the Union, the Band.' Of these subordinate companies, a brief paragraph in Franklin's Life is the only remaining record.

" While Franklin was abroad, he shows by his correspondence that he still held the institution of his youth in affectionate remembrance. This appears repeatedly in his letters to his friend Hugh Roberts. He calls it 'the good old Club,' 'the ancient Junto.' So late as 1765, he says: ' I wish you would continue to meet the Junto, notwithstanding that some effects of our political misunderstanding may sometimes appear there. It is now perhaps one of the oldest clubs, as I think it was formerly one of the best, in the king's dominions.' Even in 1766, he writes : ' Remember me affectionately to the Junto.'

" It appears, then, that the Junto continued in existence about forty years. But did it keep up its original character ? This may well be doubted. The members grew gradually to be old men, and it is hardly to be supposed that they would submit to the task of writing essays, or would formally propose questions, and afterwards debate them. Their fortunes were made, their education completed; and it is therefore much more probable that when the remnant of the once youthful and active Junto met together, they indulged themselves in social conversation and temperate conviviality. Such is said to be the tradition in the Robert's family; and it is confirmed by a letter from Dr. Franklin to their ancestor, written in 1761, in which he says: 'You tell me you sometimes visit the ancient junto. I wish you would do it oftener. Since we have held that Club till we are grown gray together, let us hold it out to the end. For my own part, I find I love company, chat, a laugh, a glass, and even a song, as well as ever; and at the same time relish better than I used to do the grave observations and wise sentences of old men's conversation; so that I am sure the Junto will be still as agreeable to me as it ever has been. I therefore hope it will not be discontinued, as long as we are able to crawl together."

exerting themselves in recommending business to us. Breintnal particularly procur'd us from the Quakers

---

In May, 1765, Hugh Roberts writes as follows to Dr. Franklin: "I sometimes visit the worthy remains of the ancient Junto, for whom I have a high esteem; but alas, the political, polemical divisions have in some measure contributed to lessen that harmony we there formerly enjoyed." To this letter Franklin answers in July following, urging his friend's attendance at the Junto, almost in the same terms used some years before, and which we have just quoted, and then closes his exhortation in the following touching words: "We loved and still love one another. We are grown gray together, and yet it is too early to part Let us sit till the evening of life is spent. The last hours are always the most joyous. When we can stay no longer, it is time enough then to bid each other good-night, separate and go quietly to bed."

The following rules for the regulation of the Junto, drawn up in 1728, will give a clearer idea of its character, and, I may add, of the character of its members. Forty years later the Junto became the nucleus of the American Philosophical Society, of which Franklin was the first President :

Have you read over these queries this morning, in order to consider what you might have to offer the Junto touching any one of them ? viz.:

1. Have you met with anything in the author you last read, remarkable or suitable to be communicated to the Junto, particularly in history, morality, poetry, physic, travels, mechanic arts, or other parts of knowledge ?
2. What new story have you lately heard, agreeable for telling in conversation ?
3. Has any citizen in your knowledge failed in his business lately, and what have you heard of the cause ?
4. Have you lately heard of any citizen's thriving well, and by what means ?
5. Have you lately heard how any present rich man, here or elsewhere, got his estate ?
6. Do you know of a fellow-citizen, who has lately done a worthy action, deserving praise and imitation; or who has lately committed an error, proper for us to be warned against and avoid ?

* *Sharks' Works of Franklin,* vol. ii. p. 9.

the printing forty sheets of their history, the rest being to be done by Keimer; and upon this wework'd exceeingly hard,for the price was low.

---

7. What unhappy effects of intemperance have you lately observed or heard; of imprudence, of passion, or of any other vice or folly?
8. What happy effects of temperance of prudence, of moderation, or of any other virtue ?
9. Have you or any of your acquaintance been lately sick or wounded? If so, what remedies were used, and what were their effects ?
10. Whom do you know that are shortly going voyages or journeys, if one should have occasion to send by them ?
11. Do you think of any thing at present in which the Junto may be serviceable to mankind, to their country, to their friends, or to themselves ?
12. Has any deserving stranger arrived in town since last meeting, that you have heard of? And what have you heard or observed of his character or merits ? And whether, think you, it lies in the power of the Junto to oblige him, or encourage him as he deserves?
13. Do you know of any deserving young beginner lately set up, whom it lies in the power *of* the Junto any way to encourage ?
14. Have you lately observed any defect in the laws of your country, of which it would be proper to move the legislature for an amendment? Or do you know of any beneficial law that is wanting?
15. Have you lately observed any encroachment on the just liberties of the people ?
16. Has anybody attacked your reputation lately? And what can the Junto do towards securing it ?
17. Is there any man whose friendship you want, and which the Junto, or any of them, can procure for you ?
18. Have you lately heard any member's character attacked, and how have you defended it ?
19. Has any man injured you from whom it is in the power of the Junto to procure redress ?
20. In what manner can the Junto, or any of them, assist you in any of your honorable designs ?
21. Have you any weighty affair on hand, in which you think the advice of the Junto may be of service ?
22. What benefits have you lately received from any man not present?

It was a folio, pro patria size, in pica, with long primer notes. I compos'd of it a sheet a day, and Meredith worked it off at press; it was often eleven at night, and sometimes later, before I had finished my distribution for the next day's work, for the little

---

23. Is there any difficulty in matters of opinion, of justice, and injustice, which you would gladly have discussed at this time ?
24. Do you see any thing amiss in the present customs or proceedings of the Junto which might be amended ?

When the Philosophical Society was instituted, a book containing some of the questions discussed by the Junto was put into the hands of Dr. William Smith, who selected from it, and published in his "Eulo-gium on Franklin" the following specimens:

Is sound an entity or body ?

How may the phenomena of vapors be explained ?

Is self-interest the rudder that steers mankind, the universal monarch to whom all are tributaries ?

Which is the best form of government, and what was that form which first prevailed among mankind ?

Can any one particular form of government suit all mankind ?

What is the reason that the tides rise higher in the Bay of Fundy than the Bay of Delaware ?

Is the emission of paper money safe ?

What is the reason that men of the greatest knowledge are not the most happy ?

How may the possessions of the Lakes be improved to our advantage?

Why are tumultuous, uneasy sensations united with our desires?

Whether it ought to be the aim of philosophy to eradicate the passions ?

How may smoky chimneys be best cured ?

Why does the flame of a candle tend upwards in a spire ?

Which is least criminal–a bad action joined with a good intention, or a good action with a bad intention ?

Is it consistent with the principles of liberty in a free government to punish a man as a libeller when he speaks the truth ?"–B.

jobbs sent in by our other friends now and then put us back. But so determin'd I was to continue doing a sheet a day of the folio, that one night, when, having impos'd my forms, I thought my day's work over, one of them by accident was broken, and two pages reduced to pi, I immediately distributed and compos'd it over again before I went to bed; and this industry, visible to our neighbors, began to give us character and credit; particularly, I was told, that mention being made of the new printing-office at the merchants' Every-night club, the general opinion was that it must fail, there being already two printers in the place, Keimer and Bradford; but Dr. Baird (whom you and I saw many years after at his native place, St. Andrew's in Scotland) gave a contrary opinion: "For the industry of that Franklin," says he, " is superior to anything I ever saw of the kind; I see him still at work when I go home from club, and he is at work again before his neighbors are out of bed." This struck the rest, and we soon after had offers from one of them to supply us with stationery; but as yet we did not chuse to engage in shop business.

I mention this industry the more particularly and the more freely, tho' it seems to be talking in my own praise, that those of my posterity, who shall read it, may know the use of that virtue, when they see its effects in my favour throughout this relation.

George Webb, who had found a female friend that lent him wherewith to purchase his time of Keimer, now came to offer himself as a journeyman to us. We could not then imploy him; but I foolishly let him know as a secret that I soon intended to begin a newspaper, and might then have work for him. My hopes of success, as I told him, were founded on this, that the then only newspaper, printed by Bradford, was a paltry thing, wretchedly manag'd, no way entertaining, and yet was profitable to him ; I therefore thought a good paper would scarcely fail of good encouragement. I requested Webb not to mention it; but he told it to Keimer, who immediately, to be beforehand with me, published proposals for printing one himself, on which Webb was to be employ'd. I resented this; and, to counteract them, as I could not yet begin our paper, I wrote several pieces of entertainment for Bradford's paper, under the title of the BUSY BODY, which Breintnal continu'd some months. By this means the attention of the publics was fixed on that paper, and Keimer's proposals, which we burlesqu'd and ridicul'd, were disregarded. He began his paper, however, and, after carrying it on three quarters of a year, with at most only ninety subscribers, he offer'd it to me for a trifle; and I, having been ready some time to go on with it, took it in hand directly; and it prov'd in a few years extremely profitable to me.*

* This paper was called *The Universal Instructor in all Arts and Sciences and Pennsylvania Gazette,* Keimer printed his last number, the 39th, on the 25th day of September, 1729.–B.

I perceive that I am apt to speak in the singular number, though our partnership still continu'd; the reason may be that, in fact, the whole management

---

Its leading articles were an installment of Chambers' Dictionary, Art *Air,* a message from Gov. Burnet of the Province of Massachusetts Bay, the reply of the Assembly, and an obituary of the governor, who had just died. The following announcement filled the rest of the sheet:

"PHILADELPHIA, *September* 25.

"It not quadrating with the circumstances of the printer hereof, S. K., to publish this Gazette any longer, he gives notice that this paper concludes his third quarter; and is the last that will be printed by him. Yet, that his generous subscribers may not be baulked or disappointed, he has agreed with B. Franklin and H. Meredith, at the new printing office, to continue it to the end of the year, having transferred the property wholly to them [D. Harry declining it],* and probably if further encouragement appears it will be continued longer. The said S. K. designs to leave this province early in the spring or sooner, if possibly he can justly accommodate his affairs with every one he stands indebted to."

The next number, 40, appeared on the 2nd of October, in new type, with the following announcement, the title " *Universal Instructor in all Arts and Sciences"* having been dropped, and with it the feature of the paper which it designated:

"The Pennsylvania Gazette being now to be carryed on by other hands, the reader may expect some account of the method we design to proceed in.

" Upon a view of Chambers' great dictionaries, from whence were taken the materials of *The Universal Instructor in all Arts and Sciences,* which usually made the first part of this paper, we find that besides their containing many things abstruse or insignificant to us, it will probably be fifty years before the whole can be gone through in this manner of publication. There are likewise in those books continual references from things under one letter of the alphabet to those under another, which relate to the same subject and are necessary to explain and complete it;

* In the previous number Keimer announced that he had made over his business to David Harry, with the design to leave this province as soon as he could get in his debts and justly balance with every one of his few creditors, etc., etc.

of the business lay upon me. Meredith was no compositor, a poor pressman, and seldom sober.

---

these taken in their turn may be ten years distant; and since it is likely that they who desire to acquaint themselves with any particular art or science would gladly have the whole before them in a much less time, we believe our readers will not think such a method of communicating knowledge to be a proper one.

"However, though we do not intend to continue the publication of those dictionaries in a regular alphabetical method, as has hitherto been done; *yet,* as several things exhibited from them in the course of these papers, have been entertaining to such of the curious who never had and cannot have the advantage of good libraries; and as there are many things still behind, which being in this manner made generally known, may perhaps become of considerable use by giving such hints to the excellent natural genius's of our country, as may contribute either to the improvement of our present manufactures or towards the invention of new ones; we propose from time to time to communicate such particular parts as appear to be of the most general consequence.

"As to the Religious Courtship, part of which has been retal'd to the public in these papers, the reader may be informed, that the whole book will probably in a little time be printed and bound by itself; and those who approve of it will doubtless be better pleased to have it entire, than in this broken, interrupted manner.

" There are many who have long desired to see a good newspaper in Pennsylvania; and we hope those gentlemen who are able, will contribute towards the making this such. We ask assistance because we are fully sensible, that to publish a good newspaper is not so easy an undertaking as many people imagine it to be. The author of a Gazette (in the opinion of the learned) ought to be qualified with an extensive acquaintance with languages, a great easiness and command of writing, and relating things clearly and intelligibly and in few words ; he should be able to speak of war both by land and sea; be well acquainted with geography, with the history of the time, with the secret interests of princes and States, the secrets of courts, and the manners and customs of all nations. Men thus accomplished are very rare in this remote part of the world; and it would be well if the writer of these papers could make up among his friends what is wanting in himself.

"Upon the whole, we may assure the public, that, as far as the encouragement we meet with will enable us, no care and pains shall be

My friends lamented my connection with him, but I was to make the best of it.

Our first papers made a quite different appearance from any before in the province; a better type, and better printed; but some spirited remarks of my writing,* on the dispute then going on between

---

omitted that may make the *Pennsylvania Gazette* as agreeable and useful an entertainment as the nature of the thing will allow."

After the publication of two numbers the Gazette was published twice a week, beginning with No. 43.—B.

* The following are the spirited remarks here referred to:

" His excellency, governor Burnet, died unexpectedly about two days after the date of this reply to his last message ; and it was thought the dispute would have ended with him, or at least have lain dormant till the arrival of a new governor from England, who possibly might or might not be inclined to enter too vigorously into the measures of his predecessor. But our last advices by the post acquaint us that his honor the lieutenant-governor (on whom the government immediately devolves upon the death or absence of the commander-in-chief) has vigorously renewed the struggle on his own account, of which the particulars will be seen in our next. Perhaps some of our readers may not fully understand the original ground of this warm contest between the governor and assembly. It seems that people have for these hundred years past, enjoyed the privilege of rewarding the governor for the time being, according to their sense of his merit and services ; and few or none of their governors have complained, or had cause to complain, of a scanty allowance. When the late governor Burnet brought with him instructions to demand a settled salary of 1000 pounds sterling per annum, on him and all his successors, and the Assembly were required to fix it immediately; he insisted on it strenuously to the last, and they as constantly refused it. It appears by their votes and proceedings that they thought it an imposition, contrary to their own charter, and to Magna Charta; and they judged that there should be a mutual dependence between the governor and governed; and that to make the governor independent would be dangerous and destructive to their liberties, and the ready way to establish tyranny. They thought likewise, that the province was not the less dependent on the crown of Great Britain, by the governor's depending immediately on them, and his own

Governor Burnet and the Massachusetts Assembly, struck the principal people, occasioned the paper and the manager of it to be much talk'd of, and in a few weeks brought them all to be our subscribers.

Their example was follow'd by many, and our number went on growing continually. This was one of the first good effects of my having learnt a little to scribble ; another was, that the leading men, seeing a newspaper now in the hands of one who

---

good conduct, for an ample support; because all acts and laws, which he might be induced to pass, must nevertheless be constantly sent home for approbation, in order to continue in force. Many other reasons were given, and arguments used in the course of the controversy, needless to particularize here, because all the material papers relating to it have been already given in our public news.

" Much deserved praise has the deceased governor received for his steady integrity in adhering to his instructions, notwithstanding the great difficulty and opposition he met with, and the strong temptations offered from time to time to induce him to give up the point. And yet, perhaps, something is due to the Assembly (as the love and zeal of that country for the present establishment is too well known to suffer any suspicion of want of loyalty), who continue thus resolutely to abide by what they think their right, and that of the people they represent; manage all the arts and menaces of a governor, famed for his cunning and politics, backed with instructions from home, and powerfully aided by the great advantage such an officer always has of engaging the principal men of a place in his party, by conferring, when he pleases, so many posts of profit and honor. Their happy mother country will perhaps observe, with pleasure, that though her gallant cocks and matchless dogs abate their natural fire and intrepidity when transported to a foreign clime (as this nation is), yet her sons in the remotest part *of* the earth, and even to the third and fourth descent, still retain that ardent spirit of liberty, and that undaunted courage, which has in every age gloriously distinguished Britons and Englishmen from the rest of mankind."—W. T. F.

could also handle a pen, thought it convenient to oblige and encourage me. Bradford still printed the votes, and laws, and other publics business. He had printed an address of the House to the governor, in a coarse, blundering manner; we reprinted it elegantly and correctly, and sent one to every member. They were sensible of the difference : it strengthened the hands of our friends in the House, and they voted us their printers for the year ensuing.

Among my friends in the House I must not forget Mr. Hamilton, before mentioned, who was then returned from England, and had a seat in it. He interested himself for me strongly in that instance, as he did in many others afterward, continuing his patronage till his death.*

Mr. Vernon, about this time, put me in mind of the debt I ow'd him, but did not press me. I wrote him an ingenuous letter of acknowledgment, crav'd his forbearance a little longer, which he allow'd me, and as soon as I was able, I paid the principal with interest, and many thanks; so that erratum was in some degree corrected.

But now another difficulty came upon me which I had never the least reason to expect. Mr. Meredith's father, who was to have paid for our printinghouse, according to the expectations given me, was able to advance only one hundred pounds currency, which had been paid; and a hundred more was due to the merchant, who grew impatient, and su'd us all. We gave bail, but saw that, if the money could not be rais'd in time, the suit must soon come to a judgment and execution, and our hopeful prospects must, with us, be ruined, as the press and letters must be sold for payment, perhaps at half price.

In this distress two true friends, whose kindness I have never forgotten, nor ever shall forget while I can remember any thing, came to me separately, unknown to each other, and, without any application from me, offering each of them to

---

* I got his son once £500 [marg. note].

advance me all the money that should be necessary to enable me to take the whole business upon myself, if that should be practicable; but they did not like my continuing the partnership with Meredith, who, as they said, was often seen drunk in the streets, and playing at low games in alehouses, much to our discredit. These two friends were William Coleman and Robert Grace. I told them I could not propose a separation while any prospect remain'd of the Merediths' fulfilling their part of our agreement, because I thought myself under great obligations to them for what they had done, and would do if they could; but, if they finally fail'd in their performance, and our partnership must be dissolv'd, I should then think myself at liberty to accept the assistance of my friends.

Thus the matter rested for some time, when I said to my partner, " Perhaps your father is dissatisfied at the part you have undertaken in this affair of ours, and is unwilling to advance for you and me what he would for you alone. If that is the case, tell me, and I will resign the whole to you, and go about my business." "No," said he, "my father has really been disappointed, and is really unable; and I am unwilling to distress him farther. I see this is a business I am not fit for. I was bred a farmer, and it was a folly in me to come to town, and put myself, at thirty years of age, an apprentice to learn a new trade. Many of our Welsh people are going to settle in North Carolina, where land is cheap. I am inclin'd to go with them, and follow my old employment. You may find friends to assist you. If you will take the debts of the company upon you; return to my father the hundred pound he has advanced ; pay my little personal debts, and give me thirty pounds and a new saddle, I will relinquish the partnership, and leave the whole in your hands." I agreed to this proposal; it was drawn up in writing, sign'd, and seal'd immediately. I gave him what he demanded, and he went soon to Carolina, from there he sent me next year two long letters, containing the best account that had been given of that country, the climate, the soil, husbandry, etc., for in those matters he was very judicious. I printed them in the papers, and they gave great satisfaction to the public.

As soon as he was gone, I recurr'd to my two friends; and because I would not give an unkind preference to either, I took half of what each had offered and I wanted of one, and half of the other; paid off the company's debts, and went on with the business in my own name, advertising that the partnership was dissolved. I think this was in or about the year 1729.*

About this time there was a cry among the people for more paper money, only fifteen thousand pounds being extant in the province, and that soon to be sunk. The wealthy inhabitants oppos'd any addition, being against all paper currency, from an apprehension that it would depreciate, as it had done in New England, to the prejudice of all creditors. We had discuss'd this point in our Junto, where I was on the side of an addition, being persuaded that the first small sum struck in 1723 had done much good by increasing the trade, employment, and number of inhabitants in the province, since I now saw all the old houses inhabited, and many new ones building : whereas I remembered well, that when I first walk'd about the streets of Philadelphia, eating my roll, I saw most of the houses in Walnut-street, between Second and Front streets, with bills on their doors, " To be letand many likewise in Chestnutstreet and other streets, which made me then think the inhabitants of the city were deserting it one after another.

Our debates possess'd me so fully of the subject, that I wrote and printed an anonymous pamphlet on it, entitled " *The Nature and Necessity of a Paper Currency.*" It was well receiv'd by the common people in general; but the rich men dislik'd it, for it increas'd and strengthen'd the clamor for more money, and they happening to have no writers among them

---

* By the agreement of dissolution, still extant, it appears that it took place on July 14th, 1730.—*Sparks.*

that were able to answer it, their opposition slacken'd, and the point was carried by a majority in the House. My friends there, who conceiv'd I had been of some service, thought fit to reward me by employing me in printing the money; a very profitable jobb and a great help to me. This was another advantage gain'd by me being able to write.

The utility of this currency became by time and experience so evident as never afterwards to be much disputed; so that it grew soon to fifty-five thousand pounds, and in 1739 to eighty thousand pounds, since which it arose during war to upwards of three hundred and fifty thousand pounds, trade, building and inhabitants all the while increasing, tho' I now think there are limits beyond which the quantity may be hurtful.

I soon after obtain'd, thro' my friend Hamilton, the printing of the Newcastle paper money, another profitable job as I then thought it; small things appearing great to those in small circumstances; and these, to me, were really great advantages, as they were great encouragements. He procured for me, also, the printing of the laws and votes of that government, which continu'd in my hands as long as I follow'd the business.

I now open'd a little stationer's shop. I had in it blanks of all sorts, the correctest that ever appear'd among us, being assisted in that by my friend Breintnal. I had also paper, parchment, chapmen's books, etc. One Whitemash, a compositor I had known in London, an excellent workman, now came to me, and work'd with me constantly and diligently ; and I took an apprentice, the son of Aquila Rose.

I began now gradually to pay off the debt I was under for the printing-house. In order to secure my credit and character as a tradesman, I took care not only to be in *reality* industrious and frugal, but to avoid all appearances to the contrary, I drest plainly ; I was seen at no places of idle diversion. I never went out a fishing or shooting; a book, indeed, sometimes debauch'd me from my work, but that was seldom, snug, and gave no scandal; and, to show that I was not above my business,

I sometimes brought home the paper I purchas'd at the stores thro' the streets on a wheelbarrow. Thus being esteem'd an industrious, thriving young man, and paying duly for what I bought, the merchants who imported stationery solicited my custom ; others proposed supplying me with books, and I went on swimmingly. In the mean time, Keimer's credit and business declining daily, he was at last forc'd to sell his printing-house to satisfy his creditors. He went to Barbadoes, and there lived some years in very poor circumstances.

His apprentice, David Harry, whom I had instructed while I work'd with him, set up in his place at Philadelphia, having bought his materials. I was at first apprehensive of a powerful rival in Harry, as his friends were very able, and had a good deal of interest. I therefore propos'd a partnership to him, which he, fortunately for me, rejected with scorn. He was very proud, dress'd like a gentleman, liv'd expensively, took much diversion and pleasure abroad, ran in debt, and neglected his business ; upon which, all business left him; and, finding nothing to do, he follow'd Keimer to Barbadoes, taking the printing-house with him. There this apprentice employ'd his former master as a journeyman ; they quarrel'd often; Harry went continually behindhand, and at length was forc'd to sell his types and return to his country work in Pensilvania. The person that bought them employ'd Keimer to use them, but in a few years he died.

There remained now no competitor with me at Philadelphia but the old one, Bradford; who was rich and easy, did a little printing now and then by straggling hands, but was not very anxious about the business. However, as he kept the post-office, it was imagined he had better opportunities of obtaining news ; his paper was thought a better distributer of advertisements than mine, and therefore had many more, which was a profitable, thing to him, and a disadvantage to me; for, tho' I did indeed receive and send papers by the post, yet the public opinion was otherwise, for what I did send was by bribing the riders, who took them privately, Bradford being unkind enough to forbid it, which occasion'd some resentment on my part; and I thought so meanly of him for it, that, when I afterward came into his situation, I took care never to imitate it.

I had hitherto continu'd to board with Godfrey, who lived in part of my house with his wife and children, and had one side of the shop for his glazier's business, he worked little, being always absorbed in his mathematics. Mrs. Godfrey projected a match for me with a relation's daughter, took opportunities of bringing us often together, till a serious courtship on my part ensu'd, the girl being in herself very deserving. The old folks encourag'd me by continual invitations to supper, and by leaving us together, till at length it was time to explain. Mrs. Godfrey manag'd our little treaty. I let her know that I expected as much money with their daughter as would pay off my remaining debt for the printing-house, which I believe was not then above a hundred pounds. She brought me word they had no such sum to spare; I said they might mortgage their house in the loan-office. The answer to this, after some days, was, that they did not approve the match; that, on inquiry of Bradford, they had been inform'd the printing business was not a profitable one; the types would soon be worn out, and more wanted; that S. Keimer and D. Harry had failed one after the other, and I should probably soon follow them; and, therefore, I was forbidden the house, and the daughter shut up.

Whether this was a real change of sentiment or only artifice, on a supposition of our being too far engaged in affection to retract, and therefore that we should steal a marriage, which would leave them at liberty to give or withhold what they pleas'd, I know not; but I suspected the latter, resented it, and went no more. Mrs. Godfrey brought me afterward some more favorable accounts of their disposition, and would have drawn me on again; but I declared absolutely my resolution to have nothing more to do with that family. This was resented by the Godfreys; we differ'd, and they removed, leaving me the whole house, and I resolved to take no more inmates.

But this affair having turned my thoughts to marriage, I look'd round me and made overtures of acquaintance in other places; but soon found that, the business of a printer being generally thought a poor one, I was not to expect money with a wife, unless with such a one as I should not otherwise think agreeable. In the mean time, that hard-to-be- governed passion of youth hurried me frequently into intrigues with low women that fell in my way, which were attended with some expense and great inconvenience, besides a continual risque to my health by a distemper which of all things I dreaded, though by great good luck I escaped it. A friendly correspondence as neighbors and old acquaintances had continued between me and Mrs. Read's family, who all had a regard for me from the time of my first lodging in their house. I was often invited there and consulted in their affairs, wherein I sometimes was of service. I piti'd poor Miss Read's unfortunate situation, who was generally dejected, seldom cheerful, and avoided company. I considered my giddiness and inconstancy when in London as in a great degree the cause of her unhappiness, tho' the mother was good enough to think the fault more her own than mine, as she had prevented our marrying before I went thither, and persuaded the other match in my absence. Our mutual affection was revived, but there were now great objections to our union. The match was indeed looked upon as invalid, a preceding wife being said to be living in England ; but this could not easily be prov'd, because of the distance ; and tho' there was a report of his death, it was not certain. Then, tho' it should be true, he had left many debts, which his successor might be call'd upon to pay. We ventured, however, over all these difficulties, I marrried her on September 1st 1730 None of the inconveniences happened that we had apprehended; she proved a good and faithful helpmate, assisted me much by attending the shop; we throve together, and have ever mutually endeavor'd to make each other happy. Thus I corrected that great *erratum* as well as I could.*

---

* Mrs. Franklin survived her marriage over forty years. She died December 19, 1774. She seems to have been a sensible woman and a devoted wife. Franklin's correspondence abounds with evidence that their union was a happy one, and in a letter to Miss Catharine Ray, afterwards wife of Gov. Green of Rhode Island, who sent him some cheese, he alludes to his wife in a way to reveal the ripened affection which subsisted between them. *Sparks,* vol. vii. p. 92 :

"Mrs. Franklin was very proud that a young lady should have so much regard for her old husband as to send him such a present. We talk of you every time it comes to table. She is sure you are a sensible girl, and a notable housewife, and talks of bequeathing me to you as a legacy; but I ought to wish you a better, and hope she will live these hundred years; for we are grown old together, and if she has any faults, I am so used to them that I don't perceive them. As the song says:

"Some faults we have all, and so has my Joan,
But then they're exceedingly small;
And, now I'm grown used to them, so like my own,
I scarcely can see them at all,
My dear friends,
I scarcely can see them at all.'

" Indeed I begin to think she has none, as I think of you. And since she is willing I should love you as much as you are willing to be loved by me, let us join in wishing the old lady a long life and a happy."

The author here quotes a stanza from one of his own " Songs," written for the Junto. It has been printed in Professor McVickar's Life of Dr. Samuel Bard:

" *My Plain Country Joan ; A Song.*

" Of their Chloes and Phyllises poets may prate,
I sing my plain country Joan,
These twelve years my wife, still the joy of my life,
Blest day that I made her my own.

" Not a word of her face, of her shape, or her air,
Or of flames or of darts you shall hear;
I beauty admire, but virtue I prize,
That fades not in seventy year.

About this time, our club meeting, not at a tavern, but in a little room of Mr. Grace's, set apart for that purpose, a proposition was made by me, that, since our books were often referr'd to in our disquisitions upon the queries, it might be convenient to us to have them altogether where we met, that upon occasion they might be consulted; and by thus clubbing our books to a common library, we should, while we lik'd to keep them together, have each of us the advantage of using the books of all the other members, which would be nearly as beneficial as iffill'd one end of the room with such books as we could best spare.

"Am I loaded with care, she takes off a large share;
That the burden ne'er makes me to reel;
Does good fortune arrive, the joy of my wife
Quite doubles the pleasure I feel.
"She defends my good name, even when I'm to blame,
Firm friend as to man e'er was given ;
Her compassionate breast feels for all the distressed,
Which draws down more blessings from heaven.
"In health a companion delightful and dear,
Still easy, engaging, and free;
In sickness no less than the carefelest nurse,
As tender as tender can be.
" In peace and good order my household she guides,
Right careful to save what I gain;
Yet cheerfully spends, and smiles on the friends
I've the pleasure to entertain.
" Some faults have we all, and so has my Joan,
But then they're exceedingly small;
And, now I'm grown used to them, so like my own,
I scarcely can see them at all.
" Were the finest young princess, with millions in purse,
To be had in exchange for my Joan,
I could not get better wife, might get a worse,
So I'll stick to my dearest old Joan."—B.

The number was not so great as we expected; and tho'each owned the whole. It was lik'd and agreed to, and we they had been of great use, yet some inconveniences occurring for want of due care of them, the collection, after about a year, was separated, and each took his books home again.

And now I set on foot my first project of a public nature, that for a subscription library. I drew up the proposals, got them put into form by our great scrivener, Brockden, and, by the help of my friends in the Junto, procured fifty subscribers of forty shillings each to begin with, and ten shillings a year for fifty years, the term our company was to continue. We afterwards obtain'd a charter, the company being increased to one hundred: this was the mother of all the North American subscription libraries, now so numerous. It is become a great thing itself, and continually increasing. These libraries have improved the general conversation of the Americans, made the common tradesmen and farmers as intelligent as most gentlemen from other countries, and perhaps have contributed in some degree to the stand so generally made throughout the colonies in defence of their privileges.

Mem⁰. Thus far was written with the intention express'd in the beginning and therefore contains several little family anecdotes of no importance to others. What follows was written many years after in compliance with the advice contain'd in these letters, and accordingly intended for the public. The affairs of the Revolution occasion'd the interruption.

Letter from Mr. Abel James with Notes of my Life (received in Paris').

MY DEAR AND HONORED FRIEND: I have often been desirous of writing to thee, but could not be reconciled to the thought, that the letter might fall into the hands of the British, lest some printer or busy-body should publish some part of the contents, and give our friend pain, and myself censure.

"Some time since there fell into my hands, to my great joy, about twenty-three sheets in thy own handwriting, containing an account of the parentage and life of thyself, directed to thy son, ending in the year 1730, with which there were notes, likewise in thy writing; a copy of which I inclose, in hopes it may be a means, if thou continued it up to a later period, that the first and latter part may be put together; and if it is not yet continued, I hope thee will not delay it. Life is uncertain, as the preacher tells us; and what will the world say if kind, humane, and benevolent Ben. Franklin should leave his friends and the world deprived of so pleasing and profitable a work; a work which would be useful and entertaining not only to a few, but to millions? The influence writings under that class have on the minds of youth is very great, and has nowhere appeared to me so plain, as in our public friend's journals. It almost insensibly leads the youth into the resolution of endeavoring to become as good and eminent as the journalist. Should thine, for instance, when published (and I think it could not fail of it), lead the youth to equal the industry and temperance of thy early youth, what a blessing with that class would such a work be ! I know of no character living, nor many of them put together, who has so much in his power as thyself to promote a greater spirit of industry and early attention to business, frugality, and temperance with the American youth. Not that I think the work would have no other merit and use in the world, far from it; but the first is of such vast importance that I know nothing that can equal it."

The foregoing letter and the minutes accompanying it being shown to a friend, I received from him the following:

Letter from Mr. Benjamin Vaughan.

" PARIS, *January* 31, 1783.

"MY DEAREST SIR : When I had read over your sheets of minutes of the principal incidents of your life, recovered for you by your Quaker acquaintance, I told you I would send you a letter expressing my reasons why I thought it would be useful to complete and publish it as he desired. Various concerns have for some time past prevented this letter being written, and I do not know whether it was worth any expectation; happening to be at leisure, however, at present, I shall by writing, at least, interest and instruct myself; but as the terms I am inclined to use may tend to offend a person of your manners, I shall only tell you how I would address any other person, who was as good and as great as yourself, but less diffident. I would say to him, Sir, I solicit the history of your life from the following motives: Your history is so remarkable, that if you do not give it, somebody else will certainly give it; and perhaps so as nearly to do as much harm, as your own management of the thing might do good. It will moreover present a table of the internal circumstances of your country, which will very much tend to invite to it settlers of virtuous and manly minds. And considering the eagerness with which such information is sought by them, and the extent of your reputation, I do not know of a more efficacious advertisement than your biography would give. All that has happened to you is also connected with the detail of the manners and situation of a rising people; and in this respect I do not think that the writings of Caesar and Tacitus can be more interesting to a true judge of human nature and society. But these, sir, are small reasons, in my opinion, compared with the chance which your life will give for the forming of future great men ; and in conjunction with your Art of Virtue (which you design to publish) of improving the features of private character, and consequently of aiding all happiness, both public and domestic. The two works I allude to, sir, will in particular give a noble rule and example of self-education. School and other education constantly proceed upon false principles, and show a clumsy apparatus pointed at a false mark; but your apparatus is simple, and the mark a true one; and while parents and young persons are left destitute of other just means of estimating and becoming prepared for a reasonable course in life, your discovery that the thing is in many a man's private power, will be invaluable! Influence upon the private character, late in life, is not only an influence late in life, but a weak influence. It is in youth that we plant our chief habits and prejudices; it is in youth that we take our party as to profession, pursuits and matrimony. In youth, therefore, the turn is given; in youth the education even of the next generation is given; in youth the private and public character is determined; and the term of life extending but from youth to age, life ought to begin well from youth, and more especially before we take our party as to our principal objects. But your biography will not merely teach selfeducation, but the education of a wise man; and the wisest man will receive lights and improve his progress, by seeing detailed the conduct of another wise man. And why are weaker men to be deprived of such helps, when we see our race has been blundering on in the dark, almost without a guide in this particular, from the farthest trace of time? Show then, sir, how much is to be done, both to sons and fathers; and invite all wise men to become like yourself, and other men to become wise. When we see how cruel statesmen and warriors can be to the human race, and how absurd distinguished men can be to their acquaintance, it will be instructive to observe the instances multiply of pacific, acquiescing manners; and to find how compatible it is to be great and domestic, enviable and yet good- humored.

"The little private incidents which you will also have to relate, will have considerable use, as we want, above all things, rules of prudence in ordinary affairs; and it will be curious to see how you have acted in these. It will be so far a sort of key to life, and explain many things that all men ought to have once explained to them, to give them a chance of becoming wise by foresight. The nearest thing to having experience of one's own, is to have other people's affairs brought before us in a shape that is interesting; this is sure to happen from your pen; our affairs and management will have an air of simplicity or importance that will not fail to strike; and I am convinced you have conducted them with as much originality as if you had been conducting discussions in politics or philosophy; and what more worthy of experiments and system (its importance and its errors considered) than human life?

" Some men have been virtuous blindly, others have speculated fantastically, and others have been shrewd to bad purposes; but you, sir, I am sure, will give under your hand, nothing but what is at the same moment, wise, practical and good. Your account of yourself (for I suppose the parallel I am drawing for Dr. Franklin, will hold not only in point of character, but of private history) will show that you are ashamed of no origin; a thing the more important, as you prove how little necessary all origin is to happiness, virtue, or greatness. As no end likewise happens without a means, so we shall find, sir, that even you yourself framed a plan by which you became considerable ; but at the same time we may see that though the event is flattering, the means are as simple as wisdom could make them ; that is, depending upon nature, virtue, thought and habit. Another thing demonstrated will be the propriety of every man's waiting for his time for appearing upon the stage of the world. Our sensations being very much fixed to the moment, we are apt to forget that more moments are to follow the first, and consequently that man should arrange his conduct so as to suit the whole of a life. Your attribution appears to have been applied to your life, and the passing moments of it have been enlivened with content and enjoyment, instead of being tormented with foolish impatience or regrets. Such a conduct is easy for those who make virtue and themselves in countenance by examples of other truly great men, of whom patience is so often the characteristic. Your Quaker correspondent, sir (for here again I will suppose the subject of my letter resembling Dr. Franklin), praised your frugality, diligence and temperance, which he considered as a pattern for all youth; but it is singular that he should have forgotten your modesty and your disinterestedness, without which you never could have waited for your advancement, or found your situation in the mean time comfortable; which is a strong lesson to show the poverty of glory and the importance of regulating our minds. If this correspondent had known the nature of your reputation as well as I do, he would have said, Your former writings and measures would secure attention to your Biography, and Art of Virtue ; this in return, would secure attention to them. This is an advantage attendant upon a various character, and which brings all that belongs to it into greater play; and it is the more useful, as perhaps more persons are at a loss for the means of improving their minds and characters, than they are for the time or the inclination to do it. But there is one concluding reflection, sir, that will shew the use of your life as a mere piece of biography. This style of writing seems a little gone out of vogue, and yet it is a very useful one; and your specimen of it may be particularly serviceable, as it will make a subject of comparison with the lives of various public cutthroats and intriguers, and with absurd monastic self-tormentors or vain literary triflers. If it encourages more writings of the same kind with your own, and induces more men to spend lives fit to be written, it will be worth all Plutarch's Lives put together. But being tired of figuring to myself a character of which every feature suits only one man in the world, without giving him the praise of it, I shall end my letter, my dear Dr. Franklin, with a personal application to your proper self. I am earnestly desirous, then, my dear sir, that you should let the world into the traits of your genuine character, as civil broils may otherwise tend to disguise or traduce it. Considering your great age, the caution of your character, and your peculiar style of thinking, it is not likely that any one besides yourself can be sufficiently master of the facts of your life, or the intentions of your mind. Besides all this, the immense revolution of the present period, will necessarily turn our attention towards the author of it, and when virtuous principles have been pretended in it, it will be highly important to shew that such have really influenced; and, as your own character will be the principal one to receive a scrutiny, it is proper (even for its effects upon your vast and rising country, as well as upon England and upon Europe) that it should stand respectable and eternal. For the furtherance of human happiness, I have always maintained that it is necessary to prove that man is not even at present a vicious and detestable animal; and still more to prove that good management may greatly amend him; and it is for much the same reason, that I am anxious to see the opinion established, that there are fair characters existing among the individuals of the race; for the moment that all men, without exception, shall be conceived abandoned, good people will cease efforts deemed to be hopeless, and perhaps think of taking their share in the scramble of life, or at least of making it comfortable principally for themselves. Take then, my dear sir, this work most speedily into your hand: shew yourself good as you are good ; temperate as you are temperate ; and above all things, prove yourself as one, who from your infancy have loved justice, liberty and concord, in a way that has made it natural and consistent for you to have acted, as we have seen you act in the last seventeen years of your life. Let Englishmen be made not only to respect, but even to love you. When they think well of individuals in your native country, they will go nearer to thinking well of your country; and when your countrymen see themselves well thought of by Englishmen, they will go nearer to thinking well of England. Extend your views even further; do not stop at those who speak the English tongue, but after having settled so many points in nature and politics, think of bettering the whole race of men. As I have not read any part of the life in question, but know only the character that lived it, I write somewhat at hazard. I am sure, however, that the life and the treatise I allude to (on the Art of Virtue) will necessarily fulfil the chief of my expectations; and still more so if you take up the measure of suiting these performances to the several views above stated. Should they even prove unsuccessful in all that a sanguine admirer of yours hopes from them, you will at least have framed pieces to interest the human mind; and whoever gives a feeling of pleasure that is innocent to man, has added so much to the fair side of a life otherwise too much darkened by anxiety and too much injured by pain. In the hope, that you will listen to the prayer addressed to you in this letter, I beg to subscribe myself, my dearest sir, etc., etc.,

" Signed, BENJ. VAUGHAN."

Continuation of the Account of my Life begun at Passy, near Paris, 1784.

It is some time since I receiv'd the above letters, but I have been too busy till now to think of complying with the request they contain. It might, too, be much better done if I were at home among my papers, which would aid my memory, and help to ascertain dates; but my return being uncertain, and having just now a little leisure, I will endeavor to recollect and write what I can ; if I live to get home, it may there be corrected and improv'd.

Not having any copy here of what is already written, I know not whether an account is given of the means I used to establish the Philadelphia public library, which, from a small beginning, is now become so considerable, though I remember to have come down to near the time of that transaction (1730). I will therefore begin here with an account of it, which may be struck out if found to have been already given.

At the time I establish'd myself in Pennsylvania, there was not a good bookseller's shop in any of the colonies to the southward of Boston. In New York and Philadelphia the printers were indeed stationers; they sold only paper, etc., almanacs, ballads, and a few common school-books. Those who lov'd reading were oblig'd to send for their books from England; the members of the Junto had each a few. We had left the alehouse, where we first met, and hired a room to hold our club in. I propos'd that we should all of us bring our books to that room, where they would not only be ready to consult in our conferences, but become a common benefit, each of us being at liberty to borrow such as he wish'd to read at home. This was accordingly done, and for some time contented us.

Finding the advantage of this little collection, I propos'd to render the benefit from books more common, by commencing a public subscription library. I drew a sketch of the plan and rules that would be necessary, and got a skilful conveyancer, Mr. Charles Brockden, to put the whole in form of articles of agreement to be subscribed, by which each subscriber engag'd to pay a certain sum for the first purchase of books, and an annual contribution for increasing them. So few were the readers at that time in Philadelphia, and the majority of us so poor, that I was not able, with great industry, to find more than fifty persons, mostly young tradesmen, willing to pay down for this purpose forty shillings each, and ten shillings per annum. On this little fund we began. The books were imported; the library was opened one day in the week for lending to the subscribers, on their promissory notes to pay double the value if not duly returned. The institution soon manifested its utility, was imitated by other towns, and in other provinces. The libraries were augmented by donations; reading became fashionable; and our people, having no public amusements to divert their attention from study, became better acquainted with books, and in a few years were observ'd by strangers to be better instructed and more intelligent than people of the same rank generally are in other countries.

When we were about to sign the above-mentioned articles, which were to be binding on us, our heirs, etc., for fifty years, Mr. Brockden, the scrivener, said to us, " You are young men, but it is scarcely probable that any of you will live to see the expiration of the term fix'd in the instrument." A number of us, however, are yet living; but the instrument was after a few years rendered null by a charter that incorporated and gave perpetuity to the company.*

The objections and reluctances I met with in soliciting the subscriptions, made me soon feel the impropriety of presenting one's self as the proposer of any useful project, that might be suppos'd to raise one's reputation in the smallest degree above that of one's neighbors, when one has need of their assistance to accomplish that project. I therefore put myself as much as I could out of sight, and stated it as a scheme of a *number of friends'* who had requested me to go about and propose it to such as they thought lovers of reading. In this way my affair went on more smoothly, and I ever after practis'd it on such occasions; and, from my frequent successes, can heartily recommend it. The present little sacrifice of your vanity will afterwards be amply repaid. If it remains a while uncertain

* This library was founded in 1731, and incorporated in 1742. By the addition made to it of the library left by Dr. James Logan, and by annual purchases, the Philadelphia Library now numbers between 70,000 and 80,000 volumes.—B.

to whom the merit belongs, some one more vain than yourself will be encouraged to claim it, and then even envy will be disposed to do you justice by plucking those assumed feathers, and restoring them to their right owner.*

This library afforded me the means of improvement by constant study, for which I set apart an hour or two each day, and thus repair'd in some degree the loss of the learned education my father once intended for me. Reading was the only amusement I allow'd myself. I spent no time in taverns games, or frolicks of any kind ; and my industry in my business continu'd as indefatigable as it was necessary. I was indebted for my printing-house; I had a young family coming on to be educated, and I had to contend with for business two printers, who were established in the place before me. My circumstances, however, grew daily easier. My original habits of frugality continuing, and my father having, among his instructions to me when a boy, frequently repeated a proverb of Solomon, "Seest thou a man diligent in his calling, he shall stand before kings, he shall not stand before mean men," I from thence considered industry as a means of obtaining wealth and distinction, which encourag'd me, tho' I did not think that I should ever literWe have an English proverb that says, "He *that would thrive, must ask his wife."* It was lucky for me that I had one as much dispos'd to industry and frugality as myself. She assistedally *stand before kings,* which, however, has since happened; for I have stood before *five,* and even had the honor of sitting down with one, the King of Denmark, to dinner.

* This was a wise application of one of the most cynical precepts of Ovid in his banishment: " *Crede mi hi, bene qui latuit bene vixit."* This line was subsequently adopted as his motto by the illustrious author of the Cartesian philosophy.– *Tristia Elegia,* iv. 25.

me cheerfully in my business, folding and stitching pamphlets, tending shop, purchasing old linen rags for the papermakers, etc., We kept no idle servants, our table was plain and simple, our furniture of the cheapest. For instance, my breakfast was a long time bread and milk (no tea), and I ate it out of a two penny earthen porringer, with a pewter spoon. But mark how luxury will enter families, and make a progress, in spite of principle: being call'd one morning to breakfast, I found it in a China bowl, with a spoon of silver! They had been bought for me without my knowledge by my wife, and had cost her the enormous sum of three and twenty shillings, for which she had no other excuse or apology to make, but that she thought *her* husband deserv'd a silver spoon and China bowl as well as any of his neighbors. This was the first appearance of plate and China in our house, which afterward, in a course of years, as our wealth increas'd, augmented gradually to several hundred pounds in value.

I had been religiously educated as a Presbyterian ; and tho' some of the dogmas of that persuasion, such as *the eternal decrees of God, election, reprobation, etc.,* appeared to me unintelligible, others doubtful, and I early absented myself from the public assemblies of the sect, Sunday being my studying day, I never was without some religious principles. I never doubted, for instance, the existence of the Deity; that he made the world, and govern'd it by his Providence; that the most acceptable service of God was the doing good to man; that our souls are immortal; and that all crime will be punished, and virtue rewarded, either here or hereafter. These I esteem'd the essentials of every religion ; and, being to be found in all the religions we had in our country, I respected them all, tho' with different degrees of respect, as I found them more or less mix'd with other articles, which, without any tendency to inspire, promote, or confirm morality, serv'd principally to divide us, and make us unfriendly to one another. This respect to all, with an opinion that the worst had some good effects, induc'd me to avoid all discourse that might tend to lessen the good opinion another might have of his own religion; and as our province increas'd in people, and new places of worship were continually wanted, and generally erected by voluntary contribution, my mite for such purpose, whatever might be the sect, was never refused.

Tho' I seldom attended any public worship, I had still an opinion of its propriety, and of its utility when rightly conducted, and I regularly paid my annual subscription for the support of the only Presbyterian minister or meeting we had in Philadelphia. He us'd to visit me sometimes as a friend, and admonish me to attend his administrations, and I was now and then prevail'd on to do so, once for five Sundays successively. Had he been in my opinion a good preacher, perhaps I might have continued, notwithstanding the occasion I had for the Sunday's leisure in my course of study; but his discourses were chiefly either polemic arguments, or explications of the peculiar doctrines of our sect, and were all to me very dry, uninteresting, and unedifying, since not a single moral principle was inculcated or enforc'd, their aim seeming to be rather to make us Presbyterians than good citizens.

At length he took for his text that verse of the fourth chapter of Philippians, "*Finally, brethren, whatsoever things are true, honest, just, pure, lovely, or of good report, if there be any virtue, or any praise, think on these things.*" And I imagin'd, in a sermon on such a text, we could not miss of having some morality. But he confin'd himself to five points only, as meant by the apostle, viz.: i. Keeping holy the Sabbath day. 2. Being diligent in reading the holy Scriptures. 3. Attending duly the public worship. 4. Partaking of the Sacrament. 5. Paying a due respect to God's ministers. These might be all good things; but, as they were not the kind of good things that I expected from that text, I despaired of ever meeting with them from any other, was disgusted, and attended his preaching no more. I had some years before compos'd a little Liturgy, or form of prayer, for my own private use (viz., in 1728), entitled, *Articles of Belief and Acts of Religion.* I return'd to the use of this, and went no more to the public assemblies. My conduct might be blameable, but I leave it, without attempting further to excuse it; my present purpose being to relate facts, and not to make apologies for them.

It was about this time I conceiv'd the bold and arduous project of arriving at moral perfection. I wish'd to live without committing any fault at any time; I would conquer all that either natural inclination, custom, or company might lead me into. As I knew, or thought, what was right and wrong, I did not see why I might not always do the one and avoid the other. But I soon found I hadundertaken a task of more difficulty than I had imagined. While my care was employ'd in guarding against one fault, I was often surprised by another; habit took the advantage of inattention; inclination was sometimes too strong for reason.

---

* Giving some advice to his daughter Sarah, in a letter written on the eve of his departure for England in 1764, the Doctor refers more at length to the subject of church ministration. He writes :

" Go constantly to church, whoever preaches. The act of devotion in the common prayer-book is your principal business there, and, if properly attended to, will do more towards amending the heart than sermons generally can do. For they were composed by men of much greater piety and wisdom than our common composers of sermons can pretend to be; and therefore I wish you would never miss the prayer days; yet I do not mean you should despise sermons even of the preachers you dislike, for the discourse is often much better than the man, as sweet and clear waters come through very dirty earth. I am the more particular on this head as you seemed to express a little before I came away, some inclination to leave our church, which I would not have you do."–*Sparks' Works of Franklin'* vol. vii. p. 269.–

I concluded, at length, that the mere speculative conviction that it was our interest to be completely virtuous, was not sufficient to prevent our slipping; and that the contrary habits must be broken, and good ones acquired and established, before we can have any dependence on a steady, uniform rectitude of conduct. For this purpose I therefore contrived the following method.

In the various enumerations of the moral virtues I had met with in my reading, I found the catalogue more or less numerous, as different writers included more or fewer ideas under the same name. Temperance, for example, was by some confined to eating and drinking, while by others it was extended to mean the moderating every other pleasure, appetite, inclination, or passion, bodily or mental, even to our avarice and ambition. I propos'd to myself, for the sake of clearness, to use rather more names, with fewer ideas annex'd to each, than a few names with more ideas; and I included under thirteen names of virtues all that at that time occurr'd to me as necessary or desirable, and annexed to each a short precept, which fully express'd the extent I gave to its meaning.

These names of virtues, with their precepts were :

1 TEMPERANCE.

Eat not to dullness ; drink not to elevation.

2. SILENCE.

Speak not but what may benefit others or yourself; avoid trifling conversation.

3. ORDER. .

Let all your things have their places; let each part of your business have its time.

4. RESOLUTION.

Resolve to perform what you ought; perform without fail what you resolve.

5. FRUGALITY.

Make no expense but to do good to others or yourself; *i.*

waste nothing.

6. INDUSTRY.

Lose no time; be always employ'd in something useful; cut off all unnecessary actions.

7. SINCERITY.

Use no hurtful deceit; think innocently and justly; and, if you speak, speak accordingly.

8. JUSTICE.

Wrong none by doing injuries, or omitting the benefits that are your duty.

9. MODERATION.

Avoid extreams; forbear resenting injuries so much as you think they deserve.

10. CLEANLINESS.

Tolerate no uncleanliness in body, cloths, or habitation.

11. TRANQUILLITY.

Be not disturbed at trifles, or at accidents common or unavoidable.

12. CHASTITY.

Rarely use venery but for health or offspring, never to dullness, weakness, or the injury of your own or another's peace or reputation.

13. HUMILITY.

Imitate Jesus and Socrates.

My intention being to acquire the *habitude* of all these virtues, I judg'd it would be well not to distract my attention by attempting the whole at once, but to fix it on one of them at a time; and, when I should be master of that, then to proceed to another, and so on, till I should have gone thro' the thirteen ; and as the previous acquisition of some might facilitate the acquisition of certain others, I arrang'd them with that view, as they stand above. Temperance first, as it tends to procure that coolness and clearness of head, which is so necessary where constant vigilance was to be kept up, and guard main tained against the unremitting attraction of ancient habits, and the force of perpetual temptations. This being acquir'd and establish'd, silence would be more easy ; and my desire being to gain knowledge at the same time that I improv'd in virtue, and considering that in conversation it was obtain'd rather by the use of the ears than of the tongue, and therefore wishing to break a habit I was getting into of prattling, punning, and joking, which only made me acceptable to trifling company, I gave *Silence* the second place. This and the next, *Order*, I expected would allow me more time for attending to my project and my studies. *Resolution,* once become habitual, would keep me firm in my endeavors to obtain all the subsequent virtues; *Frugality* and Industry freeing me from my remaining debt, and producing affluence and independence, would make more easy the practice of Sincerity and Justice, etc., Conceiving then, that, agreeably to the advice of Pythagoras in his Golden Verses,* daily exami

---

* The verses here referred to are thus given as Englished from the version of Hierocles :

" In this place you should collect together the sense of all the foregoing precepts, that so giving heed to them as to the laws of God in the inward judicature of the soul, you may make a just examination of what you have done well or ill For how will our remembrance reprehend us for doing ill, or praise us for doing well, unless the preceding meditation receive some laws, according to which the whole tenor of our life should be ordered, and to which we should conform the very private recesses of conscience all our lives long ? He requires also that this examination be daily repeated, that by continual returns of recollection we may not be deceived in our judgment The time which he recommends for this work is about evening or bed-time, that we may conclude the action of the day nation would be necessary, I contrived the following method for conducting that examination.

---

with the judgment of conscience, making the examination of our conversation an evening song to God. Wherein have I transgressed? What have I done ? What duty have I omitted ? So shall we measure our lives by the rules above mentioned, if to the law of the mind we join the judgment of reason.

" What then does the law of the mind say ? That we should honor the more excellent natures according to their essential order, that we should have our parents and relations in high esteem, love and embrace good men, raise ourselves above corporeal affections, everywhere stand in awe of ourselves, carefully observe justice, consider the frailty of riches and momentary life, embrace the lot which falls to us by divine judgment, delight in a divine frame of spirit, convert our mind to what is most excellent, love good discourses, not lie open to impostures, not be servilely affected in the possession of virtue, advise before action to prevent repentance, free ourselves from uncertain opinions, live with knowledge, and lastly, that we should adapt our bodies and the things without to the exercise of virtue. These are the things which the lawgiving mind has implanted in the souls of men, which when reason admits; it becomes a most vigilant judge of itself, in this manner, Wherein have I transgressed ? what have I done ? and if afterwards she finds herself to have spent the whole day agreeably to the foregoing rules, she is rewarded with a divine complacency. And if she find anything done amiss, she corrects herself by the restorative of an after admonition.

" Wherefore he would have us keep off sleep by the readiness and alacrity of reason. And this the body will easily endure, if temperately dieted it has not contracted a necessity of sleeping. By which means even our most natural appetites are subjected to the empire of reason.

" Do not admit sleep (says he) till you have examin'd every action of the day. And what is the form of examination ? Wherein have I transgress'd? what have I done? what duty have I omitted? For we sin two ways. By doing what we should not, and by not doing what we should. For 'tis one thing not to do well, and another thing to commit evil. One is a sin of omission, and the other of commission.

" For instance, 'tis our duty to pray, but not to blaspheme; to nourish our parents, but not to revile them. He that does the former of these does what he ought, he that does the latter what he ought not Though there is as much guilt in a sin of omission as in a sin of commission.

I made a little book, in which I allotted a page for each of the virtues. I rul'd each page with red ink, so as to have seven columns, one for each day of the week, marking each column with a letter for the day. I cross'd these columns with thirteen red lines, marking the beginning of each line with the first letter of one of the virtues, on which line, and in its proper column, I might mark, by a little black spot, every fault I found upon examination to have been committed respecting that virtue upon that day.*

" He exhorts also that we proceed methodically in our examination from the beginning to the end, leaving nothing out in the middle, which is implied by the word, runover. For oftentimes change of order deceives the judgment, and makes us favorable to our ill actions through disorder of memory. Besides, a daily recollection of our actions begets care and studiousness of conversation, and a sense of our immortality. And this is worth our admiration, that when he bid us recollect everything, yet he added not, Wherein have I done well ? or what duty have I perform'd ? But he turn'd the memory to what was a less occasion of pride, requiring a scrutiny only of our sins. And as for the judge, he has constituted that which is most just and impartial, and most intimate and domestics, the conscience, right reason, or a man's self, which he had before caution'd us to stand in awe of above all things. For who can so admonish another as every man can himself ? For he that is at his own liberty will use the freedom of nature, and shake off the admonitions of others, when he is not minded to follow them. But reason, which is within us, cannot choose but here itself God has set this over us as a guardian, instructor and schoolmaster. And this the verse makes the judge of the day's action, acquiesces in its determination whether it condemns or approves itself. For when it reads over what is done in the register of memory, then, looking to the exemplar of the law, it pronounces itself worthy of honor or dishonor. This course, if daily follow'd, perfects the divine image in them that use it, leading them by additions and subtractions to the beauty of virtue, and all attainable perfection. For here end the instructions about civil virtue."–

* This "little book" is dated on 1st of July, 1733.–W. T. F.

Form of the Pages.

TEMPERANCE.							
EAT NOT TO DULNESS; DRINK NOT TO ELEVATION.							
	S.	M.	T.	W.	T.	F.	S.
T.							
S.	*	*		*		*	
O.	**	*	*		*	*	*
R.			*			*	
F.		*			*		
I.			*				
S.							
J.							
M.							
C.							
T.							
C.							
H.							

I determined to give a week's strict attention to each of the virtues successively. Thus, in the first week, my great guard was to avoid every the least offence against *Temperance,* leaving the other virtues to their ordinary chance, only marking evening the faults of the day. Thus, if in the first week I could keep my first line, marked T, clear of spots, I suppos'd the habit of that virtue so much strengthen'd, and its opposite weaken'd, that I might venture extending my attention to include the next, and for the following week keep both lines clear of spots. Proceeding thus to the last, I could go thro' a course complete in thirteen weeks, and four courses in a year. And like him who, having a garden to weed, does not attempt to eradicate all the bad herbs at once, which would exceed his reach and his strength, but works on one of the beds at a time, and, having accomplish'd the first, proceeds to a second, so I should have, I hoped, the encouraging pleasure of seeing on my pages the progress I made in virtue, by clearing successively my lines of their spots, till in the end, by a number of courses, I should be happy in viewing a clean book, after a thirteen weeks' daily examination.

This my little book had for its motto these lines from Addison's *Cato :*

> "Here will I hold. If there's a powerabove us
> (And that there is, all nature cries aloud
> Thro' all her works), He must delight invirtue;
> And that which he delights in must be happy."

Another from Cicero,

"O vitae Philosophia dux ! O virtutum indagatrix expultrixque vitio- rum ! Unus dies, bene et ex praeceptis tuis actus, peccanti immortalitati est anteponendus."

Another from the Proverbs of Solomon, speaking of wisdom or virtue:

" Length of days is in her right hand, and in her left hand riches and honour. Her ways are ways of pleasantness, and all her paths are peace." iii. 16, 17.

And conceiving God to be the fountain of wisdom, I thought it right and necessary to solicit his assistance for obtaining it; to this end I formed the following little prayer, which was prefix'd to my tables of examination, for daily use.

" *O powerful Goodness ! bountiful Father! merciful Guide! Increase in me that wisdom which discovers my truest interest. Strengthen my resolutions to perform what that wisdom dictates. Accept my kind offices to thy other children as the only return in my power for thy continual favours to me.*"

I used also sometimes a little prayer which I took from Thomson's Poems, viz.:

> " Father of light and life, thou Good Supreme !
> O teach me what is good; teach me Thyself!
> Save me from folly, vanity, and vice,
> From every low pursuit; and fill my soul
> With knowledge, conscious peace, and virtue pure;
> Sacred, substantial, never-fading bliss !"

The precept of *Order* requiring that *every part of my business should have its allotted time,* one page in my little book contain'd the following scheme of employment for the twenty-four hours of a natural day.

The Morning. *Question.* What good shall I do this day ?	5, 6	Rise, wash, and address *powerful Goodness!* Contriveday's business, and take the resolution of the day;
	7	prosecute the present study, and breakfast
	8, 9, 10, 11	Work
NOON	12, 1	Read, or overlook my accounts, and dine
	2, 3, 4, 5	Work
Evening .	6	Put things in their places.
Question. What good have I done to-day ?	7, 8, 9, 10	Supper. Music or diversion. or conversation. Examination
Night.	11, 12	
	1, 2, 3, 4	Sleep.

I enter'd upon the execution of this plan for selfexamination, and continu'd it with occasional intermissions for some time. I was surpris'd to find myself so much fuller of faults than I had imagined ; but I had the satisfaction of seeing them diminish. To avoid the trouble of renewing now and then my little book, which, by scraping out the marks on the paper of old faults to make room for new ones in a new course, became full of holes, I transferr'd my tables and precepts to the ivory leaves of a memorandum book, on which the lines were drawn with red ink, that made a durable stain, and on those lines I mark'd my faults with a black-lead pencil, which marks I could easily wipe out with a wet sponge. After a while I went thro' one course only in a year, and afterward only one in several years, till at length I omitted them entirely, being employ'd in voyages and business abroad, with a multiplicity of affairs that interfered; but I always carried my little book with me.

My scheme of ORDER gave me the most trouble; and I found that, tho' it might be practicable where a man's business was such as to leave him the disposition of his time, that of a journeyman printer, for instance, it was not possible to be exactly observed by a master, who must mix with the world, and often receive people of business at their own hours. *Order,* too, with regard to places for things, papers, etc., I found extreamly difficult to acquire. I had not been early accustomed to it, and, having an exceeding good memory, I was not so sensible of the inconvenience attending want of method. This article, therefore, cost me so much painful attention, and my faults in it vexed me so much, and I made so little progress in amendment, and had such frequent relapses, that I was almost ready to give up the attempt, and content myself with a faulty character in that respect, like the man who, in buying an ax of a smith, my neighbour, desired to have the whole of its surface as bright as the edge. The smith consented to grind it bright for him if he would turn the wheel; he turn'd, while the smith press'd the broad face of the ax hard and heavily on the stone, which made the turning of it very fatiguing. The man came every now and then from the wheel to see how the work went on, and at length would take his ax as it was, without farther grinding. "No," said the smith, "turn on, turn on ; we shall have it bright by-and by; as yet, it is only speckled." " Yes," says the man,

" *but I think I like a speckled ax best.*"

And I believe this may have been the case with many, who, having, for want of some such means as I employ'd, found the difficulty of obtaining good and breaking bad habits in other points of vice and virtue, have given up the struggle, and concluded that " *a speckled ax was best;*" for something, that pretended to be reason, was every now and then suggesting to me that such extream nicety as I exacted of myself might be a kind of foppery in morals, which, if it were known, would make me ridiculous; that a perfect character might be attended with the inconvenience of being envied and hated; and that a benevolent man should allow a few faults in himself, to keep his friends in countenance.

In truth, I found myself incorrigible with respect to Order; and now I am grown old, and my memory bad, I feel very sensibly the want of it. But, on the whole, tho' I never arrived at the perfection I had been so ambitious of obtaining, but fell far short of it, yet I was, by the endeavour, a better and a happier man than I otherwise should have been if I had not attempted it; as those who aim at perfect writing by imitating the engraved copies, tho' they never reach the wish'd for excellence of those copies, their hand is mended by the endeavor, and is tolerable while it continues fair and legible.

It may be well my posterity should be informed that to this little artifice, with the blessing of God, their ancestor ow'd the constant felicity of his life, down to his 79th year,* in which this is written. What reverses may attend the remainder is in the hand of Providence; but, if they arrive, the reflection on

* This was written, therefore, in 1785, the year the Doctor returned from Paris.–

past happiness enjoy'd ought to help his bearing them with more resignation. To Temperance he ascribes his long-continued health, and what is still left to him of a good constitution; to Industry and Frugality, the early easiness of his circumstances and acquisition of his fortune, with all that knowledge that enabled him to be a useful citizen, and obtained for him some degree of reputation among the learned; to Sincerity and Justice, the confidence of his country, and the honorable employs it conferred upon him ; and to the joint influence of the whole mass of the virtues, even in the imperfect state he was able to acquire them, all that evenness of temper, and that cheerfulness in conversation, which makes his company still sought for, and agreeable even to his younger acquaintance. I hope, therefore, that some of my descendants may follow the example and reap the benefit.

It will be remark'd that, tho' my scheme was not wholly without religion, there was in it no mark of any of the distinguishing tenets of any particular sect. I had purposely avoided them; for, being fully persuaded of the utility and excellency of my method, and that it might be serviceable to people in all religions, and intending some time or other to publish it, I would not have any thing in it that should prejudice any one, of any sect, against it. I purposed writing a little comment on each virtue, in which I would have shown the advantages of possessing it, and the mischiefs attending its opposite vice; and I should have called my book THE ART OF VIRTUE,* because it would have shown the means and manner of obtaining virtue, which would have distinguished it from the mere exhortation to be good, that does not instruct and indicate the means, but is like the apostle's man of verbal charity, who only without showing to the naked and hungry how or where they might get clothes or victuals, exhorted them to be fed and clothed.– James ii. 15, 16.

---

* Nothing so likely to make a man's fortune as virtue.–*Marg. note.*

But it so happened that my intention of writing and publishing this comment was never fulfilled. I did, indeed, from time to time, put down short hints of the sentiments, reasonings, etc., to be made use of in it, some of which I have still by me; but the necessary close attention to private business in the earlier part of my life, and public business since, have occasioned my postponing it ; for, it being connected in my mind with *a great and extensive 'project,* that required the whole man to execute, and which an unforeseen succession of employs prevented my attending to, it has hitherto remain'd unfinish'd.

In this piece it was my design to explain and enforce this doctrine, that vicious actions are not hurtful because they are forbidden, but forbidden because they are hurtful, the nature of man alone considered; that it was, therefore, every one's interest to be virtuous who wish'd to be happy even in this world; and I should, from this circumstance (there being always in the world a number of rich merchants, nobility, states, and princes, who have need of honest instruments for the management of their affairs, and such being so rare), have endeavored to convince young persons that no qualities were so likely to make a poor man's fortune as those of probity and integrity.

My list of virtues contain'd at first but twelve; but a Quaker friend having kindly informed me that I was generally thought proud; that my pride show'd itself frequently in conversation ; that I was not content with being in the right when discussing any point, but was overbearing, and rather insolent, of which he convinc'd me by mentioning several instances ; I determined endeavouring to cure myself, if I could, of this vice or folly among the rest, and I added *Humility* to my list, giving an extensive meaning to the word.

I cannot boast of much success in acquiring the *reality* of this virtue, but I had a good deal with regard to the *appearance* of it. I made it a rule to forbear all direct contradiction to the sentiments of others, and all positive assertion of my own. I even forbid myself, agreeably to the old laws of our Junto, the use of every word or expression in the language that imported a fix'd opinion, such as *certainly, undoubtedly,* etc., and I adopted, instead of them, *I conceive, I apprehend,* or *I imagine* a thing to be so or so; or it *so appears to me at present.* When another asserted something that I thought an error, I deny'd myself the pleasure of contradicting him abruptly, and of showing immediately some absurdity in his proposition; and in answering I began by observing that in certain cases or circumstances his opinion would be right, but in the present case there *appear'd* or *seem'd* to me some difference, etc. I soon found the advantage of this change in my manner; the conversations I engag'd in went on more pleasantly. The modest way in which I propos'd my opinions procur'd them a readier reception and less contradiction; I had less mortification when I was found to be in the wrong, and I more easily prevail'd with others to give up their mistakes and join with me when I happened to be in the right.

And this mode, which I at first put on with some violence to natural inclination, became at length so easy, and so habitual to me, that perhaps for these fifty years past no one has ever heard a dogmatical expression except me. And to this habit (after my character of integrity) I think it principally owing that I had early so much weight with my fellowcitizens when I proposed new institutions, or altera- tions in the old, and so much influence in public councils when I became a member; for I was but a bad speaker, never eloquent, subject to much hesitation in my choice of words, hardly correct in language, and yet I generally carried my points.

In reality, there is, perhaps, no one of out natural passions so hard to subdue as *pride.* Disguise it, struggle with it, beat it down, stifle it, mortify it as much as one pleases, it is still alive, and will every now and then peep out and show itself; you will see it, perhaps, often in this history; for, even if I could conceive that I had completely overcome it, I should [Thus far written at Passy, 1784.]

["I am now about to write at home, August, 1788, *but can not have the help expected from my papers, many of them being lost in the war. I have, however, found the following"]*

HAVING mentioned *a great and extensive project* which I had conceiv'd, it seems proper that some account should be here given of that project and its object. Its first rise in my mind appears in the following little paper, accidentally preserv'd, viz.:

Observations on my reading history, in Library, May 19th, 1731.

"That the great affairs of the world, the wars, revolutions, etc., are carried on and effected byparties.

That the view of these parties is their present general interest, or what they take to be such.

That the different views of these different parties occasion all confusion.

That while a party is carrying on a general design, each man has his particular private interest in view.

That as soon as a party has gain'd its general point, each member becomes intent upon his particular interest; which, thwarting others, breaks that party into divisions, and occasions more confusion.

That few in public affairs act from a meer view of the good of their country, whatever they may pretend; and, tho' their actings bring real good to their country, yet men primarily considered that their own and their country's interestwas united and did not act from a principle of benevolence.

That fewer still, in public affairs, act with a view to the good of mankind.

---

* This is a marginal memorandum.–

There seems to me at present to be great occasion for raising a United Party for Virtue, by forming the virtuous and good men of all nations into a regular body, to be govern'd by suitable good and wise rules, which good and wise men may probably be more unanimous in their obedience to, than common people are to common laws.

I at present think that whoever attempts this aright, and is well qualified, can not fail of pleasing God, and of meeting with success.

B. F."

Revolving this project in my mind, as to be undertaken hereafter, when my circumstances should afford me the necessary leisure, I put down from time to time, on pieces of paper, such thoughts as occurr'd to me respecting it. Most of these are lost; but I find one purporting to be the substance of an intended creed, containing, as I thought, the essentials of every known religion, and being free of every thing that might shock the professors of any religion. It is express'd in these words, viz.:

" That there is one God, who made all things.

" That he governs the world by his providence.

" That he ought to be worshiped by adoration, prayer, and thanksgiving.

" But that the most acceptable service of God is doing good to man.

" That the soul is immortal.

"And that God will certainly reward virtue and punish vice, either here or hereafter."*

My ideas at that time were, that the sect should be begun and spread at first among young and single men only; that each person to be initiated should not only declare his assent

---

* In the Middle Ages, if such a phenomenon of Franklin were possible then he would probably the founder of monastic order.

to such creed, but should have exercised himself with the thirteen weeks' examination and practice of the virtues, as in the be- fore-mention'd model; that the existence of such asociety should be kept a secret, till it was become
considerable, to prevent solicitations for the admission of improper persons, but that the members should each of them search among his acquaintance for ingenuous, welldisposed youths, to whom, with prudent caution, the scheme should be gradually communicated; that the members should engage to afford their advice, assistance, and support to each other in promoting one another's interests, business, and advancement in life; that, for distinction, we should be call'd *The Society of the Free and Easy:* free, as being, by the general practice and habit of the virtues, free from the dominion of vice; and particularly by the practice of industry and frugality, free from debt, which exposes a man to confinement, and a species of slavery to his creditors.

This is as much as I can now recollect of the project, except that I communicated it in part to two young men, who adopted it with some enthusiasm; but my then narrow circumstances, and the necessity I was under of sticking close to my business, occasion'd my postponing the further prosecution of it at that time ; and my multifarious occupations, public and private, induc'd me to continue postponing, so that it has been omitted till I have no longer strength or activity left sufficient for such an enterprise ; tho' I am still of opinion that it was a practicable scheme and might have been very useful, by forming a great number of good citizens; I was not discourag'd by the seeming magnitude of the undertaking, as I have always thought that one man of tolerable abilities may work great changes, and accomplish great affairs among mankind, if he first forms a good plan and cutting off all amusements or other employments that would divert his attention, makes the execution of that same plan his sole study and business.

In 1732 I first publish'd my Almanack, under the name of *Richard Saunders;* it was continu'd by me about twenty-five years, commonly call'd *Poor Richard's Almanac.* I endeavor'd to make it both entertaining and useful, and it accordingly came to be in such demand, that I reap'd considerable profit from it, vending annually near ten thousand.* And observing that it was generally read, scarce any neighborhood in the province being without it, I consider'd it as a proper vehicle for conveying instruction among the common people, who bought scarcely any other books; I therefore filled all the little spaces that occurr'd between the remarkable days in the calendar with proverbial sentences, chiefly such as inculcated industry and frugality as the means of procuring wealth, and thereby securing virtue; it being more difficult for a man in want, to act always honestly, as, to use here one of those proverbs, *it is hardfor an empty sack to stand upright.*

---

* The advertisement to the first number of this the most celebrated of Almanacs was printed in the Pennsylvania Gazette on the 19th of December, 1732. Though appearing thus late in the season, three editions of No. 1 were sold before the end of January. The advertisement ran as follows:

"Just published, for 1733, An Almanack, containing the Lunations, Eclipses, Planets' Motions and Aspects, Weather, Sun and Moon's Rising and Setting, High Water, etc.; besides many pleasant and witty Verses, Jests, and Sayings ; Author's Motive of Writing; Prediction of the Death of his Friend, Mr. Titan Leeds; Moon no Cukold; Bachelor's Folly; Parson's Wine and Baker's Pudding; Short Visits : Kings and Bears ; New Fashions ; Game for Kisses; Katherine's Love ; Different Sentiments; Signs of a Tempest; Death of a Fisherman; Conjugal Debate ; Men and Melons; The Prodigal; Breakfast in Bed; Oyster Lawsuit, etc. By Richard Saunders, Philomat Printed and Sold by B. Franklin."

I believe that is no complete collection of this Almanac is in existence. The most complete one that I have any knowledge of was made by Mr. for some years the publisher of a New York Directory.

At his death, however, the collection, I am told, became dispersed.–

These proverbs, which contained the wisdom of many ages and nations, I assembled and form'd into a connected discourse prefix'd to the Almanack of 1757, as the harangue of a wise old man to the people attending an auction. The bringing. all these scatter'd counsels thus into a focus enabled them to make greater impression. The piece, being universally approved, was copied in all the newspapers of the Continent; reprinted in Britain on a broad side, to be stuck up in houses; two translations were made of it in French, and great numbers were bought by the clergy and gentry, to distribute gratis among their poor parishioners and tenants. In Pennsylvania, as it discouraged useless expense in foreign superfluities, some thought it had its share of influence in producing that growing plenty of money which was observable for several years after its publication.

I considered my newspaper, also, as another means of communicating instruction, and in that view frequently reprinted in it extracts from the Spectator, and other moral writers; and sometimes publish'd little pieces of my own, which had been first compos'd for reading in our Junto. Of these are a Socratic dialogue, tending to prove that, whatever might be his parts and abilities, a vicious man could not properly be called a man of sense; and a discourse on selfdenial, showing that virtue was not secure till its practice became a habitude, and was free from the opposition of contrary inclinations. These may be found in the papers about the beginning of 1735.

In the conduct of my newspaper, I carefully excluded all libelling and personal abuse, which is of late years become so disgraceful to our country. Whenever I was solicited to insert any thing of that kind, and the writers pleaded, as they generally did, the liberty of the press, and that a newspaper was like a stage-coach, in which any one who would pay had a right to a place, my answer was, that I would print the piece separately if desired, and the author might have as many copies as he pleased to distribute himself, but that I would not take upon me to spread his detraction; and that, having contracted with my subscribers to furnish them with what might be either useful or entertaining, I could not fill their papers with private altercation, in which they had no concern without doing them manifest injustice.

Now, many of our printers make no scruple of gratifying the malice of individuals by false accusations of the fairest characters among ourselves, augmening animosity even to the producing of duels; and are, moreover, so indiscreet as to print scurrilous reflections on the government of neighboring states, and even on the conduct of our best national allies, which may be attended with the most pernicious consequences. These things I mention as a caution to young printers, and that they may be encouraged not to pollute their presses and disgrace their profession by such infamous practices, but refuse steadily, as they may see by my example that such a course of conduct will not, on the whole, be injurious to their interests.

In 1733 I sent one of my journeymen to Charleston, South Carolina, where a printer was wanting. I furnish'd him with a press and letters, on an agreement of partnership, by which I was to receive one-third of the profits of the business, paying one-third of the expense. He was a man of learning, and honest but ignorant in matters of account and tho' he sometimes made me remittances, I could get no account from him, nor any satisfactory state of our partnership while he lived. On his decease, the business was continued by his widow, who, being born and bred in Holland, where, as I have been inform'd, the knowledge of accounts makes a part of female education, she not only sent me as clear a state as she could find of the transactions past, but continued to account with the greatest regularity and exactness every quarter afterwards, and managed the business with such success, that she not only brought up reputably a family of children, but, at the expiration of the term, was able to purchase of me the printing-house and establish she her son in it.

I mention this affair chiefly for the sake of recommending that branch of education for our young females, as likely to be of more use to them and for their children, in case of widowhood, than either music or dancing, by preserving them from losses by imposition of crafty men, and enabling them to continue, perhaps, a profitable mercantile house, with establish'd correspondence, till a son is grown up fit to undertake and go on with it, to the lasting advantage and enriching of the family.

About the year 1734 there arrived among us from Ireland a young Presbyterian preacher, named Hemphill, who delivered with a good voice, and apparently extempore, most excellent discourses, which drew together considerable numbers of different persuasions, who join'd in admiring them. Among the rest, I became one of his constant hearers, his sermons pleasing me, as they had little of the dogmatical kind, but inculcated strongly the practice of virtue, or what in the religious stile are called good works. Those, however, of our congregation, who considered themselves as orthodox Presbyterians, disapprov'd his doctrine and were join'd by most of the old clergy, who arraign'd him of heterodoxy before the synod, in order to have him silenc'd. I became his zealous partisan, and contributed all I could to raise a party in his favour, and we combated for him a while with some hopes of success. There was much scribbling pro and con upon the occasion; and finding that, tho' an elegant preacher, he was but a poor writer, I lent him my pen and wrote for him two or three pamphlets, and one piece in the Gazette of April, 1735. Those pamphlets, as is generally the case with controversial writings, tho' eagerly read at the time, were soon out of vogue, and I question whether a single copy of them now exists.

During the contest an unlucky occurrence hurt his cause exceedingly. One of our tersaries having heard him preach a sermon that was much admired, he thought that had somewhere read the sermon before, or at least a part of it. On search, he found that part quoted at length, in one of the British Reviews, from a discourse of Dr. Foster's. This detection gave many of our party disgust, who accordingly abandoned his cause, and occasion'd our more speedy discomfiture in the synod. I stuck by him, however, as I rather approv'd his giving us good sermons compos'd by others, than bad ones of his own manufacture, tho' the latter was the practice of our common teachers. He afterward acknowledg'd to me that none of those he preach'd were his own; adding, that his memory was such as enabled him to retain and repeat any sermon after one reading only. On our defeat, he left us in search elsewhere of better fortune, and I quitted the congregation, never joining it after, tho' I continu'd my subscription in the support of its ministers for many years.

I had begun in 1733 to study languages; I soon made myself so much a master of the French as to be able to read the books with ease. I then undertook the Italian. An acquaintance, who was also learning it, us'd often to tempt me to play chess with him. Finding this took up too much of the time I had to spare for study, I at length refus'd to play any more, unless on this condition, that the victor in every game should have a right to impose a task, either in parts of the grammar to be got by heart or in translations, etc., which tasks that the vanquish'd was to perform upon honour, before our next meeting. As we play'd pretty equally, we thus beat one another into that language. I afterwards with a little painstaking, acquir'd so much spanish books to read.

I have already mention'd that I had only one year's instruction in a Latin school, and that when very young, after which I neglected that language entirely. But, when I had attained an acquaintance with the French, Italian, and Spanish, I was surpriz'd to find, on looking over a Latin Testament, that I understood so much more of that language than I had imagined, which encouraged me to apply myself again to the study of it, and I met with more success as those preceding languages had greatly smooth'd my way.

From these circumstances, I have thought that there is some inconsistency in our common mode of teaching languages. We are told that it is proper to begin first with the Latin, and, having acquir'd that, it will be more easy to attain those modern languages which are deriv'd from it; and yet we do not begin with the Greek, in order more easily to acquire the Latin. It is true that, if you can clamber and get to the top of a staircase without using the steps, you will more easily gain them in descending; but certainly, if you begin with the lowest you will with more ease ascend to the top; and I would therefore offer it to the consideration of those who superintend the education of our youth, whether, since many of those who begin with the Latin quit the same after spending some years without having made any great proficiency, and what they have learnt becomes almost useless, so that their time has been lost, it would not have been better to have begun with the French, proceeding to the Italian, etc.; for, tho', after spending the same time, they should quit the study of languages and never arrive at the Latin, they would, however, have acquired another tongue or two, that, being in modern use, might be serviceable to them in common life.*

---

* It may be doubted whether any thing more wise than this has been written upon the much-vexed question to which it relates. The au

After ten years' absence from Boston, and having become easy in my circumstances, I made a journey thither to visit my relations, which I could not sooner well afford. In returning, I call'd at Newport to see my brother, then settled there with his printinghouse. Our former differences were forgotten, and our meeting was very cordial and affectionate. He was fast declining in his health, and requested of me that, in case of his death, which he apprehended not far distant, I would take home his son, then but ten years of age, and bring him up to the printing business.

---

thority of Franklin, the most eminently practical man of his age, in favor of reserving the study of the dead languages until the mind has reached a certain maturity, is confirmed by the confession of one of the most eminent scholars of any age.

"Our seminaries of learning," says Gibbon, " do not exactly correspond with the precept of a Spartan king, ' that the child should be instructed in the arts which will be useful to the man;' since a finished scholar may emerge from the head of Westminster or Eton, in total ignorance of the business and conversation of English gentlemen in the latter end of the eighteenth century. But these schools may assume the merit of teaching all that they pretend to teach, the Latin and Greek languages: they deposit in the hands of a disciple the keys of two valuable chests; nor can he complain, if they are afterwards lost or neglected by his own fault. The necessity of leading in equal ranks so many unequal powers of capacity and application, will prolong to eight or ten years the juvenile studies, which might be despatched in half that time by the skilful master of a single pupil. Yet even the repetition of exercise and discipline contributes to fix in a vacant mind the verbal science of grammar and prosody: and the private or voluntary student, who possesses the sense and spirit of the classics, may offend, by a false quantity, the scrupulous ear of a well-flogged critic. For myself, I must be content with a very small share of the civil and literary fruits of a public school. In the space of two years (1749, 1750), interrupted by danger and debility, I painfully climbed into the third form; and my riper age was left to acquire the beauties of the Latin and the rudiments of the Greek tongue."–B.

This I accordingly perform'd, sending him a few years to school before I took him into the office. His mother carried on the business till he was grown up, I assisted him with an assortment of new types, those of his father being in a manner worn out. Thus it was that I made my brother ample amends for the service I had depriv'd him of by leaving him so early.

In 1736 I lost one of my sons, a fine boy of four years old, by the small-pox, taken in the common way. I long regretted bitterly, and still regret that I had not given it to him by inoculation. This I mention for the sake of parents who omit that operation, on the supposition that they should never forgive themselves if a child died under it; my example showing that the regret may be the same either way, and that, therefore, the safer should be chosen.

Our club, the Junto, was found so useful, and afforded such satisfaction to the members, that several were desirous of introducing their friends, which could not well be done without exceeding what we had settled as a convenient number, viz., twelve. We had from the beginning made it a rule to keep our institution a secret, which was pretty well observ'd; the intention was to avoid applications of improper persons for admittance, some of whom, perhaps, we might find it difficult to refuse. I was one of those who were against any addition to our number, but, instead of it, made in writing a proposal, that every member separately should endeavor to form a subordinate club, with the same rules respecting queries, etc., and without informing them of the connection with the Junto. The advantages proposed were, the improvement of so many more young citizens by the use of our institutions; our better acquaintance with the general sentiments of the inhabitants on any occasion, as the Junto member might propose what queries we should desire, and was to report to the Junto what pass'd in his separate club; the promotion of our particular interests in business by more extensive recommendation, and the increase of our influence in public affairs, and our power of doing good by spreading thro' the several clubs the sentiments of the Junto.

The project was approv'd, and every member undertook to form his club, but all of them did not succeed. Five or six only were compleated, which were called by different names, as the Vine, the Union, the Band, etc. They were useful to themselves and afforded us a good deal of amusement, information and instruction, besides answering, in some considerable degree, our views of influencing the public opinion on particular occasions, of which I shall give some instances in course of time as they happened.

My first promotion was my being chosen, in 1736, as clerk of the General Assembly. The choice was made that year without opposition; but the year following, when I was again propos'd (the choice, like that of the members, being annual), a new member made a long speech against me, in order to favour some other candidate. I was, however chosen, which was the more agreeable to me, as, besides the pay for the immediate service as clerk, the place gave me a better opportunity of keeping up an interest among the members, which secur'd to me the business of printing the votes, laws, paper money, and other occasional jobbs for the public, that, on the whole, were very profitable.

I therefore did not like the opposition of this new member, who was a gentleman of fortune and education, with talents that were likely to give him, in time, great influence in the House, which, indeed, afterwards happened. I did not, however, aim at gaining his favour by paying any servile respect to him, but, after some time, took this other method. Having heard that he had in his library a certain very scarce and curious book, I wrote a note to him, expressing my desire of perusing that book, and requesting he would do me the favour of lending it to me for a few days. He sent it immediately, and I return'd it in about a week with another note, expressing strongly my sense of the favour. When we next met in the House, he spoke to me (which he had never done before), with great civility; and he ever after manifested a readiness to serve me on all occasions, so that we became great friends, and our friendship continued to his death.

This is another instance of the truth of an old maxim I had learned, which says, "*He that has once done you a kindness will be more ready to do you another , than he whom you yourself have obliged*". And it shows how much more profitable it is prudently to remove, than to resent, return, and continue inimical proceedings.

In 1737, Colonel Spotswood, late governor of Virginia, and then postmaster-general, being dissatisfied with the conduct of his deputy at Philadelphia, respecting some negligence in rendering, and inexactitude of his accounts, took from him the commission and offered it to me. I accepted it readily, and found it of great advantage; for, tho' the salary was small, it facilitated the correspondence that improv'd my newspaper, increas'd the number demanded, as well as the advertisements to be inserted, so that it came to afford me a considerable income. My old competitor's newspaper declin'd proportionably, and I was satisfy'd without retaliating his refusal, while postmaster, to permit my papers being carried by the riders. Thus he suffer'd greatly from his neglect in due accounting; and I mention it as a lesson to those young men who may be employ'd in managing affairs for others, that they should always render accounts, and make remittances, with great clearness and punctuality. The character of observing such a conduct is the most powerful of all recommendations to new employments and increase of business.

I began now to turn my thoughts a little to public affairs, beginning, however, with small matters. The city watch was one of the first things that I conceiv'd to want regulation. It was managed by the constables of the respective wards in turn

; the constable warned a number of housekeepers to attend him for the night. Those who chose never to attend, paid him six shillings a year to be excus'd, which was suppos'd to be for hiring substitutes, but was, in reality, much more than was necessary for that purpose, and made the constableship a place of profit; and the constable, for a little drink, often got such ragamuffins about him as a watch, that respectable housekeepers did not choose to mix with. Walking the rounds, too, was often neglected, and most of the nights spent in tippling. I thereupon wrote a paper to be read in Junto, representing these irregularities, but insisting more particularly on the inequality of this six shilling tax of the constables, respecting the circumstances of those who paid it, since a poor widow housekeeper, all whose property to be guarded by the watch did not perhaps exceed the value of fifty pounds, paid as much as the wealthiest merchant, who had thousands of pounds' worth of goods in his stores.

On the whole, I proposed as a more effectual watch, the hiring of proper men to serve constantly in that business; and as a more equitable way of supporting the charge, the levying a tax that should be proportion'd to the property. This idea, being approv'd by the Junto, was communicated to the other clubs, but as arising in each of them; and though the plan was not immediately carried into execution, yet, by preparing the minds of people for the change, it paved the way for the law obtained a few years after, when the members of our clubs were grown into more influence.

About this time I wrote a paper (first to be read in Junto, but it was afterward publish'd) on the different accidents and carelessnesses by which houses were set on fire, with cautions against them, and means proposed of avoiding them. This was much spoken of as a useful piece, and gave rise to a project, which soon followed it, of forming a company for the more ready extinguishing of fires, and mutual assistance in removing and securing of goods when in danger. Associates in this scheme were presently found, amounting to thirty. Our articles of agreement oblig'd every member to keep always in good order, and fit for use, a certain number of leather buckets, with strong bags and baskets (for packing and transporting of goods), which were to be brought to every fire; and we agreed to meet once a month and spend a social evening together, in discoursing and communicating such ideas as occurred to us upon the subject of fires, as might be useful in our conduct on such occasions.

The utility of this institution soon appeared, and many more desiring to be admitted than we thought convenient for one company, they were advised to form another, which was accordingly done ; and this went on, one new company being formed after another, till they became so numerous as to include most of the inhabitants who were men of property ; and now, at the time of my writing this, tho' upward of fifty years since its establishment, that which I first formed, called the Union Fire Company, still subsists and flourishes, tho' the first members are all deceas'd but myself and one, who is older by a year than I am. The small fines that have been paid by members for absence at the monthly meetings have been apply'd to the purchase of fireengines, ladders, firehooks, and other useful implements for each company, so that I question whether there is a city in the world better provided with the means of putting a stop to beginning conflagrations; and, in fact, since these institutions, the city has never lost by fire more than one or two houses at a time, and the flames have often been extinguished before the house in which they began has been half consumed.*

---

* This fire company was formed on Dec. 7, 1736. It was designed primarily for the security of the property of its members, though they did not limit their usefulness to their own members when their property

In 1739 arrived among us from Ireland the Reverend Mr. Whitefield, who had made himself re-markable there as an itinerant preacher.

---

was not in danger. The Union Fire Company was active till 1791. In a role of the companies of that day we find it heading the list, having thirty members, one engine, two hundred and fifty buckets, thirteen ladders, two hooks, no bags, and one eighty-foot rope.

It will be seen by the articles of association which follow that the number of members was restricted to thirty. The applicants in a year or two much exceeded this number, and there being no possibility of uniting with it, measures were taken to form a new company, which resulted in 1738 in the establishment of the second voluntary fire company.

" The Fellowship." See a series of interesting sketches of the fire apparatus and the Philadelphia Fire Department, between the years 1701 and 1802, written for the Philadelphia *Sunday Dispatch,* by Thompson Westcott.

" *Articles of the Union Fire Company of Philadelphia, originally formed Dec.* 7, 1736.

" I. That we will each of us, at his own proper charge, provide six leather buckets and two bags, the bags to be made of good ozenburgs or wider linen, whereof each bag shall contain four yards at least, and shall have a running cord near the mouth, which said buckets and bags shall be marked with their own names respectively and company, and shall be kept ready at hand, and shall be applied to no other use than for preserving our own and our fellow-citizens' houses, goods and effects, in case of fire as aforesaid.

" II. That if any of us shall neglect to provide his buckets and bags as aforesaid, or when so provided shall neglect to keep them ready for the uses herein mentioned, or shall apply them to any other purpose, he shall forfeit and pay to the clerk for the time being, for the use of the company, the sum of VIIIth of a dollar for each bucket or bag misapplied or wanting, except any of them happen to be lost at a fire.

He was at first permitted to preach in some of ourchurches; but the clergy, taking a dislike to him, soon refus'd him their pulpits,

---

"III. That if any of the buckets or bags so marked as aforesaid shall be lost or damaged at any fire, the same shall be supplied or repaired out of the stock of the company, provided notice be given thereof to the company within four months after such loss or damage.

" IV. That we will, all of us, upon hearing of FIRE breaking out, immediately repair to the same with at least one-half of our buckets and bags, and there exert our best endeavors to extinguish such fire, and preserve the goods and effects of such of us as may be in danger. And if more than one of us shall be in danger at one time, we will divide ourselves with the remainder of our buckets and bags as nearly as may be, to be equally helpful. And.to prevent suspicious persons from coming into or carrying any goods out of such houses as may be in danger, two of our members shall constantly attend at the doors until all the goods and effects that can be saved are packed up and carried to a place of safety. And upon hearing the cry of FIRE in the night-time we will immediately cause sufficient lights to be distributed in such parts of the houses of such of our company as may be thought in danger, in order to prevent confusion and enable their friends to give them more speedy and effectual assistance. And moreover, as this association is intended for a general benefit, we do further agree, that whenever a FIRE breaks out in any part of the city, though none of our houses, goods or effects may be in apparent danger, we will nevertheless repair thither with our buckets and bags as before mentioned, and give our utmost assistance to such of our fellow-citizens as may stand in need of it, in the same manner as if they belonged to this company.

" V. Provides for eight meetings during the year, and every member shall pay three shillings for his share of the reckoning of the evening. Members not there at the commencement of the evening to pay one shilling; those not there during the entire evening to pay four shilling.

" VI. Provides that each of us, in our turns, agreeable to the order of our subscriptions, serve the company as clerk or get some other and he was oblig'd to preach in the fields. The multitudes of all sects and denominations that attended his sermons were enormous,and it was matter of speculation to me, who was one of the number, to observe the extraordinary influence of his oratory on his hearers, and how much they admir'd and respected him, notwithstanding his common abuse of them, by assuring them they were naturally *half beasts and half devils.* It was wonderful to see the change soon made in the manners of our inhabitants. From being thoughtless or indifferent about religion, it seem'd as if all the world were growing religious, so that one could not walk thro' the town in an evening without hearing psalms sung in different families of every street.And it being found inconvenient to assemble in the open air, subject to its inclemencies, the building of a house to meet

---

member to serve in our stead, whose duty shall be to inspect the condition of all our buckets, bags, ladders and engine, and make report at each meeting. The article also sets out the duties of the clerk, such as giving notice of meetings, keeping minutes, etc.

"VII. Provides for the election of treasurer and prescribes his duties.

"VIII. Provides that the company shall not consist of more than thirty members, etc.

" IX. Provides that each member shall keep a copy of these articles and a list of all the members' names fixed in open view near his buckets, on pain of forfeiture for each, as often as the same is reported to the company.

" X. Provides that all fines shall be paid to the treasurer for the use of the company.

" XI. That upon the death of any of our company the survivors shall, in time of danger as aforesaid, be aiding and assisting the widow of such decedent during her widowhood, as if her husband had been living–she only keeping her buckets and bags in repair, and causing them to be sent to every fire aforesaid."–B.

in was no sooner propos'd, and persons appointed to receive contributions, but sufficient sums were soon receiv'd to procure the ground and erect the building, which was one hundred feet long and seventy broad, about the size of Westminster Hall; and the work was carried on with such spirit as to be finished in a much shorter time than could have been expected. Both house and ground were vested in trustees, expressly for the use of any preacher of any religious persuasion who might desire to say something to the people at Philadelphia; the design in building not being to accommodate any particular sect, but the inhabitants in general; so that even if the Mufti of Constantinople were to send a missionary to preach Mohammedanism to us, he would find a pulpit at his service.

Mr. Whitefield, in leaving us, went preaching all the way thro' the colonies to Georgia. The settlement of that province had lately been begun, but, instead of being made with hardy, industrious husbandmen, accustomed to labor, the only people fit for such an enterprise, it was with families of broken shopkeepers and other insolvent debtors, many of indolent and idle habits, taken out of the jails, who, being set down in the woods, unqualified for clearing land, and unable to endure the hardships of a new settlement, perished in numbers, leaving many helpless children unprovided for. The sight of their miserable situation inspir'd the benevolent heart of Mr. Whitefield with the idea of building an Orphan House there, in which they might be supported and educated. Returning northward, he preach'd up this charity, and made large collections, for his eloquence had a wonderful power over the hearts and purses of his hearers, of which I myself was an instance.

I did not disapprove of the design, but, as Georgia was then destitute of materials and workmen, and it was proposed to send them from Philadelphia at a great expense. I thought it would have been better to have built the house here, and brought the children to it. This I advis'd; but he was resolute in his first project, rejected my counsel, and I therefore refus'd to contribute. I happened soon after to attend one of his sermons, in the course of which I perceived he intended to finish with a collection, and I silently resolved he should get nothing from me. I had in my pocket a handful of copper money, three or four silver dollars, and five pistoles in gold. As he proceeded I began to soften, and concluded to give the coppers. Another stroke of his oratory made me asham'd of that, and determin'd me to give the silver; and he finish'd so admirably, that I empty'd my pocket wholly into the collector's dish, gold and all. At this sermon there was also one of our club, who, being of my sentiments respecting the building in Georgia, and suspecting a collection might be intended, had, by precaution, emptied his pockets before he came from home. Towards the conclusion of the discourse, however, he felt a strong desire to give, and apply'd to a neighbour, who stood near him, to borrow some money for the purpose. The application was unfortunately [made] to perhaps the only man in the company who had the firmness not to be affected by the preacher. His answer was, *"At any other time, Friend Hopkinson, I would lend to thee freely; but not now, for thee seems to be out of thy right senses".*

Some of Mr. Whitefield's enemies affected to suppose that he would apply these collections to his own private emolument; but I, who was intimately acquainted with him (being employed in printing his Sermons and Journals, etc.), never had the least suspicion of his integrity, but am to this day decidedly of opinion that he was in all his conduct a perfectly *honest man;* and methinks my testimony in his favour ought to have the more weight, as we had no religious connection. He us'd, indeed, sometimes to pray for my conversion, but never had the satisfaction of believing that his prayers were heard. Ours was a mere civil friendship, sincere on both sides, and lasted to his death.

The following instance will show something of the terms on which we stood. Upon one of his arrivals from England at Boston, he wrote to me that he should come soon to Philadelphia, but knew not where he could lodge when there, as he understood his old friend and host, Mr. Benezet, was removed to Germantown. My answer was, "You know my house; if you can make shift with its scanty accommodations, you will be most heartily welcome." He reply'd, that if I made that kind offer for Christ's sake, I should not miss of a reward. And I returned, *"Don't let me be mistaken; it was not for Christs sake, but for your sake."* One of our common acquaintance jocosely remark'd, that, knowing it to be the custom of the saints, when they received any favour, to shift the burden of the obligation from off their own shoulders, and place it in heaven, I had contriv'd to fix it on earth.

The last time I saw Mr. Whitefield was in London, when he consulted me about his Orphan House concern, and his purpose of appropriating it to the establishment of a college.

He had a loud and clear voice, and articulated his words and sentences so perfectly, that he might be heard and understood at a great distance, especially as his auditories, however numerous, observ'd the most exact silence. He preach'd one evening from the top of the Court-house steps, which are in the middle of Market street, and on the west side of Second-street, which crosses it at right angles. Both streets were fill'd with his hearers to a considerable distance. Being among the hindmost in Market-street, I had the curiosity to learn how far he could be heard, by retiring backwards down the street towards the river; and I found his voice distinct till I came near Frontstreet, when some noise in that street obscur'd it. Imagining then a semicircle, of which my distance should be the radius, and that it were fill'd with auditors, to each of whom I allow'd two square feet, I computed that he might well be heard by more than thirty thousand. This reconcil'd me to the newspaper accounts of his having preach'd to twenty-five thousand people in the fields, and to the antient histories of generals haranguing whole armies, of which I had sometimes doubted.

By hearing him often, I came to distinguish easily between sermons newly compos'd, and those which he had often preach'd in the course of his travels. His delivery of the latter was so improv'd by frequent repetitions that every modulation of voice, was so perfectly well turn'd and well plac'd, that, without being interested in the subject, one could not help being pleas'd with the discourse; a pleasure of much the same kind with that receiv'd from an excellent piece of music. This is an advantage itinerant preachers have over those who are stationary, as the latter can not well improve their delivery of a sermon by so many rehearsals.

His writing and printing from time to time gave great advantage to his enemies; unguarded expressions, and even erroneous opinions, delivered in preaching, might have been afterwards explain'd or qualifi'd by supposing others that might have accompani'd them, or they might have been deny'd; but *litera scripta manet.* Critics attack'd his writings violently, and with so much appearance of reason as to diminish the number of his votaries and prevent their encrease; so that I am of opinion if he had never written any thing, he would have left behind him a much more numerous and important sect, and his reputation might in that case have been still growing, even after his death, as there being nothing of his writing on which to found a censure and give him a lower character, his proselytes would be left at liberty to feign for him as great a variety of excellences as their enthusiastic admiration might wish him to have possessed.

My business was now continually augmenting and my circumstances growing daily easier, my newspaper having become very profitable, as being for a time almost the only one in this and the neighbouring provinces. I experienced, too, the truth of the observation, " *that after getting the first hundred pound, it is more easy to get the second"* money itself being of a prolific nature.

The partnership at Carolina having succeeded, I was encourag'd to engage in others, and to promote several of my workmen, who had behaved well, by establishing them with printing-houses in different colonies, on the same terms with that in Carolina, Most of them did well, being enabled at the end of our term, six years, to purchase the types of me and go on working for themselves, by which means several families were raised. Partnerships often finish in quarrels; but I was happy in this, that mine were all carried on and ended amicably, owing, I think, a good deal to the precaution of having very explicitly settled, in our articles, every thing to be done by or expected from each partner, so that there was nothing to dispute, which precaution I would therefore recommend to all who enter into partnerships; for, whatever esteem partners may have for, and confidence in each other at the time of the contract, little jealousies and disgusts may arise, with ideas of inequality in the care and burden of the business, etc., which are attended often with breach of friendship and of the connection, perhaps with lawsuits and other disagreeable consequences.

I had, on the whole, abundant reason to be satisfied with my being established in Pennsylvania. There were, however, two things that I regretted, there being no provision for defense, nor for a complete education of youth; no militia, nor any college. I therefore, in 1743, drew up a proposal for establishing an academy ; and at that time, thinking the Reverend Mr. Peters, who was out of employ, a fit person to superintend such an institution, I communicated the project to him; but he, having more profitable views in the service of the proprietaries, which succeeded, declin'd the undertaking; and, not knowing another at that time suitable for such a trust, I let the scheme lie a while dormant. I succeeded better the next year, 1744, in proposing and establishing a Philosophical Society. The paper I wrote for that purpose will be found among my writings, when collected.* With respect to defense, Spain having been several years at war against Great Britain, and being

---

The paper here referred to will be found in the 4th vol. of Sparks * Works of Franklin , p. 14. It bears date the 14th of May, 1743, Old Style. It is entitled, " A proposal for promoting useful knowledge among the British Plantations in America." It commences by speaking of the great extent of the colonial possessions, "having different cli- mates and different soils, producing different plants, mines, and minerals, and capable of different improvements, manufactures," etc.

It then says: "The first drudgery of settling new colonies, which confines the attention of people to mere necessaries, is now pretty well over ; and there are many in every province in circumstances that set them at ease, and afford leisure to cultivate the finer arts, and improve the common stock of knowledge. To such of these who are men of speculation, many hints must from time to time arise, many observations occur, which if well examined, pursued, and improved, might produce discoveries to the advantage of some or all of the British Plantations, or to the benefit of mankind in general. . .But as, from the extent of the country, such persons are widely separated, and seldom can see and converse or be acquainted with each other, so that many useful particulars remain uncommunicated, die with the discoverers, and are lost to mankind; it is to remedy this inconvenience for the future, proposed–

" That one society be formed of virtuosi, or ingenious men, residing in the several colonies, to be called The American Philosophical Society, who are to maintain constant correspondence."

With respect to defense, Spain having been several years at war against Great Britain, and being

---

"That Philadelphia, being the city nearest to the centre of the continent colonies, communicating with all of them northward and southward by post, and with all the islands by sea, and having the advantage of a good growing library, be the centre of the Society."

"That at Philadelphia there be always at least seven members, viz. a physician, a botanist, a mathematician, a chemist, a mechanician, a geographer, and a general natural philosopher, besides a president, treasurer and secretary.

" That these members meet once a month, or oftener, at their own expense, to communicate to each other their observations and experiments ; to receive, read, and consider such letters, communications, or queries as shall be sent from distant members; to direct the dispersing of the copies of such communications as are valuable, to other distant members, in order to procure their sentiments thereupon."

Then follows an enumeration, made with some detail, of the subjects on which it was proposed that the Society should be occupied: including investigations in botany; in medicine; in mineralogy and mining; in mathematics; in chemistry; in mechanics; in arts, trades, and manufactures; in geography and topography; in agriculture; and " all philosophical experiments that let light into the nature of things, tend to increase the power of man over matter, and multiply the conveniences or pleasures of life."

The circular proposes that "a correspondence be kept up with the Royal Society of London, and the Dublin Society; that abstracts of the communications be sent quarterly to all the members; and that, at the end of every year, collections be made and printed of such experiments, discoveries, and improvements, as may be thought of public advantage."

at length join'd by France, which brought us into great danger; and the laboured and long-continued

---

The duties of the secretary are particularly laid down, and they are very arduous; requiring that he attend to all the correspondence, " abstract, correct, and methodize such papers as require it, and as he shall be directed to do by the president, after they have been considered, debated, and digested in the Society; to enter copies thereof in the Society's books, and make out copies for distant members." And after enumerating these difficult duties, the circular closes by saying:

"Benjamin Franklin, the writer of this proposal, offers himself to serve the Society as their secretary. till they shall be provided with one more capable."

In this projet will be found all the leading features of the present American Philosophical Society. There can be no doubt that from the day when it was proposed the necessary measures for carrying it into execution were taken. Dr. Thomas Bond (himself one of the original members), in an oration delivered before the Society in 1782, says:– "Franklin gradually established many necessary institutions, among which was this Philosophical Society, so early as 1743, when the plan was formed and published, the members chosen, and an invitation given to all ingenious persons to cooperate and correspond with them on the laudable occasion." It is true that Franklin, in his Autobiography, gives the date 1744, saying, "in that year I succeeded in proposing and establishing a Philosophical Society. The paper I wrote for that purpose will be found among my writings, if not lost with many others." But Franklin wrote from memory, and the date of the paper referred to, which was doubtless the proposal of 1743, shows that he had made a mistake in the year.

In a letter to Cadwallader Colden, dated New York, 5th April, 1744, Dr. Franklin acquaints him " that the Society, as far as relates to Philadelphia, was actually formed, and had several meetings to mutual satisfaction."

In this letter the following list is presented of the original members:

Dr. Thomas Bond, as Physician.

Mr. John Bartram, as Botanist

Mr. Thomas Godfrey, as Mathematician.

Mr. Samuel Rhoads, as Mechanician.

Mr. William Parsons, as Geographer.

endeavour of our governor, Thomas, to prevail with our Quaker Assembly to pass a militia law, and make other provisions for the security of the province, having proved abortive, I determined to try what might be done by a voluntary association of the people. To promote this, I first wrote and published a pamphlet, entitled PLAIN TRUTH, in which I stated our defenceless situation in strong lights, with the necessity of union and discipline for our defense, and promis'd to propose in a few days an association, to be generally signed for that purpose. The pamphlet had a sudden and surprising effect. I was call'd upon for the instrument of association, and having settled the draft of it with a few friends, I appointed a meeting of the citizens in the large building before mentioned. The house was pretty full; I had prepared a number of printed copies and provided pens and ink dispers'd all over the room. I

Dr. PHINEAS BOND, as General Natural Philosopher.
Mr. THOMAS HOPKINSON, President.
Mr. WILLIAM COLEMAN, Treasurer.
BENJAMIN FRANKLIN, Secretary.

Though the American Philosophical Society was not, strictly speaking, the organic continuation of the Junto, there can be no doubt that the plan of establishing it had been often brought before the Junto for consideration, for we know that it was the practice of Franklin, when he had new projects to propose, to have them first discussed in the Club. But a stronger evidence still of the part which they took in forming the new institution is presented by the fact that of the nine original members of the Philosophical Society, six, including the three officers, are known to have belonged to the Junto,–namely, Franklin, Hopkinson, Coleman, Godfrey, Rhoads and Parsons.–B.

harangued them a little on the subject, read the paper, and explained it, and then distributed the copies, which were eagerly signed, not the least objection being made.

When the company separated, and the papers were collected, we found above twelve hundred hands; and, other copies being dispersed in the country, the subscribers amounted at length to upward of ten thousand. These all furnished themselves as soon as they could with arms formed themselves into companies and regiments, chose their own officers, and met every week to be instructed in the manual exercise, and other parts of military discipline. The women, by subscriptions among themselves, provided silk colors, which they presented to the companies, painted with different devices and mottos, which I supplied.

The officers of the companies composing the Philadelphia regiment, being met, chose me for their colonel; but, conceiving myself unfit, I declin'd that station, and recommended Mr. Lawrence, a fine person, and man of influence, who was accordingly appointed. I then propos'd a lottery to defray the expense of building a battery below the town, and furnishing it with cannon. It filled expeditiously, and the battery was soon erected, the merlons being fram'd of logs and fill'd with earth. We bought some old cannon from Boston, but, these not being sufficient, we wrote to England for more, soliciting, at the same time, our proprietaries for some assistance, tho' without much expectation of obtaining it.

Meanwhile, Colonel Lawrence, William Allen, Abram Taylor, Esqr., and myself were sent to New York by the associators, commission'd to borrow some cannon of Governor Clinton. He at first refus'd us peremptorily; but at dinner with his council, where there was great drinking of Madeira wine, as the custom of that place then was, he softened by degrees, and said he would lend us six. After a few more bumpers he advanc'd to ten ; and at length he very good-naturedly conceded eighteen. They were fine cannon, eighteenpounders, with their carriages, which we soon transported and mounted on our battery, where the associators kept a nightly guard while the war lasted, and among the rest I regularly took my turn of duty there as a common soldier.

My activity in these operations was agreeable to the governor and council; they took me into confidence, and I was consulted by them in every measure wherein their concurrence was thought useful to the association. Calling in the aid of religion, I propos'd to them the proclaiming a fast, to promote reformation, and implore the blessing of Heaven on our undertaking. They embrac'd the motion ; but, as it was the first fast ever thought of in the province, the secretary had no precedent from which to draw the proclamation. My education in New England, where a fast is proclaimed every year, was here of some advantage : I drew it in the accustomed style ; it was translated into German, printed in both languages, and divulg'd thro' the province. This gave the clergy of the different sects an opportunity of influencing their congregations to join in the association, and it would probably have been general among all but Quakers if the peace had not soon interven'd.

It was thought by some of my friends that, by my activity in these affairs, I should offend that sect, and thereby lose my interest in the Assembly of the province, where they formed a great majority. A young gentleman who had likewise some friends in the House, and wished to succeed me as their clerk, acquainted me that it was decided to displace me at the next election; and he, therefore, in good will, advis'd me to resign, as more consistent with my honour than being turn'd out. My answer to him was, that I had read or heard of some public man who made it a rule never to ask for an office, and never to refuse one when offer'd to him. "I approve," says I, "of his rule, and will practice it with a small addition; I shall never *ask,* never *refuse,* nor ever *resign* an office. If they will have my office of clerk to dispose of to another, they shall take it from me. I will not, by giving it up, lose my right of some time or other making reprisals on my adversaries." I heard, however, no more of this; I was chosen again unanimously as usual at the next election. Possibly, as they dislik'd my late intimacy with the members of council, who had join'd the governors in all the disputes about military preparations, with which the House had long been harass'd, they might have been pleas'd if I would voluntarily have left them; but they did not care to displace me on account merely of my zeal for the association, and they could not well give another reason.

Indeed I had some cause to believe that the defense of the country was not disagreeable to any of them, provided they were not requir'd to assist in it. And I found that a much greater number of them than I could have imagined, tho' against offensive war, were clearly for the defensive. Many pamphlets *pro* and *con* were publish'd on the subject, and some by good Quakers, in favour of defense, which I believe convinc'd most of their younger people.

A transaction in our fire company gave me some insight into their prevailing sentiments. It had been propos'd that we should encourage the scheme for building a battery by laying out the present stock, then about sixty pounds, in tickets of the lottery. By our rules, no money could be dispos'd of till the next meeting after the proposal. The company consisted of thirty members, of which twenty-two were Quakers, and eight only of other persuasions. We eight punctually attended the meeting; but, tho' we thought that some of the Quakers would join us, we were by no means sure of a majority. Only one Quaker, Mr. James Morris, appear'd to oppose the measure. He expressed much sorrow that it had ever been propos'd, as he said *Friends* were all against it, and it would create such discord as might break up the company. We told him that we saw no reason for that; we were the minority, and if *Friends* were against the measure, and outvoted us, we must and should, agreeably to the usage of all societies, submit. When the hour for business arriv'd it was mov'd to put the vote; he allow'd we might then do it by the rules, but, as he could assure us that a number of members intended to be present for the purpose of opposing it, it would be but candid to allow a little time for their appearing.

While we were disputing this, a waiter came to tell me two gentlemen below desir'd to speak with me. I went down, and found they were two of our Quaker members. They told me there were eight of them assembled at a tavern just by; that they were determin'd to come and vote with us if there should be occasion, which they hop'd would not be the case, and desir'd we would not call for their assistance if we could do without it, as their voting for such a measure might embroil them with their elders and friends. Being thus secure of a majority, I went up, and after a little seeming hesitation, agreed to a delay of another hour. This Mr. Morris allow'd to be extreamly fair. Not one of his opposing friends appear'd, at which he express'd great surprize; and, at the expiration of the hour, we carry'd the resolution eight to one; and as, of the twentytwo Quakers, eight were ready to vote with us, and thirteen, by their absence, manifested that they were not inclin'd to oppose the measure, I afterward estimated the proportion of Quakers sincerely against defense as one to twenty-one only; for these were all regular members of that society, and in good reputation among them, and had due notice of what was propos'd at that meeting.

The honorable and learned Mr. Logan, who had always been of that sect, was one who wrote an address to them, declaring his approbation of defensive war, and supporting his opinion by many strong arguments. He put into my hands sixty pounds to be laid out in lottery tickets for the battery, with directions to apply what prizes might be drawn wholly to that service. He told me the following anecdote of his old master, William Penn, respecting defense. He came over from England, when a young man, with that proprietary, and as his secretary. It was wartime, and their ship was chas'd by an armed vessel, suppos'd to be an enemy. Their captain prepar'd for defense; but told William Penn, and his company of Quakers, that he did not expect their assistance, and they might retire into the cabin, which they did, except James Logan, who chose to stay upon deck, and was quarter'd to a gun. The suppos'd enemy prov'd a friend, so there was no fighting; but when the secretary went down to communicate the intelligence, William Penn rebuk'd him severely for staying upon deck, and undertaking to assist in defending the vessel, contrary to the principles of *Friends,* especially as it had not been required by the captain. This reproof, being before all the company, piqu'd the secretary, who answer'd, "*I being thy servant, why did thee not order me to come down ? But thee was willing enough that I should stay and help to fight the ship when thee thought there was danger.*"

My being many years in the Assembly, the majority of which were constantly Quakers, gave me frequent opportunities of seeing the embarrassment given them by their principle against war, whenever application was made to them, by order of the crown, to grant aids for military purposes. They were unwilling to offend government, on the one hand, by a direct refusal; and their friends, the body of the Quakers, on the other, by a compliance contrary to their principles; hence a variety of evasions to avoid complying, and modes of disguising the compliance when it became unavoidable. The common mode at last was, to grant money under the phrase of its being "*for the kings use*" and never to inquire how it was applied.

But, if the demand was not directly from the crown, that phrase was found not so proper, and some other was to be invented. As, when powder was wanting (I think it was for the garrison at Louisburg), and the government of New England solicited a grant of some from Pennsilvania, which was much urg'd on the House by Governor Thomas, they could not grant money to buy powder, because that was an ingredient of war; but they voted an aid to New England of three thousand pounds, to be put into the hands of the governor, and appropriated it for the purchasing of bread, flour, wheat, or *other grain*. Some of the council, desirous of giving the House still further embarrassment, advis'd the governor not to accept provision, as not being the thing he had demanded; but he reply'd, " I shall take the money, for I understand very well their meaning; other grain is gunpowder," which he accordingly bought, and they never objected to it.*

It was in allusion to this fact that, when in our fire company we feared the success of our proposal in favour of the lottery, and I had said to my friend Mr. Syng, one of our members, "If we fail, let us move the purchase of a fireengine with the money; the Quakers can have no objection to that; and then, if you nominate me and I you as a committee for that purpose, we will buy a great gun, which is certainly a *fireengine.*" "I see," says he, "you have improv'd by being so long in the Assembly; your equivocal project would be just a match for their wheat or *other grain*".

These embarrassments that the Quakers suffer'd from having establish'd and published it as one of their principles that no kind of war was lawful, and which, being once published, they could not afterwards, however they might change their minds, easily get rid of, reminds me of what I think a more prudent conduct in another sect among us, that of the Dunkers. I was acquainted with one of its founders, Michael Welfare, soon after it appear'd. He complain'd to me that they were grievously calumniated by the zealots of other persuasions, and charg'd with abominable principles and practices, to which they were utter strangers. I told him this had always been the case with new sects, and that, to put a stop to such abuse,

---

* See the votes.–[Marg, note].

I imagin'd it might be well to publish the articles of their belief, and the rules of their discipline. He said that it had been propos'd among them, but not agreed to, for this reason : " When we were first drawn together as a society," says he, " it had pleased God to enlighten our minds so far as to see that some doctrines, which we once esteemed truths, were errors; and that others, which we had esteemed errors, were real truths. From time to time He has been pleased to afford us farther light, and our principles have been improving, and our errors diminishing. Now we are not sure that we are arrived at the end of this progression, and at the perfection of spiritual or theological knowledge; and we fear that, if we should once print our confession of faith, we should feel ourselves as if bound and confin'd by it, and perhaps be unwilling to receive farther improvement, and our successors still more so, as conceiving what we their elders and founders had done, to be something sacred, never to be departed from."

This modesty in a sect is perhaps a singular instance in the history of mankind, every other sect supposing itself in possession of all truth, and that those who differ are so far in the wrong; like a man travelling in foggy weather, those at some distance before him on the road he sees wrapped up in the fog, as well as those behind him, and also the people in the fields on each side, but near him all appears clear, tho' in truth he is as much in the fog as any of them. To avoid this kind of embarrassment, the Quakers have of late years been gradually declining the public service in the Assembly and in the magistracy, choosing rather to quit their power than their principle.

In order of time, I should have mentioned before, that having, in 1742, invented an open stove for the better warming of rooms, and at the same time saving fuel, as the fresh air admitted was warmed in entering, I made a present of the model to Mr. Robert Grace, one of my early friends, who, having an iron-furnace, found the casting of the plates for these stoves a profitable thing, as they were growing in demand. To promote that demand, I wrote and published a pamphlet, entitled *"An Account of the new-invented Pennsylvania Fireplaces; wherein their Construction and Manner of Operation is particularly explained; their Advantages above every other Method of warming Rooms demonstrated; and all Objections that have been raised against the Use of them answered and obviated"* etc. This pamphlet had a good effect. Gov'r. Thomas was so pleas'd with the construction of this stove, as described in it, that he offered to give me a patent for the sole vending of them for a term of years; but I declin'd it from a principle which has ever weighed with me on such occasions, viz., *That, as we enjoy great advantages from the inventions of others, we should be glad of an opportunity to serve others by any invention of ours; and this we should do freely and generously.*

An ironmonger in London however, assuming a good deal of my pamphlet, and working it up into his own, and making some small changes in the machine, which rather hurt its operation, got a patent for it there, and made, as I was told, a little fortune by it. And this is not the only instance of patents taken out for my inventions by others, tho' not always with the same success, which I never contested, as having no desire of profiting by patents myself, and hating disputes. The use of these fireplaces in very many houses, both of this and the neighboring colonies, has been, and is, a great saving of wood to the inhabitants.

Peace being concluded, and the association business therefore at an end, I turn'd my thoughts again to the affair of establishing an academy. The first step I took was to associate in the design a number of active friends, of whom the Junto furnished a good part; the next was to write and publish a pamphlet, entitled *Proposals relating to the Education of Youth in Pennsylvania.* This I distributed among the principal inhabitants gratis; and as soon as I could suppose their minds a little prepared by the perusal of it, I set on foot a subscription for opening and supporting an academy: it was to be paid in quotas yearly for five years; by so dividing it, I judg'd the subscription might be larger, and I believe it was so, amounting to no less, if I remember right, than five thousand pounds.

In the introduction to these proposals, I stated their publication, not as an act of mine, but of some *public-spirited gentlemen* avoiding as much as I could, according to my usual rule, the presenting myself to the public as the author of any scheme for their benefit.

The subscribers, to carry the project into immediate execution, chose out of their number twenty- four trustees, and appointed Mr. Francis, then attorney-general, and myself to draw up constitutions for the government of the academy; which being done and signed, a house was hired, masters engag'd, and the schools opened, I think, in the same year, 1749.

The scholars increasing fast, the house was soon found too small, and we were looking out for a piece of ground, properly situated, with intention to build, when Providence threw into our way a large house ready built, which, with a few alterations, might well serve our purpose. This was the building before mentioned, erected by the hearers of Mr. Whitefield, and was obtained for us in the following manner.

It is to be noted that the contributions to this building being made by people of different sects, care was taken in the nomination of trustees, in whom the building and ground was to be vested, that a predominancy should not be given to any sect, lest in time that predominancy might be a means of appropriating the whole to the use of such sect, contrary to the original intention. It was therefore that one of each sect was appointed, viz., one Church-of-England man, one

Presbyterian, one Baptist, one Moravian, etc., those, in case of vacancy by death, were to fill it by election from among the contributors. The Moravian happen'd not to please his colleagues, and on his death they resolved to have no other of that sect. The difficulty then was, how to avoid having two of some other sect, by means of the new choice.

Several persons were named, and for that reason not agreed to. At length one mention'd me, with the observation that I was merely an honest man, and of no sect at all, which prevail'd with them to choose me. The enthusiasm which existed when the house was built had long since abated, and its trustees had not been able to procure fresh contributions for paying the ground-rent, and discharging some other debts the building had occasion'd, which embarrass'd them greatly. Being now a member of both setts of trustees, that for the building and that for the academy, I had a good opportunity of negotiating with both, and brought them finally to an agreement, by which the trustees for the building were to cede it to those of the academy, the latter undertaking to discharge the debt, to keep for ever open in the building a large hall for occasional preachers, according to the original intention, and maintain a freeschool for the instruction of poor children. Writings were accordingly drawn, and on paying the debts the trustees of the academy were put in possession of the premises; and by dividing the great and lofty hall into stories, and different rooms above and below for the several schools, and purchasing some additional ground, the whole was soon made fit for our purpose, and the scholars remov'd into the building. The care and trouble of agreeing with the workmen, purchasing materials, and superintending the work, fell upon me; and I went thro' it the more cheerfully, as it did not then interfere with my private business, having the year before taken a very able, industrious, and honest partner, Mr. David Hall, with whose character I was well acquainted, as he had work'd for me four years. He took off my hands all care of the printing-office, paying me punctually my share of the profits. This partnership continued for eighteen years, successfully for both of us.

The trustees of the academy, after a while, were incorporated by a charter from the governor; their funds were increas'd by contributions in Britain and grants of land from the proprietaries, to which the Assembly has since made considerable addition; and thus was established the present University of Philadelphia. I have been continued one of its trustees from the beginning, now near forty years, and have had the very great pleasure of seeing a number of the youth who have receiv'd their education in it, distinguish'd by their improv'd abilities, serviceable in public stations, and ornaments to their country.*

When I disengaged myself, as above mentioned, from private business, I flatter'd myself that, by the sufficient tho' moderate fortune I had acquir'd, I had secured leisure during the rest of my life for philosophical studies and amusements. I purchased all Dr. Spence's apparatus, who had come from England to lecture here, and I proceeded in my electrical experiments with great alacrity ; but the public, now considering me as a man of leisure, laid hold of me for their purposes, every part of our civil government, and almost at the same time, imposing some duty upon me. The governor put me into the commission of the peace; the corporation of the city chose me of the common council, and soon after an aiderman ; and the citizens at large chose me a burgess to represent them in Assembly. This latter station was the more agreeable to me, as I was at length tired with sitting there to hear debates, in which, as

---

* The old "Academy," as the building of which Franklin speaks has given place to a new and tasteful edifice. For many years the new building had been occupied as an academy, preparatory to the University, commodious buildings for which, were erected in South Ninth street, near Chestnut.

clerk, I could take no part, and which were often so unentertaining that I was induc'd to amuse myself with making magic squares or circles, or any thing to avoid weariness; and I conceiv'd my becoming a member would enlarge my power of doing good. I would not, however, insinuate that my ambition was not flatter'd by all these promotions ; it certainly was; for, considering my low beginning, they were great things to me; and they were still more pleasing, as being so many spontaneous testimonies of the public good opinion, and by me entirely unsolicited.

The office of justice of the peace I try'd a little, by attending a few courts, and sitting on the bench to hear causes; but finding that more knowledge of the common law than I possess'd was necessary to act in that station with credit, I gradually withdrew from it, excusing myself by my being oblig'd to attend the higher duties of a legislator in the Assembly. My election to this trust was repeated every year for ten years, without my ever asking any elector for his vote, or signifying, either directly or indirectly, any desire of being chosen. On taking my seat in the House, my son was appointed their clerk.

The year following, a treaty being to be held with the Indians at Carlisle, the governor sent a message to the House, proposing that they should nominate some of their members, to be join'd with some members of council, as commissioners for that purpose.* The House named the speaker (Mr. Norris) and myself; and, being commission'd, we went to Carlisle, and met the Indians accordingly.

As those people are extreamly apt to get drunk, and, when so, are very quarrelsome and disorderly, we strictly forbad the selling any liquor to them; and when they complain'd of this restriction, we told them that if they would continue sober during the treaty, we would give them plenty of rum when business was over. They promis'd this, and they kept their

---

* See the votes to have this more correctly.—[Marg, note.]

promise, because they could get no liquor, and the treaty was conducted very orderly, and concluded to mutual satisfaction. They then claim'd and receiv'd the rum; this was in the afternoon: they were near one hundred men, women, and children, and were lodg'd in temporary cabins, built in the form of a square, just without the town. In the evening, hearing a great noise among them, the commissioners walk'd out to see what was the matter. We found they had made a great bonfire in the middle of the square; they were all drunk, men and women, quarreling and fighting. Their darkcolour'd bodies, half naked, seen only by the gloomy light of the bonfire, running after and beating one another with firebrands, accompanied by their horrid yellings, form'd a scene the most resembling our ideas of hell that could well be imagin'd; there was no appeasing the tumult, and we retired to our lodging. At midnight a number of them came thundering at our door, demanding more rum, of which we took no notice.

The next day, sensible they had misbehav'd in giving us that disturbance, they sent three of their old counselors to make their apology. The orator acknowledg'd the fault, but laid it upon the rum; and then endeavored to excuse the rum by saying, "*The Great Spirit, who made all things, made every thing for some use, and 'whatever use he design'd any thing for, that use it should always be put to. Now, when he made rum, he said, 'Let this be for the Indians to get drunk with' and it must be so.*" And, indeed, if it be the design of Providence to extirpate these savages in order to make room for cultivators of the earth, it seems not improbable that rum may be the appointed means. It has already annihilated all the tribes who formerly inhabited the sea-coast.

In 1751, Dr. Thomas Bond, a particular friend of mine, conceived the idea of establishing a hospital in Philadelphia (a very beneficent design, which has been ascrib'd to me, but was originally his), for the reception and cure of poor sick persons, whether inhabitants of the province or strangers. He was zealous and active in endeavouring to procure subscriptions for it, but the proposal being a novelty in America, and at first not well understood, he met but with small success.

At length he came to me with the compliment that he found there was no such thing as carrying a public-spirited project through without my being concern'd in it. " For," says he, " I am often ask'd by those to whom I propose subscribing, Have you consulted Franklin upon this business? And what does he think of it? And when I tell them that I have not (supposing it rather out of your line), they do not subscribe, but say they will consider of it." I enquired into the nature and probable utility of his scheme, and receiving from him a very satisfactory explanation, I not only subscrib'd to it myself, but engag'd heartily in the design of procuring subscriptions from others. Previously, however, to the solicitation, I endeavoured to prepare the minds of the people by writing on the subject in the newspapers, which was my usual custom in such cases, but which he had omitted.

The subscriptions afterwards were more free and generous; but, beginning to flag, I saw they would be insufficient without some assistance from the Assembly, and therefore propos'd to petition for it, which was done. The country members did not at first relish the project; they objected that it could only be serviceable to the city, and therefore the citizens alone should be at the expense of it; and they doubted whether the citizens themselves generally approv'd of it. My allegation on the contrary, that it met with such approbation as to leave no doubt of our being able to raise two thousand pounds by voluntary donations, they considered as a most extravagant supposition, and utterly impossible.

On this I form'd my plan; and, asking leave to bring in a bill for incorporating the contributors according to the prayer of their petition, and granting them a blank sum of money, which leave was obtained chiefly on the consideration that the House could throw the bill out if they did not like it, I drew it so as to make the important clause a conditional one, viz., " And be it enacted, by the authority aforesaid, that when the said contributors shall have met and chosen their managers and treasurer, *and shall have raised by their contributions a capital stock of*-------------- *value* (the yearly interest of which is to be applied to the accommodating of the sick poor in the said hospital, free of charge for diet, attendance, advice, and medicines), *and shall make the same afpear to the satisfaction of the speaker of the Assembly for the time being,* that *then* it shall and may be lawful for the said speaker, and he is hereby required, to sign an order on the provincial treasurer for the payment of twothousand pounds, in two yearly payments, to the treasurer of the said hospital, to be applied to the founding, building, and finishing of the same."

This condition carried the bill through; for the members, who had oppos'd the grant, and now conceiv'd they might have the credit of being charitable without the expence, agreed to its passage; and then, in soliciting subscriptions among the people, we urg'd the conditional promise of the law as an additional motive to give, since every man's donation would be doubled; thus the clause work'd both ways. The subscriptions accordingly soon exceeded the requisite sum, and we claim'd and receiv'd the public gift, which enabled us to carry the design into execution. A convenient and handsome building was soon erected; the institution has by constant experience been found useful, and flourishes to this day; and I do not remember any of my political manoeuvres, the success of which gave me at the time more pleasure, or wherein, after thinking of it, I more easily excus'd myself for having made some use of cunning.

It was about this time that another projector, the Rev. Gilbert Tennent, came to me with a request that I would assist him in procuring a subscription for erecting a new meeting-house. It was to be for the use of a congregation he had gathered among the Presbyterians, who were originally disciples of Mr. Whitefield. Unwilling to make myself disagreeable to my fellow-citizens by too frequently soliciting their contributions, I absolutely refus'd. He then desired I would furnish him with a list of the names of persons I knew by experience to be generous and public-spirited. I thought it would be unbecoming in me, after their kind compliance with my solicitations, to mark them out to be worried by other beggars, and therefore refus'd also to give such a list. He then desir'd I would at least give him my advice. " That I will readily do," said I; " and, in the first place, I advise you to apply to all those whom you know will give something; next, to those whom you are uncertain whether they will give any thing or not, and show them the list of those who have given; and, lastly, do not neglect those who you are sure will give nothing, for in some of them you may be mistaken." He laugh'd and thank'd me, and said he would take my advice. He did so, for he ask'd of *everybody,* and he obtain'd a much larger sum than he expected, with which he erected the capacious and very elegant meeting-house that stands in Arch-street.

Our city, tho' laid out with a beautiful regularity, the streets were large Straight and crossing each othet at right angles, had the disgrace of suffering those streets to remain long unpav'd, and in wet weather the wheels of heavy carriages plough'd them into a quagmire, so that it was difficult to cross them; and in dry weather the dust was offensive. I had liv'd near what was call'd the Jersey Market, and saw with pain the inhabitants wading in mud while purchasing their provisions. A strip of ground down the middle of that market was at length pav'd with brick, so that, being once in the market, they had firm footing, but were often over shoes in dirt to get there. By talking and writing on the subject, I was at length instrumental in getting the street pav'd with stone between the market and the brick'd foot-pavement, that was on each side next the houses. This, for some time, gave an easy access to the market dryshod; but, the rest of the street not being pav'd, whenever a carriage came out of the mud upon this pavement, it shook off and left its dirt upon it, and it was soon cover'd with mire, which was not remov'd, the city as yet having no scavengers.

After some inquiry, I found a poor, industrious man, who was willing to undertake keeping the pavement clean, by sweeping it twice a week, carrying off the dirt from before all the neighbours' doors, for the sum of sixpence per month, to be paid by each house. I then wrote and printed a paper setting forth the advantages to the neighbourhood that might be obtain'd by this small expense; the greater ease in keeping our houses clean, so much dirt not being brought in by people's feet; the benefit to the shops by more custom, etc., etc., as buyers could more easily get at them; and by not having, in windy weather, the dust blown in upon their goods, etc., etc. I sent one of these papers to each house, and in a day or two went round to see who would subscribe an agreement to pay these sixpences; it was unanimously sign'd, and for a time well executed. All the inhabitants of the city were delighted with the cleanliness of the pavement that surrounded the market, it being a convenience to all, and this rais'd a general desire to have all the streets paved, and made the people more willing to submit to a tax for that purpose.

After some time I drew a bill for paving the city, and brought it into the Assembly. It was just before I went to England, in 1757, and did not pass till I was gone,* and then with an alteration in the mode of assessment, which I thought not for the better, but with an additional provision for lighting as well as paving the streets, which was a great improvement. It was by a private person, the late Mr. John Clifton, his giving a sample of the utility of lamps, by placing one at his door, that the people were first impress'd with the idea of enlighting all the city. The honour of this public benefit has also been ascrib'd to me, but it belongs truly to that gentleman. I did but follow

* See votes.

his example, and have only some merit to claim respecting the form of our lamps, as differing from the globe lamps we were at first supply'd with from London. Those we found inconvenient in these respects: they admitted no air below; the smoke, therefore, did not readily go out above, but circulated in the globe, lodg'd on its inside, and soon obstructed the light they were intended to afford; giving, besides, the daily trouble of wiping them clean; and an accidental stroke on one of them would demolish it, and render it totally useless. I therefore suggested the composing them of four flat panes, with a long funnel above to draw up the smoke, and crevices admitting air below, to facilitate the ascent of the smoke; by this means they were kept clean, and did not grow dark in a few hours, as the London lamps do, but continu'd bright till morning, and an accidental stroke would generally break but a single pane, easily repair'd. I have sometimes wonder'd that the Londoners did not, from the effect holes in the bottom of the globe lamps us'd at Vauxhall have in keeping them clean, learn to have such holes in their street lamps. But, these holes being made for another purpose, viz., to communicate flame more suddenly to the wick by a little flax hanging down thro' them, the other use, of letting in air, seems not to have been thought of; and therefore, after the lamps have been lit a few hours, the streets of London are very poorly illuminated.

The mention of these improvements puts me in mind of one I propos'd, when in London, to Dr. Fothergill, who was among the best men I have known, and a great promoter of useful projects. I had observ'd that the streets, when dry, were never swept, and the light dust carried away; but it was suffer'd to accumulate till wet weather reduc'd it to mud, and then, after lying some days so deep on the pavement that there was no crossing but in paths kept clean by poor people with brooms, it was with great labour rak'd together and thrown up into carts open above, the sides of which suffer'd some of the slush at every jolt on the pavement to shake out and fall, sometimes to the annoyance of foot-passengers. The reason given for not sweeping the dusty streets was, that the dust would fly into the windows of shops and houses.

An accidental occurrence had instructed me how much sweeping might be done in a little time. I found at my door in Cravenstreet, one morning, a poor woman sweeping my pavement with a birch broom; she appeared very pale and feeble, as just come out of a fit of sickness. I ask'd who employ'd her to sweep there ; she said, " Nobody ; but am very poor and in distress, and I sweeps before gentlefolkses doors, and hopes they will give me something." I bid her sweep the whole street clean, and I would give her a shilling ; this was at nine o'clock ; at 12 she came for the shilling. From the slowness I saw at first in her working, I could scarce believe that the work was done so soon, and sent my servant to examine it, who reported that the whole street was swept perfectly clean, and all the dust plac'd in the gutter, which was in the middle; and the next rain wash'd it quite away, so that the pavement and even the kennel were perfectly clean.

I then judg'd that, if that feeble woman could sweep such a street in three hours, a strong, active man might have done it in half the time. And here let me remark the convenience of having but one gutter in such a narrow street, running down its middle, instead of two, one on each side, near the footway; for where all the rain that falls on a street runs from the sides and meets in the middle, it forms there a current strong enough to wash away all the mud it meets with ; but when divided into two channels, it is often too weak to cleanse either, and only makes the mud it finds more fluid, so that the wheels of carriages and feet of horses throw and dash it upon the foot-pavement, which is thereby rendered foul and slippery, and sometimes splash it upon those who are walking. My proposal, communicated to the good doctor, was as follows:

" For the more effectual cleaning and keeping clean the streets of London and Westminster, it is proposed that the several watchmen be contracted with to have the dust swept up in dry seasons, and the mud rak'd up at other times, each in the several streets and lanes of his round ; that they be furnish'd with brooms and other proper instruments for these purposes, to be kept at their respective stands, ready to furnish the poor people they may employ in the service.

" That in the dry summer months the dust be all swept up into heaps at proper distances, before the shops and windows of houses are usually opened, when the scavengers, with close-covered carts, shall also carry it all away.

" That the mud, when rak'd up, be not left in heaps to be spread abroad again by the wheels of carriages and trampling of horses, but that the scavengers be provided with bodies of carts, not plac'd high upon wheels, but low upon sliders, with lattice bottoms, which, being cover'd with straw, will retain the mud thrown into them, and permit the water to drain from it, whereby it will become much lighter, water making the greatest part of its weight; these bodies of carts to be plac'd at convenient distances, and the mud brought to them in wheelbarrows ; they remaining where plac'd till the mud is drain'd, and then horses brought to draw them away."

I have since had doubts of the practicability of the latter part of this proposal, on account of the narrowness of some streets, and the difficulty of placing the draining-sleds so as not to encumber too much the passage; but I am still of opinion that the former, requiring the dust to be swept up and carry'd away before the shops are open, is very practicable in the summer, when the days are long; for, in walking thro' the Strand and Fleet-street one morning at seven o'clock, I observ'd there was not a single shop open, tho' it had been daylight and the sun up above three hours ; the inhabitants of London chusing voluntarily to live much by candle-light and sleep by sunshine, and yet often complain, a little absurdly, of the duty on candles, and the high price of tallow.

Some may think these trifling matters not worth minding or relating; but when they consider that tho' dust blown into the eyes of a single person, or into a single shop on a windy day, is but of small importance, yet the great number of the instances in a populous city, and its frequent repetitions give it weight and consequence, perhaps they will not censure very severely those who bestow some attention to affairs of this seemingly low nature. Human felicity is produc'd not so much by great pieces of good fortune that seldom happen, as by little advantages that occur every day. Thus, if you teach a poor young man to shave himself, and keep his razor in order, you may contribute more to the happiness of his life than in giving him a thousand guineas. The money may be soon spent, the regret only remaining of having foolishly consumed it; but in the other case, he escapes the frequent vexation of waiting for barbers, and of their sometimes dirty fingers, offensive breaths, and dull razors; he shaves when most convenient to him, and enjoys daily the pleasure of its being done with a good instrument. With these sentiments I have hazarded the few preceding pages, hoping that they may afford hints which some time or other may be useful to a city I love, having lived many years in it very happily, and perhaps to some of our towns in America.

Having been for some time employed by the postmaster-general of America as his comptroller in regulating several offices, and bringing the officers to account, I was, upon his death in 1753, appointed, jointly with Mr. William Hunter, to succeed him, by a commission from the postmaster-general in England. The American office never had hitherto paid any thing to that of Britain. We were to have six hundred pounds a year between us, if we could make that sum out of the profits of the office. To do this, a variety of improvements were necessary; some of these were inevitably at first expensive, so that in the first four years the office became above nine hundred pounds in debt to us. But it soon after began to repay us; and before I was displac'd by a freak of the ministers, of which I shall speak hereafter, we had brought it to yield *three times* as much clear revenue to the crown as the postoffice of Ireland. Since that imprudent transaction, they have receiv'd from it—not one farthing !

The business of the postoffice occasion'd my taking a journey this year to New England, where the College of Cambridge, of their own motion, presented me with the degree of Master of Arts. Yale College, in Connecticut, had before made me a similar compliment. Thus, without studying in any college, I came to partake of their honours. They were conferr'd in consideration of my improvements and discoveries in the electric branch of natural philosophy.

In 1754, war with France being again apprehended, a congress of commissioners from the different colonies was, by an order of the Lords of Trade, to be assembled at Albany, there to confer with the chiefs of the Six Nations concerning the means of defending both their country and ours. Governor Hamilton, having receiv'd this order, acquainted the House with it, requesting they would furnish proper presents for the Indians, to be given on this occasion ; and naming the speaker (Mr. Norris) and myself to join Mr. Thomas Penn and Mr. Secretary Peters as commissioners to act for Pennsylvania. The House approv'd the nomination, and provided the goods for the present, and tho' they did not much like treating out of the provinces; and we met the other commissioners at Albany about the middle of June.

In our way thither, I projected and drew a plan for the union of all the colonies under one government, so far as might be necessary for defense, and for other important general purposes. As we pass'd thro' New York, I had there shown my project to Mr. James Alexander and Mr. Kennedy, two gentlemen of great knowledge in public affairs, and, being fortified by their approbation, I ventur'd to lay it before the Congress. It then appeared that several of the commissioners had form'd plans of the same kind. A previous question was first taken, whether a union should be established, which pass'd in the affirmative unanimously. A committee was then appointed, one member from each colony, to consider the several plans and report. Mine happen'd to be preferr'd, and, with a few amendments, was accordingly reported.

By this plan the general government was to be administered by a president-general, appointed and supported by the crown, and a grand council was to be chosen by the representatives of the people of the several colonies, met in their respective assemblies. The debates upon it in Congress went on daily, hand in hand with the Indian business. Many objections and difficulties were started, but at length they were all overcome, and the plan was unanimously agreed to, and copies ordered to be transmitted to the Board of Trade and to the assemblies of the several provinces. Its fate was singular : the assemblies did not adopt it, as they all thought there was too much *prerogative* in it, and in England it was judg'd to have too much of the *democratic*. The Board of Trade therefore did not approve of it, nor recommend it for the approbation of his majesty; but another scheme was form'd, supposed to answer the same purpose better, whereby the governors of the provinces, with some members of their respective councils, were to meet and order the raising of troops, building of forts, etc., and to draw on the treasury of Great Britain for the expense, which was afterwards to be refunded by an act of Parliament laying a tax on America. My plan, with my reasons in support of it, is to be found among my political papers that are printed.*

Being the winter following in Boston, I had much conversation with Governor Shirley upon both the plans. Part of what passed between us on the occasion may also be seen among those papers. The different and contrary reasons of dislike to my plan makes me suspect that it was really the true medium ; and I am still of opinion it would have been happy for both sides the water if it had been adopted. The colonies, so united, would have been sufficiently strong to have defended themselves; there would then have been no need of troops from England; of course, the subsequent pretence for taxing

---

* See *Sparks' Works of Franklin'* vol. iii. pp. 22-55.

America, and the bloody contest it occasioned, would have been avoided. But such mistakes are not new: history is full of the errors of states and princes.

> " Look round the habitable world, how few
> Know their own good, or, knowing it, pursue !"

Those who govern, having much business on their hands, do not generally like to take the trouble of considering and carrying into execution new projects. The best public measures are therefore seldom *adopted from previous wisdom, but forc'd by the occasion.*

The Governor of Pennsylvania, in sending it down to the Assembly, express'd his approbation of the plan, " as appearing to him to be drawn up with great clearness and strength of judgment, and therefore recommended it as well worthy of their closest and most serious attention." The House, however, by the management of a certain member, took it up when I happen'd to be absent, which I thought not very fair, and reprobated it without paying any attention to it at all, to my no small mortification.

In my journey to Boston this year, I met at New York with our new governor, Mr. Morris, just arriv'd there from England, with whom I had been before intimately acquainted. He brought a commission to supersede Mr. Hamilton, who tir'd with the disputes his proprietary instructions subjected him to, had resign'd. Mr. Morris ask'd me if I thought he must expect as uncomfortable an administration. I said, "No; you may, on the contrary, have a very comfortable one, if you will only take care not to enter into any dispute with the Assembly." "My dear friend," says he, pleasantly, "how can you advise my avoiding disputes? You know I love disputing; it is one of my greatest pleasures ; however, to show the regard I have for your counsel, I promise you I will, if possible, avoid them." He had some reason for loving to dispute, being eloquent, an acute sophister, and, therefore, generally successful in argumentative conversation. He had been brought up to it from a boy, his father, as I have heard, accustoming his children to dispute with one another for his diversion, while sitting at table after dinner; but I think the practice was not wise; for, in the course of my observation, these disputing, contradicting, and confuting people are generally unfortunate in their affairs. They get victory sometimes, but they never get good will, which would be of more use to them. We parted, he went to Philadelphia, and I to Boston.

In returning, I met at New York with the votes of the Assembly, by which it appear'd that, notwithstanding his promise to me, he and the House were already in high contention; and it was a continual battle between them as long as he retain'd the government. I had my share of it; for, as soon as I got back to my seat in the Assembly, I was put on every committee for answering his speeches and messages, and by the committees always desired to make the drafts. Our answers, as well as his messages, were often tart, and sometimes indecently abusive ; and, as he knew I wrote for the Assembly, one might have imagined that, when we met, we could hardly avoid cutting throats; but he was so good-natur'd man that no personal difference between him and me was occasion'd by the contest, and we often din'd together.

One afternoon, in the height of this public quarrel, we met in the street. "Franklin," says he, "you must come home with me and spend the evening; I to have some company that you will likeand, taking me by the arm, he led me to his house. In gay conversation over our wine, after supper, he told us, jokingly, that he much admir'd the idea of Sancho Panza, who, when it was proposed to give him a government, requested it might be a government of *blacks,* as then, if he could not agree with his people, he might sell them. One of his friends, who sat next to me, says, "Franklin, why do you continue to side with these damn'd Quakers? Had not you better sell them? The proprietor would give you a good price." "The governor," says I, " has not yet *blacked* them enough." He, indeed, had labored hard to blacken the Assembly in all his messages, but they wip'd off his coloring as fast as he laid it on, and plac'd it, in return, thick upon his own face; so that, finding he was likely to be negrofied himself, he as well as Mr. Hamilton, grew tir'd of the contest, and quitted the government.

* These public quarrels were all at bottom owing to the proprietaries, our hereditary governors, who, when any expense was to be incurred for the defense of their province, with incredible meanness instructed their deputies to pass no act for levying the necessary taxes, unless their vast estates were in the same act expressly excused; and they had even taken bonds of these deputies to observe such instructions. The Assemblies for three years held out against this injustice, tho' constrained to bend at last. At length Captain Denny, who was Governor Morris's successor, ventured to disobey those instructions: how that was brought about I shall show hereafter.

But I am got forward too fast withi my story : there are still some transactions to be mention'd that happened during the administration of Governor Morris.

War being in a manner commenced with France, the government of Massachusetts Bay projected an attack upon Crown Point, and sent Mr. Quincy to Pennsylvania, and Mr. Pownall, afterward Governor Pownall, to New York, to solicit assistance. As I was in the Assembly, knew its temper, and was Mr. Quincy's countryman, he appli'd to me for my influence and assistance. I dictated his address to them, which was well receiv'd. They voted an aid of ten thousand pounds, to be laid out in provisions. But the governor refusing his assent to their bill (which included this with other sums granted for the use of the crown), unless a clause were inserted exempting the proprietary estate from bearing any part of the tax that would be necessary, the Assembly, tho' very desirous of making their grant to New England effectual, were at a loss how to accomplish it. Mr. Quincy labored hard with the governor to obtain his assent, but he was obstinate.

---

* My acts in Morris's time, military, etc.–*(Marg. note)*

I then suggested a method of doing the business without the governor, by orders on the trustees of the Loan Office, which, by law, the Assembly had the right of drawing. There was, indeed, little or no money at that time in the office, and therefore I propos'd that the orders should be payable in a year, and to bear an interest of five per cent. With these orders I suppos'd the provisions might easily be purchas'd. The Assembly, with very little hesitation, adopted the proposal. The orders were immediately printed, and I was one of the committee directed to sign and dispose of them. The fund for paying them was the interest of all the paper currency then extant in the province upon loan, together with the revenue arising from the excise, which being known to be more than sufficient, they obtain'd instant credit, and were not only receiv'd in payment for the provisions, but many money'd people, who had cash lying by them, vested it in those orders, which they found advantageous, as they bore interest while upon hand, and might on any occasion be used as money; so that they were eagerly all bought up, and in a few weeks none of them were to be seen. Thus this important affair was by my means compleated. Mr. Quincy return'd thanks to the Assembly in a handsome memorial, went home highly pleas'd with the success of his embassy, and ever after bore for me the most cordial and affectionate friendship.

The British government, not chusing to permit the union of the colonies as propos'd at Albany, and to trust that union with their defense, lest they should thereby grow too military, and feel their own strength, suspicions and jealousies at this time being entertain'd of them, sent over General Braddock with two regiments of regular English troops for that purpose. He landed at Alexandria, in Virginia, and thence march'd to Fredetictown, in Maryland, where he halted for carriages. Our Assembly apprehending, from some information, that he had conceived violent prejudices against them, as averse to the service, wish'd me to wait upon him, not as from them, but as postmaster-general, under the guise of proposing to settle with him the mode of conducting with most celerity and certainty the despatches between him and the governors of the several provinces, with whom he must necessarily have continual correspondence, and of which they propos'd to pay the expense. My son accompanied me on this journey.

We found the general at Frederictown, waiting impatiently for the return of those he had sent thro' the back parts of Maryland and Virginia to collect waggons. I stayed with him several days, din'd with him daily, and had full opportunity of removing all his prejudices, by the information of what the Assembly had before his arrival actually done, and were still willing to do, to facilitate his operations. When I was about to depart, the returns of waggons to be obtained were brought in, by which it appear'd that they amounted only to twenty-five, and not all of those were in serviceable condition. The general and all the officers were surpris'd, declar'd the expedition was then at an end, being impossible ; and exclaim'd against the ministers for ignorantly landing them in a country destitute of the means of conveying their stores, baggage, etc., not less than one hundred and fifty waggons being necessary.

I happen'd to say I thought it was pity they had not been landed rather in Pennsylvania, as in that country almost every farmer had his waggon. The general eagerly laid hold of my words, and said, " Then you, sir, who are a man of interest there, can probably procure them for us; and I beg you will undertake it." I ask'd what terms were to be offer'd the owners of the waggons; and I was desir'd to put on paper the terms that appeared to me necessary. This I did, and they were agreed to, and a commission and instructions accordingly prepar'd immediately. What those terms were will appear in the advertisement I publish'd as soon as I arriv'd at Lancaster, which being, from the great and sudden effect it produc'd, a piece of some curiosity, I shall insert it at length, as follows:

ADVERTISEMENT.

LANCASTER, *April* 26, 1755.

"Whereas, one hundred and fifty waggons, with four horses to each waggon, and fifteen hundred saddle or pack horses, are wanted for the service of his majesty's forces now about to rendezvous at Will's Creek, and his excellency General Braddock having been pleased to empower me to contract for the hire of the same, I hereby give notice that I shall attend for that purpose at Lancaster from this day to next Wednesday evening, and at York from next Thursday morning till Friday evening, where I shall be ready to agree for waggons and teams, or single horses, on the following terms, viz.: 1. That there shall be paid for each waggon, with four good horses and a driver, fifteen shillings per diem ; and for each able horse with a pack-saddle, or other saddle and furniture, two shillings per diem; and for each able horse without a saddle, eighteen pence per diem.

2. That the pay commence from the time of their joining the forces at Will's Creek, which must be on or before the 20th of May ensuing, and that a reasonable allowance be paid over and above for the time necessary for their travelling to Will's Creek and home again after their discharge. 3. Each waggon and team, and every saddle or pack horse, is to be valued by indifferent persons chosen between me and the owner; and in case of the loss of any waggon, team, or other horse in the service, the price according to such valuation is to be allowed and paid. 4. Seven days' pay is to be advanced and paid in hand by me to the owner of each waggon and team, or horse, at the time of contracting, if required, and the remainder to be paid by General Braddock, or by the paymaster of the army,

at the time of their discharge, or from time to time, as it shall be demanded. 5. No drivers of waggons, or persons taking care of the hired horses, are on any account to be called upon to do the duty of soldiers, or be otherwise employed than in conducting or taking care of their carriages or horses. 6. All oats, Indian corn, or other forage that waggons or horses bring to the camp, more than is necessary for the subsistence of the horses, is to be taken for the use of the army, and a reasonable price paid for the same.

"Note.–My son, William Franklin, is empowered to enter into like contracts with any person in Cumberland county.

B.FRANKLIN."

"To the inhabitants of the Counties of Lancaster york) and Cumberland.

"Friends and Countrymen,

"Being occasionally at the camp at Frederic a few days since, I found the general and officers extremely exasperated on account of their not being supplied with horses and carriages, which had been expected from this province, as most able to furnish them; but, through the dissensions between our governor and Assembly, money had not been provided, nor any steps had been taken for that purpose.

It was proposed to send an armed force immediately into these counties, to seize as many of the best carriages and horses as should be wanted, and compel as many persons into the service as would be necessary to drive and take care of them.

"1 apprehended that the progress of British soldiers through these counties on such an occasion, especially considering the temper they are in, and their resentment against us, would be attended with many and great inconveniences to the inhabitants, and therefore more willingly took the trouble of trying first what might be done by fair and equitable means. The people of these back counties have lately complained to the Assembly that a sufficient currency was wanting ; you have an opportunity of receiving and dividing among you a very considerable sum; for, if the service of this expedition should continue, as it is more than probable it will, for one hundred and twenty days, the hire of these waggons and horses will amount to upward of thirty- thousand pounds, which will be paid you in silver and gold of the king's money.

The service will be light and easy, for the army will scarce march above twelve miles per day, and the waggons and baggage-horses, as they carry those things that are absolutely necessary to the welfare of the army, must march with the army, and no faster; and are for the army's sake, always placed where they can be most secure, whether in a march or in a camp.

If you are really, as I believe you are, good and loyal subjects to his majesty, you may now do a most acceptable service, and make it easy to yourselves ; for three or four of such as can not separately spare from the business of their plantations a waggon and four horses and a driver, may do it together, one furnishing the waggon, another one or two horses, and another the driver, and divide the pay proportionately between you ; but if you do not give this service to your king and country voluntarily, when such good pay and reasonable terms are offered to you, your loyalty will be strongly suspected. The king's business must be done; so many brave troops, come so far for your defense, must not stand idle through your backwardness to do what may be reasonably expected from you; waggons and horses must be had; violent measures will probably be used, and you will be left to seek for a recompense where you can find it, and your case, perhaps, be little pitied or regarded.

" I have no particular interest in this affair, as, except the satisfaction of endeavoring to do good, I shall have only my labor for my pains. If this method of obtaining the waggons and horses is not likely to succeed, I am obliged to send word to the general in fourteen days; and I suppose Sir John St. Clair, the hussar, with a body of soldiers, will immediately enter the province for the purpose, which I shall be sorry to hear, because I am very sincerely and truly your friend and well-wisher.

"B. FRANKLIN."

I received of the general about eight hundred pounds, to be disbursed in advance-money to the waggon owners, etc.; but that sum being insufficient, I advanc'd upward of two hundred pounds more, and in two weeks the one hundred and fifty
waggons, with two hundred and fiftynine carrying horses, were on their march for the camp. The advertisement promised payment according to the valuation, in case any waggon or horse should be lost. The owners, however, alleging they did not know General Braddock, or what dependence might be had on his promise, insisted on my bond for the performance, which I accordingly gave them.

While I was at the camp, supping one evening with the officers of Colonel Dunbar's regiment, he represented to me his concern for the subalterns, who, he said, were generally not in affluence, and could ill afford, in this dear country, to lay in the stores that might be necessary in so long a march, thro' a wilderness, where nothing was to be purchas'd. I commiserated their case, and resolved to endeavor procuring them some relief. I said nothing, however, to him of my intention, but wrote the next morning to the committee of the Assembly, who had the disposition of somepublic money, warmly recommending the case of these officers to their consideration, and proposing that a present should be sent them of necessaries and refreshments. My son, who had some experience of a camp life, and of its wants, drew up a list for me, which I enclos'd in my letter. The committee approv'd, and used such diligence that, conducted by my son, the stores arrived at the camp as soon as the waggons. They consisted of twenty parcels, each containing

6 lbs. loaf sugar.
6 lbs. good Muscovado do.
1 lb. good green tea.
1 lb. good bohea do.
6 lbs. good ground coffee.
6 lbs. chocolate.
1-2 cwt best white biscuit
1-2 lb. pepper.
I quart best white wine vinegar.
1 Gloucester cheese.
1 kegg containing 20 lbs.goodbutter.
2 doz. old Madeira wine.
2 gallons Jamaica spirits.
1 bottle flour of mustard.
2 well-cur'd hams.
1-2 dozen dry'd tongues.
6 lbs. rice.
6 lbs. raisins.

These twenty parcels, well pack'd, were placed on as many horses, each parcel, with the horse, being intended as a present for one officer. They were very thankfully receiv'd, and the kindness ac knowledg'd by letters to me from the colonels of both regiments, in the most grateful terms. The general, too, was highly satisfied with my conduct in procuring him the waggons, etc., and readily paid my account of disbursements, thanking me repeatedly, and requesting my farther assistance in sending provisions after him. I undertook this also, and was busily employ'd in it till we heard of his defeat, advancing for the service of my own money, upwards of one thousand pounds sterling, of which I sent him an account. It came to his hands, luckily for me, a few days before the battle, and he return'd me immediately an order on the paymaster for the round sum of one thousand pounds, leaving the remainder to the next account. I consider this payment as good luck, having never been able to obtain that remainder, of which more hereafter.

This general was, I think, a brave man, and might probably have made a figure as a good officer in some European war. But he had too much selfconfidence, too high an opinion of the validity of regular troops, and too mean a one of both Americans and Indians. George Croghan, our Indian interpreter, join'd him on his march with one hundred of those people, who might have been of great use to his army as guides, scouts, etc., if he had treated them kindly; but he slighted and neglected them, and they gradually left him.

In conversation with him one day, he was giving me some account of his intended progress. " After taking Fort Duquesne," says he, " I am to proceed to Niagara; and, having taken that, to Frontenac, if the season will allow time; and I suppose it will, for Duquesne can hardly detain me above three or four days; and then I see nothing that can obstruct my march to Niagara." Having before revolv'd in my mind the long line his army must make in their march by a very narrow road, to be cut for them thro' the woods and bushes, and also what I had read of a former defeat of fifteen hundred French, who invaded the Iroquois country, I had conceiv'd some doubts and some fears for the event of the campaign. But I ventur'd only to say, "To be sure, sir, if you arrive well before Duquesne, with these fine troops, so well provided with artillery, that place not yet compleatly fortified, and as we hear with no very strong garrison, can probably make but a short resistance. The only danger I apprehend of obstruction to your march is from ambuscades of Indians, who, by constant practice, are dexterous in laying and executing them; and the slender line, near four miles long, which your army must make, may expose it to be attack'd by surprise . in its flanks, and to be cut like a thread into several pieces, which, from their distance, can not come up in time to support each other."

He smil'd at my ignorance, and reply'd, "These savages may, indeed, be a formidable enemy to your raw American militia, but upon the king's regular and disciplin'd troops, sir, it is impossible they should make any impression." I was conscious of an impropriety in my disputing with a military man in matters of his profession, and said no more. The enemy, however, did not take the advantage of his army which I apprehended its long line of march exposd it to, but let it advance without interruption till within nine miles of the place; and then, when more in a body (for it had just passed a river, where the front had halted till all were come over), and in a more open part of the woods than any it had pass'd, attackd its advanced guard by a heavy fire from behind trees and bushes, which was the first intelligence the general had of an enemy's being near him. This guard being disordered, the general hurried the troops up. to their assistance, which was done in great confusion, thro waggons, baggage, and cattle; and presently the fire came upon their flank: the officers, being on horseback, were more easily distinguish'd, pick'd out as marks, and fell very fast; and the soldiers were crowded together in a huddle, having or hearing no orders, and standing to be shot at till two-thirds of them were killed; and then, being seiz'd with a panick, the whole fled with precipitation.

The waggoners took each a horse out of his team and scamper'd ; their example was immediately followed by others ; so that all the waggons, provisions, artillery, and stores were left to the enemy. The general, being wounded, was brought off with difficulty ; his secretary, Mr. Shirley, was killed by his side ; and out of eighty-six officers, sixty-three were killed or wounded, and seven hundred and fourteen men killed out of eleven hundred. These eleven hundred had been picked by men from the whole army; the rest had been left behind with Colonel Dunbar, who was to follow with the heavier part of the stores, provisions, and baggage. The flyers, not being pursu'd, arriv'd at Dunbar's camp, and the panick they brought with them instantly seiz'd him and all his people; and, tho' he had now above one thousand men, and the enemy who had beaten Braddock did not at most exceed four hundred Indians and French together, instead of proceeding, and endeavoring to recover some of the lost honour, he ordered all the stores, ammunition, etc., to be destroy'd, that he might have more horses to assist his flight towards the settlements, and less lumber to remove. He was there met with requests from the governors of Virginia, Maryland, and Pennsylvania, that he would post his troops on the frontiers, so as to afford some protection to the inhabitants; but he continu'd his hasty march thro' all the country, not thinking himself safe till he arriv'd at Philadelphia, where the inhabitants could protect him. This whole transaction gave us Americans the first suspicion that our exalted ideas of the prowess of British regulars had not been well founded.

In their first march, too, from their landing till they got beyond the settlements, they had plundered and stripped the inhabitants, totally ruining some poor families, besides insulting, abusing, and confining the people if they remonstrated. This was enough to put us out of conceit of such defenders, if we had really wanted any. How different was the conduct of our French friends in 1781, who, during a march thro' the most inhabited part of our country from Rhode Island to Virginia, near seven hundred miles, occasioned not the smallest complaint for the loss of a pig, a chicken, or even an apple.

Captain Orme, who was one of the general's aids-de-camp, and, being grievously wounded, was brought off with him, and continu'd with him to his death, which happen'd in a few days, told me that he was totally silent all the first day, and at night only said, " *Who would have thought it?"* That he was silent again the following day, saying only at last, " *We shall better know how to deal with them another time;"* and dy'd in a few minutes after.

The secretary's papers, with all the general's orders, instructions and correspondence, falling into the enemy's hands, they selected and translated into French a number of the articles, which they printed, to prove the hostile intentions of the British court before the declaration of war. Among these I saw some letters of the general to the ministry, speaking highly of the great service I had rendered the army, and recommending me to their notice. David Hume, too, who was some years after secretary to Lord Hertford, when minister in France, and afterward to General Conway, when secretary of state, told me he had seen among the papers in that office, letters from Braddock highly recommending me. But, the expedition having been unfortunate, my service, it seems, was not thought of much value, for those recommendations were never of any use to me.

As to rewards from himself, I ask'd only one, which was, that he would give orders to his officers not to enlist any more of our bought servants, and that he would discharge such as had been already enlisted. This he readily granted, and several were accordingly return'd to their masters, on my application. Dunbar, when the command devolv'd on him, was not so generous. He being at Philadelphia, on his retreat, or rather flight, I apply'd to him for the discharge of the servants of three poor farmers of Lancaster county that he had enlisted, reminding him of the late general's orders on that head. He promised me that, if the masters would come to him at Trenton, where he should be in a few days on his march to New York, he would there deliver their men to them. They accordingly were at the expense and trouble of going to Trenton, and there he refus'd to perform his promise, to their great loss and disappointment.

As soon as the loss of the waggons and horses was generally known, all the owners came upon me for the valuation which I had given bond to pay. Their demands gave me a great deal of trouble, my acquainting them that the money was ready in the paymaster's hands, but that orders for paying it must first be otained from General Shirley, and my assuring them that I had apply'd to that general by letter; but, he being at a distance, an answer could not soon be receiv'd, and they must have patience, all this was not sufficient to satisfy, and some began to sue me. General Shirley at length relieved me from this terrible situation by appointing commissioners to examine the claims, and ordering payment. They amounted to near twenty thousand pound, which to pay would have ruined me.

Before we had the news of this defeat, the two Doctors Bond came to me with a subscription paper for raising money to defray the expense of a grand firework, which it was intended to exhibit at a rejoicing on receipt of the news of our taking Fort Duquesne. I looked grave, and said it would, I thought, be time enough to prepare for the rejoicing when we knew we should have occasion to rejoice.

They seem'd surpris'd that I did not immediately comply with their proposal. "Why the d–1!" says one of them, " you surely don't suppose that the fort will not be taken?" " I don't know that it will not be taken, but I know that the events of war are subject to great uncertainty." I gave them the reasons of my doubting; the subscription was dropt, and the projectors thereby missed the mortification they would have undergone if the firework had been prepared. Dr. Bond, on some other occasion afterward, said that he did not like Franklin's forebodings.

Governor Morris, who had continually worried the Assembly with message after message before the defeat of Braddock, to beat them into the making of acts to raise money for the defense of the province, without taxing among others, the proprietary estates, and had rejected all their bills for not having such an exempting clause, now redoubled his attacks with more hope of success, the danger and necessity being greater. The Assembly, however, continu'd firm, believing they had justice on their side, and that it would be giving up an essential right if they suffered the governor to amend their money-bills. In one of the last, indeed, which was for granting fifty thousand pounds, his propos'd amendment was only of a single word. The bill express'd " that all estates, real and personal, were to be taxed, those of the proprietaries *not* excepted." His amendment was, for *not* read *only:* a small, but very material alteration. However, when the news of this disaster reached England, our friends there, whom we had taken care to furnish with all the Assembly's answers to the governor's messages, rais'd a clamor against the proprietaries for their meanness and injustice in giving their governor such instructions; some going so far as to say that, by obstructing the defense of their province, they forfeited their right to it. They were intimidated by this, and sent orders to their receiver-general to add five thousand pounds of their money to whatever sum might be given by the Assembly for such purpose.

This, being notified to the House, was accepted in lieu of their share of a general tax, and a new bill was form'd, with an exempting clause, which passed accordingly. By this act I was appointed one of the commissioners for disposing of the money, sixty thousand pounds. I had been active in modelling the bill and procuring its passage, and had, at the same time, drawn a bill for establishing and disciplining a voluntary militia, which I carried thro' the House without much difficulty, as care was taken in it to leave the Quakers at their liberty. To promote the association necessary to form the militia, I wrote a dialogue,* stating and answering all the objections I could think of to such a militia, which was printed, and had, as I thought, great effect.

While the several companies in the city and country were forming, and learning their exercise, the governor prevail'd with me to take charge of our North-western frontier, which was infested by the enemy, and provide for the defense of the inhabitants by raising troops and building a line of forts. I undertook this military business, tho' I did not conceive myself well qualified for it. He gave me a commission with full powers, and a parcel of blank commissions for officers, to be given to whom I thought fit. I had but little difficulty in raising men, having soon five hundred and sixty under my command. My son, who had in the preceding war been an officer in the army rais'd against Canada, was my aid-de-camp, and of great use to me. The Indians had burned Gnadenhut, a village settled by the Moravians, and massacred the inhabitants ; but the place was thought a good situation for one of the forts.

In order to march thither, I assembled the companies at Bethlehem, the chief establishment of those people. I was surprised to find it in so good a posture of defense; the destruction of Gnadenhut had made them apprehend danger. The principal buildings were defended by a stockade;

* This dialogue and the militia act are in the Gentleman's Magazine for February and March, 1756.—*[Marg, note.]*

they had purchased a quantity of arms and ammunition from New York, and had even plac'd quantities of small pavirig stones between the windows of their high stone houses, for their women to throw down upon the heads of any Indians that should attempt to force into them. The armed brethren, too, kept watch, and reliev'd as methodically as in any garrison town. In conversation with the bishop, Span- genberg, I mention'd this my surprise; for, knowing they had obtained an act of Parliament exempting them from 'military duties in the colonies, I had suppos'd they were conscientiously scrupulous of bearing arms. He answer'd me that it was not one of their established principles, but that, at the time of their obtaining that act it was thought to be a principle with many of their people. On this occasion, however, they, to their surprise, found it adopted by but a few. It seems they were either deceiv'd in themselves, or deceiv'd the Parliament; but common sense, aided by present danger, will sometimes be too strong for whimsical opinions.

It was the beginning of January when we set out upon this business of building forts. I sent one detachment toward the Minisink, with instructions to erect one for the security of that upper part of the country, and another to the lower part, with similar instructions; and I concluded to go myself with the rest of my force to Gnadenhut, where a fort was tho't more immediately necessary. The Moravians procur'd me five waggons for our tools, stores, baggage, etc.

Just before we left Bethlehem, eleven farmers, who had been driven from their plantations by the Indians, came to me requesting a supply of firearms, that they might go back and fetch off their cattle. I gave them each a gun with suitable ammunition. We had not march'd many miles before it began to rain, and it continued raining all day; there were no habitations on the road to shelter us, till we arriv'd near night at the house of a German, where, in his barn, we were all huddled together, as wet as water could make us. It was well that we were not attack'd in our march, for our arms were of the most ordinary sort, and our men could not keep their gun locks dry. The Indians are dextrous in contrivances for that purpose, which we had not. They met that day the eleven poor farmers above mentioned, and killed ten of them. The one who escap'd inform'd that his and his companions' guns would not go off, the priming being wet with the rain.

The next day being fair, we continu'd our march, and arriv'd at the desolated Gnadenhut. There was a saw-mill near, round which were left several piles of boards, with which we soon hutted ourselves; an operation the more necessary at that inclement season, as we had no tents. Our first work was to bury more effectually the dead we found there, who had been half interr'd by the country people.

The next morning our fort was plann'd and mark'd out, the circumference measuring four hundred and fifty-five feet, which would require as many palisades to be made of trees, one with another, of a foot diameter each. Our axes, of which we had seventy were immediately set to work to cut down trees, and, our men being dextrous in the use of them, great despatch was made. Seeing the trees fall so fast, I had the curiosity to look at my watch when two men began to cut at a pine; in six minutes they had it upon the ground, and I found it of fourteen inches diameter. Each pine made three palisades of eighteen feet long, pointed at one end. While these were preparing, our other men dug a trench all round, of three feet deep in which the palisades were to be planted; and, our waggons, the bodys being taken off, and the fore and hind wheels separated by taking out the pin which united the two parts of the perch, we had ten carriages, with two horses each, to bring the palisades from the woods to the spot. When they were set up, our carpenters built a stage of boards all round within, about six feet high, for the men to stand on when to fire thro' the loopholes. We had one swivel gun, which we mounted on one of the angles, and fir'd it as soon as fix'd, to let the Indians know, if any were within hearing, that we had such pieces ; and thus our fort, if such a magnificent name may be given to so miserable a stockade, was finish'd in a week, though it rain'd so hard every other day the men could not work.

This gave me occasion to observe, that, when men are employ'd, they are best content'd; for on the days they worked they were good-natur'd and cheerful, and, with the consciousness of having done a good day's work, they spent the evening jollily; but on our idle days they were mutinous and quarrelsome, finding fault with their pork, the bread, etc., and in continual ill-humor, which put me in mind of a sea-captain, whose rule it was to keep his men constantly at work; and, when his mate once told him that they had done every thing, and there was nothing further to employ them about, *"Oh" says he " make them scour the anchor".*

This kind of fort, however contemptible, is a sufficient defense against Indians, who have no cannon. Finding ourselves now posted securely, and having a place to retreat to on occasion, we ventur'd out in parties to scour the adjacent country. We met with no Indians, but we found the places on the neighboring hills where they had lain to watch our proceedings. There was an art in their contrivance of those places that seems worth mention. It being winter, a fire was necessary for them; but a common fire on the surface of the ground would by its light have discover'd their position at a distance. They had therefore dug holes in the ground about three feet diameter, and somewhat deeper; we saw where they had with their hatchets cut off the charcoal from the sides of burnt logs lying in the woods. With these coals they had made small fires in the bottom of the holes, and we observ'd among the weeds and grass the prints of their bodies, made by their laying all round, with their legs hanging down in the holes to keep their feet warm, which, with them, is an essential point. This kind of fire, somanag'd, could not discover them, either by its light, flame, sparks, or even smoke : it appear'd that their number was not great, and it seems they saw we were too many to be attacked by them with prospect of advantage.

We had for our chaplain a zealous Presbyterian minister, Mr. Beatty, who complained to me that the men did not generally attend his prayers and exhortations. When they enlisted, they were promised, besides pay and provisions, a gill of rum a day, which was punctually serv'd out to them, half in the morning, and the other half in the evening; and I observ'd they were as punctual in attending to receive it; upon which I said to Mr. Beatty, " It is, perhaps, below the dignity of your profession to act as steward of the rum, but if you were to deal it out and only just after prayers, you would have them all about you." He liked the tho't, undertook the office, and, with the help of a few hands to measure out the liquor, executed it to satisfaction, and never were prayers more generally and more punctually attended; so that I thought this method preferable to the punishment inflicted by some military laws for non-attendance on divine service.

I had hardly finish'd this business, and got my fort well stor'd with provisions, when I receiv'd a letter from the governor, acquainting me that he had call'd the Assembly, and wished my attendance there, if the posture of affairs on the frontiers was such that my remaining there was no longer necessary. My friends, too, of the Assembly, pressing me by their letters to be, if possible, at the meeting, and my three intended forts being now compleated, and the inhabitants contented to remain on their farms under that protection, I resolved to return ; the more willingly, as a New England officer, Colonel Clapham, experienced in Indian war, being on a visit to our establishment, consented to accept the command. I gave him a commission, and, parading the garrison, had it read before them, and introduc'd him to them as an officer who, from his skill in military affairs, was much more fit to command them than myself; and, giving them a little exhortation, took my leave. I was escorted as far as Bethlehem, where I rested a few days to recover from the fatigue I had undergone. The first night, being in a good bed, I could hardly sleep, it was so different from my hard lodging on the floor of our hut at Gnaden wrapt only in a blanket or two.

While at Bethlehem, I inquir'd a little into the practice of the Moravians: some of them had accompanied me, and all were very kind to me. I found they work'd for a common stock, eat at common tables, and slept in common dormitories, great numbers together. In the dormitories I observed loopholes, at certain distances all along just under the ceiling, which I thought judiciously placed for change of air. I was at their church, where I was entertain'd with good music, the organ being accompanied with violins, hautboys, flutes, clarinets, etc. I understood that their sermons were not usually preached to mixed congregations of men, women, and children, as is our common practice, but that they assembled sometimes the married men, at other times their wives, then the young men, the young women, and the little children, each division by itself. The sermon I heard was to the latter, who came in and were plac'd in rows on benches; the boys under the conduct of a young man, their tutor, and the girls conducted by a young woman. The discourse seem'd well adapted to their capacities, and was delivered in a pleasing, familiar manner, coaxing them, as it were, to be good. They behav'd very orderly, but looked pale and unhealthy, which made me suspect they were kept too much within doors, or not allow'd sufficient exercise.

I inquir'd concerning the Moravian marriages, whether the report was true that they were by lot. I was told that lots were us'd only in particular cases; that generally, when a young man found himself dispos'd to marry, he inform'd the elders of his class, who consulted the elder ladies that govern'd the young women. As these elders of the different sexes were well acquainted with the tempers and dispositions of their respective pupils, they could best judge what matches were suitable, and their judgments were generally acquiesc'd in; but if, for example, it should happen that two or three young women were found to be equally proper for the young man, the lot was then recurred to. I objected, if the matches are not made by the mutual choice of the parties, some of them may chance to be very unhappy. "And so they may," answer'd my informer, " if you let the parties choose for themselves which, indeed, I could not deny.

Being returned to Philadelphia, I found the association went on swimmingly, the inhabitants that were not Quakers having pretty generally come into it, formed themselves into companies, and chose their captains, lieutenants, and ensigns, according to the new law. Dr. B. visited me, and gave me an account of the pains he had taken to spread a general good liking to the law, and ascribed much to those endeavors. I had the vanity to ascribe all to my *Dialogue;* however, not knowing but that he might be in the right, I let him enjoy his opinion, which I take to be generally the best way in such cases. The officers meeting, chose me to be colonel of the regiment, which I this time accepted. I forget how many companies we had, but we paraded about twelve hundred well-looking men, with a company of artillery, who had been furnished with six brass field-pieces, which they had become so expert in the use of as to fire twelve times in a minute. The first time I reviewed my regiment they accompanied me to my house, and would salute me with some rounds fired before my door, which shook down and broke several glasses of my electrical apparatus. And my new honour proved not much less brittle; for all our commissions were soon after broken by a repeal of the law in England.

During this short time of my colonelship, being about to set out on a journey to Virginia, the officers of my regiment took it into their heads that it would be proper for them to escort me out of town, as far as the Lower Ferry. Just as I was getting on horseback they came to my door, between thirty and forty, mounted, and all in their uniforms. I had not been previously acquainted with the project, or I should have prevented it, being naturally averse to the assuming of state on any occasion ; and I was a good deal chagrin'd at their appearance, as I could not avoid their accompanying me. What made it worse was, that, as soon as we began to move, they drew their swords and rode with them naked all the way. Somebody wrote an account of this to the proprietor, and it gave him great offense. No such honor had been paid him when in the province, nor to any of his governors; and he said it was only proper to princes of the blood royal, which may be true for aught I know, who was, and still an ignorant of the etiquette in such cases.

This silly affair, however, greatly increased his rancour against me, which was before not a little, on account of my conduct in the Assembly respecting the exemption of his estate from taxation, which I had always oppos'd very warmly, and not without severe reflections on his meanness and injustice of contending for it. He accused me to the ministry as being the great obstacle to the king's service, preventing, by my influence in the House, the proper form of the bills for raising money, and he instanced this parade with my officers as a proof of my having an intention to take the government of the province out of his hands by force. He also applied to Sir Everard Fawkener, the postmaster-general, to deprive me of my office; but it had no other effect than to procure from Sir Everard a gentle admonition.

Notwithstanding the continual wrangle between the governor and the House, in which I, as a member, had so large a share, there still subsisted a civil intercourse between that gentleman and myself, and we never had any personal difference. I have sometimes since thought that his little or no resentment against me, for the answers it was known I drew up to his messages, might be the effect of professional habit, and that, being bred a lawyer, he might consider us both as merely advocates for contending clients in a suit, he for the proprietaries and I for the Assembly. He would, therefore, sometimes call in a friendly way to advise with me on difficult points, and sometimes, tho' not often, take my advice.

We acted in concert to supply Braddock's army with provisions; and, when the shocking news arrived of his defeat, the governor sent in haste for me, to consult with him on measures for preventing the desertion of the back counties. I forget now the advice I gave; but I think it was, that Dunbar should be written to, and prevail'd with, if possible, to post his troops on the frontiers for their protection, till, by reenforcements from the colonies, he might be able to proceed on the expedition. And, after my return from the frontier, he would have had me undertake the conduct of such an expedition with provincial troops, for the reduction of Fort Duquesne, Dunbar and his men being otherwise employed ; and he proposed to commission me as general. I had not so good an opinion of my military abilities as he profess'd to have, and I believe his professions must have exceeded his real sentiments ; but probably he might think that my popularity would facilitate the raising of the men, and my influence in Assembly, the grant of money to pay them, and that, perhaps, without taxing the proprietary estate. Finding me not so forward to engage as he expected, the project was dropt, and he soon after left the government, being superseded by Captain Denny.

Before I proceed in relating the part I had in public affairs under this new governor's administration, it may not be amiss here to give some account of the rise and progress of my philosophical reputation.

In 1746, being at Boston, I met there with a Dr. Spence, who was lately arrived from Scotland, and show'd me some electric experiments. They were imperfectly perform'd, as he was not very expert; but, being on a subject quite new to me, they equally surpris'd and pleased me. Soon after my return to Philadelphia, our library company receiv'd from Mr. P. Collinson, Fellow of the Royal Society of London, a present of a glass tube, with some account of the use of it in making such experiments. I eagerly seized the opportunity of repeating what I had seen at Boston; and, by much practice, acquir'd great readiness in performing those, also, which we had an account of from England, adding a number of new ones. I say much practice, for my house was continually full, for some time, with people who came to see these new wonders.

To divide a little this incumbrance among my friends, I caused a number of similar tubes to be blown at our glass-house, with which they furnish'd themselves, so that we had at length several performers. Among these, the principal was Mr. Kinnersley, an ingenious neighbor, who, being out of business, I encouraged to undertake showing the experiments for money, and drew up for him two lectures, in which the experiments were rang'd in such order, and accompanied with explanations in such method, as that the foregoing should assist in comprehending the following. He procur'd an elegant apparatus for the purpose, in which all the little machines that I had roughly made for myself were nicely form'd by instrument-makers. His lectures were well attended, and gave great satisfaction ; and after some time he went thro' the colonies, exhibiting them in every capital town, and pick'd up some money. In the West India islands, indeed, it was with difficulty the experiments could be made, from the general moisture of the air.

Oblig'd as we were to Mr. Collinson for his present of the tube, etc., I thought it right he should be inform'd of our success in using it, and wrote him several letters containing accounts of our experiments. He got them read in the Royal Society, where they were not at first thought worth so much notice as to be printed in their Transactions. One paper, which I wrote for Mr. Kinnersley, on the sameness of lightning with electricity, I sent to Dr. Mitchel, an acquaintance of mine, and one of the members also of that society, who wrote me word that it had been read, but was laughed at by the connoisseurs. The papers, however, being shown to Dr. Fothergill, he thought them of too much value to be stifled, and advis'd the printing of them. Mr. Collinson then gave them to cave for publication in his Gentleman's Magazine; but he chose to print them separately in a pamphlet, and Dr. Fothergill wrote the preface. Cave, it seems, judged rightly for his profit, for by the additions that arrived afterward, they swell'd to a quarto volume, which has had five editions, and cost him nothing for copy-money.

It was, however, some time before those papers were much taken notice of in England. A copy of them happening to fall into the hands of the Count de Button, philosopher deservedly of great reputation in France, and, indeed, all over Europe, he prevailed with M. Dalibard to translate them into French, and they were printed at Paris. The publication offended the Abbe Nollets preceptor in Natural Philosophy to the royal family, and an able experimenter, who had form'd and publish'd- a theory of electricity, which then had the general vogue. He could not at first believe that such a work came from America, and said it must have been fabricated by his enemies at Paris, to decry his system. Afterwards, having been assur'd that there really existed such a person as Franklin at Philadelphia, which he had doubted, he wrote and published a volume of Letters, chiefly address'd to-me, defending his theory, and denying the verity of my experiments, and of the positions deduc'd from them.

I once purpos'd answering the abbe, and actually began the answer; but, on consideration that my writings contain'd a description of experiments which any one might repeat and verify, and if not to be verifi'd, could not be defended ; or of observations offer'd as conjectures, and not delivered dogmatically, therefore not laying me under any obligation to defend them; and reflecting that a dispute between two persons, writing in different languages, might be lengthened greatly by mistranslations, and thence misconceptions of one another's meaning, much of one of the abbe's letters being founded on an error in the translation, I concluded to let my papers shift for themselves, believing it was better to spend what time I could spare from public business in making new experiments, than in disputing about those already made. I therefore never answered M. Nollet, and the event gave me no cause to repent my silence; for my friend M. le Roy, of the Royal Academy of Sciences, took up my cause and refuted him; my book was translated into the Italian, German, and Latin languages ; and the doctrine it contain'd was by degrees universally adopted by the philosophers of Europe, in preference to that of the abbe ; so that he lived to see himself the last of his sect, except Monsieur B, of Paris, his *eleve* and immediate disciple.

What gave my book the more sudden and general celebrity, was the success of one of its proposed experiments, made by Messrs. Dalibard and De Lor at Marly, for drawing lightning from the clouds. This engag'd the public attention every where. M. de Lor, who had an apparatus for experimental philosophy, and lectur'd in that branch of science, undertook to repeat what he called the *Philadelphia Experiments;* and, after they were performed before the king and court, all the curious of Paris flocked to see them. I will not swell this narrative with an account of that capital experiment, nor of the infinite pleasure I receiv'd in the success of a similar one I made soon after with a kite at Philadelphia, as both are to be found in the histories of electricity.

Dr. Wright, an English physician, when at Paris, wrote to a friend, who was of the Royal Society, an account of the high esteem my experiments were in among the learned abroad, and of their wonder that my writings had been so little noticed in England. The society, on this, resum'd the consideration of the letters that had been read to them; and the celebrated Dr. Watson drew up a summary account of them, and of all I had afterwards sent to England on the subject, which he accompained with some praise of the writer. This summary was then printed in their Transactions; and some members of the society in London, particularly the very ingenious Mr. Canton, having verified the experiment of procuring lightning from the clouds by a pointed rod, and acquainting them with the success, they soon made me more than amends for the slight with which they had before treated me. Without my having made any application for that honor, they chose me a member, and voted that I should be excus'd the customary payments, which would have amounted to twenty-five guineas; and ever since have given me their Transactions gratis.*

---

* Dr. Franklin gives a further account of his election in a letter to his son, Governor Franklin, from which the following is an extract:

LONDON, 19 *December,* 1767.

"We have had an ugly affair at the Royal Society lately. On

They also presented me with the gold medal of Sir Godfrey Copley for the year 1753, the delivery of which was accompanied by a very handsome speech* of the president, Lord Macclesfield, wherein I was highly honoured.

Our new governor, Captain Denny, brought over

Dacosta, a Jew, who, as our clerk, was intrusted with collecting our moneys, has been so unfaithful as to embezzle near thirteen hundred pounds in four years. Being one of the Council this year, as well as the last, I have been employed all the last week in attending the inquiry into, and unravelling, his accounts, in order to come at a full knowledge of his frauds. His securities are bound in one thousand pounds to the Society, which they will pay, but we shall probably lose the rest. He had this year received twenty-six admission payments of twenty-five guineas each, which he did not bring to account.

"While attending to this affair, I had an opportunity of looking over the old Council books and journals of the Society, and, having a curiosity to see how I came in, of which I had never been informed, I looked back for the minutes relating to it. You must know, it is not usual to admit persons that have not requested to be admitted ; and a recommendatory certificate in favor of the candidate, signed by at least three of the members, is by our rule to be presented to the Society, expressing that he is desirous of that honor, and is so and so qualified. As I never had asked or expected the honor, I was, as I said before, curious to see how the business was managed. I found that the certificate, worded very advantageously for me, was signed by Lord Maccles field, then president, Lord Parker, and Lord Willoughby; that the election was by a unanimous vote; and, the honor being voluntarily conferred by the Society, unsolicited by me, it was thought wrong to demand or receive the usual fees or composition ; so that my name was entered on the list, with a vote of Council that I was not to pay any thing, and accordingly nothing has ever been demanded of me. Those who are admitted in the common way, pay five guineas admission fees, and two guineas and a half yearly contribution, or twenty-five guineas down in lieu of it. In my case a substantial favor accompanied the honor."—W. T. F.

* See this speech in vol. v. p. 499, *Sparks' Works of Franklin.*—B.

for me the before-mentioned medal from the Royal Society, which he presented to me at an entertainment given him by the city. He accompanied it with very polite expressions of his esteem for me, having, as he said, been long acquainted with my character. After dinner, when the company, as was customary at that time, were engag'd in drinking, he took me aside into another room, and acquainted me that he had been advis'd by his friends in England to cultivate a friendship with me, as one who was capable of giving him the best advice, and of contributing most effectually to the making his administration easy ; that he therefore desired of all things to have a good understanding with me, and he begg'd me to be assur'd of his readiness on all occasions to render me every service that might be in his power. He said much to me, also, of the proprietor's good disposition towards the province, and of the advantage it might be to us all, and to me in particular, if the opposition that had been so long continu'd to his measures was dropt, and harmony restor'd between him and the people; in effecting which, it was thought no one could be more serviceable than myself; and I might depend on adequate acknowledgments and recompenses, etc. The drinkers, finding we did not return immediately to the table, sent us a decanter of Madeira, which the governor made liberal use of, and in proportion became more profuse of his solicitations and promises.

My answers were to this purpose: that my circumstances, thanks to God, were such as to make proprietary favours unnecessary to me; and that, being a member of the Assembly, I could not possibly accept of any; that, however, I had no personal enmity to the proprietary, and that, whenever the public measures he propos'd should appear to be for the good of the people, no one should espouse and forward them more zealously than myself; my past opposition having been founded on this, that the measures which had been urged were evidently intended to serve the proprietary interest, with great prejudice to that of the people; that I was much obliged to him (the governor) for his professions of regard to me, and that he might rely on every thing in my power to make his administration as easy as possible, hoping at the same time that he had not brought with him the same unfortunate instruction his predecessor had been hamper'd with.

On this he did not then explain himself; but when he afterwards came to do business with the Assembly, they appear'd again, the disputes were renewed, and I was as active as ever in the opposition, being the penman, first, of the request to have a communication of the instructions, and then of the remarks upon them, which may be found in the votes of the time, and in the Historical Review I afterward publish'd. But between us personally no enmity arose ; we were often together; he was a man of letters, had seen much of the world, and was very entertaining and pleasing in conversation. He gave me the first information that my old friend Jas. Ralph was still alive; that he was esteem'd one of the best political writers in England; had been employ'd in the dispute between Prince Frederic and the king, and had obtain'd a pension of three hundred a year; that his reputation was indeed small as a poet, Pope having damned his poetry in the Dunciad; but his prose was thought as good as any man's.

* The Assembly finally finding the proprietary obstinately persisted in manacling their deputies with instructions inconsistent not only with the privileges of the people, but with the service of the crown, resolv'd to petition the king against them, and appointed me their agent to go over to England, to present and support the petition. The House had sent up a bill to the governor, granting a sum of sixty thousand

---

* The many unanimous resolves of the Assembly–what date ?– *[Marg. note.]*

pounds for the king's use (ten thousand pounds of which was subjected to the orders of the then general, Lord Loudoun), which the governor absolutely refus'd to pass, in compliance with his instructions.

I had agreed with Captain Morris, of the paquet at New York, for my passage, and my stores were put on board, when Lord Loudoun arriv'd at Philadelphia, expressly, as he told me, to endeavor an accommodation between the governor and Assembly, that his majesty's service might not be obstructed by their dissensions. Accordingly, he desir'd the governor and myself to meet him, so that he might hear what was to be said on both sides. We met and discuss'd the business. In behalf of the Assembly, I urg'd all the various arguments that may be found in the public papers of that time, which were of my writing, and are printed with the minutes of the Assembly ; and the governor pleaded his instructions; the bond he had given to observe them, and his he will ruin if he disobey'd, yet seemed not unwilling to hazard himself if Lord Loudoun would advise it. This his lordship did not choose to do, though I once thought I had nearly prevail'd with him to do it; but finally he rather chose to urge the compliance of the Assembly ; and he entreated me to use my endeavours with them for that purpore, declaring that he would spare none of the king's troops for the defense of our frontiers, and that, if we did not continue to provide for that defense ourselves, they must remain expos'd to the enemy.

I acquainted the House with what had pass'd, and, presenting them with a set of resolutions I had drawn up, declaring our rights, and that we did not relinquish our claim to those rights, but only suspended the exercise of them on this occasion thro' *force* against which we protested, they at length agreed to drop that bill, and frame another conformable to the proprietary instructions. This of course the governor pass'd, and I was then at liberty to proceed on my voyage.

But, in the mean time, the paquet had sailed with my sea-stores, which was some loss to me, and my only recompense was his lordship's thanks for my service, all the credit of obtaining the accommodation falling to his share.

He set out for New York before me; and, as the time for dispatching the paquet-boats was at his disposition, and there were two then remaining there, one of which, he said, was to sail very soon, I requested to know the precise time, that I might not miss her by any delay of mine. His answer was, " I have given out that she is to sail on next Saturday but I may let you know, *entre nous,* that if you are there by Monday morning, you will be in time, but do not delay longer." By some accidental hinderance at a ferry, it was Monday noon before I arrived, and I was much afraid she might have sailed, as the wind was fair; but I was soon made easy by the information that she was still in the harbor, and would not move till the next day. One would imagine that I was now on the very point of departing for Europe. I thought so ; but I was not then so well acquainted with his lordship's character, of which *indecision* was one of the strongest features. I shall give some instances. It was about the beginning of April that I came to New York, and I think it was near the end of June before we sail'd. There were then two of the paquet-boats, which had been long in port, but were detained for the general's letters, which were always to be ready tomorrow. Another paquet arriv'd; she too was detain'd; and, before we sail'd, a fourth was expected. Ours was the first to be dispatch'd, as having been there longest. Passengers were engag'd in all, and some extremely impatient to be gone, and the merchants uneasy about their letters, and the orders they had given for insurance (it being war time) for fall goods; but their anxiety avail'd nothing; his lordship's letters were not ready ; and yet whoever waited on him found him always at his desk, pen in hand and concluded he must needs write abundantly.

Going myself one morning to pay my respects, I found in his chamber one Innis, a messenger of Philadelphia, who had come from thence express with a paquet from Governor Denny for the General. He delivered to me some letters from my friends there, which occasion'd my inquiring when he was to return, and where he lodg'd, that I might send some letters by him. He told me he was order'd to call tomorrow at nine for the general's answer to the governor, and should set off immediately. I put my letters into his hands the same day. A fortnight after I met him again in the same place. " So, you are soon return'd, Innis ?" "*Return'd!* no, I am not *gone* yet." " How so?" " I have called here by order every morning these two weeks past for his lordship's letter, and it is not yet ready." "Is it possible, when he is so great a writer? for I see him constantly at his escritoire." " Yes," says Innis, " but he is like St. George on the signs, *always on horseback, and never rides on".* This observation of the messenger was, it seems, well founded; for, when in England, I understood that Mr. Pitt gave it as one reason for removing this general, and sending Generals Amherst and Wolfe, *that the minister never heard from him, and could not know what he was doing.*

This daily expectation of sailing, and all the three paquets going down to Sandy Hook, to join the fleet there, the passengers thought it best to be on board, lest by a sudden order the ships should sail, and they be left behind. There, if I remember right, we were about six weeks, consuming our sea-stores, and oblig'd to procure more. At length the fleet sail'd, the General and all his army on board, bound to Louisburg, with intent to besiege and take that fortress; all the paquetboats in company ordered to attend the General's ship ready to receive his dispatches when they should be ready. We were out five days before we got a letter with leave to part, and then our ship quitted the fleet and steered for England. The other two paquets he still detained, carried them with him to Halifax, where he stayed some time to exercise the men in sham attacks upon sham forts, then alter'd his mind as to besieging Louisburg, and return'd to New York, with all his troops, together with the two paquets above mentioned, and all their passengers ! During his absence the French and savages had taken Fort George, on the frontier of that province, and the savages had massacred many of the garrison after capitulation.

I saw afterwards in London Captain Bonnell, who commanded one of those paquets. He told me that, when he had been detain'd a month, he acquainted his lordship that his ship was grown foul, to a degree that must necessarily hinder her fast sailing, a point of consequence for a paquet-boat, and requested an allowance of time to heave her down and clean her bottom. He was asked how long time he would require He answer'd, three days. The general replied, " If you can do it in one day, I will give leave ; otherwise not; for you must certainly sail the day after to-morrow." So he never obtain'd leave, though detained afterwards from day to day during full three months.

I saw also in London one of Bonnell's passengers, who was so enrag'd against his lordship for deceiving and detaining him so long at New York, and then carrying him to Halifax and back again, that he swore he would sue him for damages. Whether he did or not, I never heard; but, as he represented the injury to his affairs, it was very considerable.

On the whole, I wonder'd much how such a man came to be intrusted with so important a business as the conduct of a great army; but, having since seen more of the great world, and the means of obtaining, and motives for giving places, my wonder is diminished. General Shirley, on whom the command of the army devolved upon the death of Braddock, would, in my opinion, if continued in place, have made a much better campaign than that of Loudoun in 1757, which was frivolous, expensive, and disgraceful to our nation beyond conception; for, tho' Shirley was not a bred soldier, he was sensible and sagacious in himself, and attentive to good advice from others, capable of forming judicious plans, and quick and active in carrying them into execution. Loudoun, instead of defending the colonies with his great army, left them totally expos'd, while he paraded idly at Halifax, by which means Fort George was lost, besides, he derang'd all our mercantile operations, and distress'd our trade, by a long embargo on the exportation of provisions, on pretence of keeping supplies from being obtain'd by the enemy, but in reality for beating down their price in favor of the contractors, in whose profits, it was said, perhaps from suspicion only, he had a share. And, when at length the embargo was taken off, by neglecting to send notice of it to Charlestown, the Carolina fleet was detain'd near three months longer, whereby their bottoms were so much damaged by the worm that a great part of them foundered in their passage home.

Shirley was, I believe, sincerely glad of being relieved from so burdensome a charge as the conduct of an army must be to a man unacquainted with military business. I was at the entertainment given by the city of New York to Lord Loudoun, on his taking upon him the command- Shirley, tho' thereby superseded, was present also. There was a great company of officers, citizens, and strangers, and, some chairs having been borrowed in the neighborhood, there was one among them very low, which fell to the lot of Mr. Shirley. Perceiving it as I sat by him, I said, " They have given you, sir, too low a seat." " No matter," says he, " Mr. Franklin, I find *a low seat* the easiest."

While I was, as before mention'd, detain'd at New York, I receiv'd all the accounts of the provisions, etc., that I had furnish'd to Braddock, some of which accounts could not sooner be obtain'd from the different persons I had employ'd to assist in the business. I presented them to Lord Loudoun, desiring to be paid the balance. He caus'd them to be regularly examined by the proper officer, who, after comparing every article with its voucher, certified them to be right; and the balance due for which his lordship promis'd to give me an order on the paymaster. This was, however, put off from time to time; and, tho' I call'd often for it by appointment, I did not get it. At length, just before my departure, he told me he had, on better consideration, concluded not to mix his accounts with those of his predecessors. "And you," says he, " when in England, have only to exhibit your accounts at the treasury, and you will be paid immediately.

I mention'd, but without effect, the great and unex-pected expense I had been put to by being detain'd so long at New York, as a reason for my desiring to be presently paid; and on my observing that it was not right I should be put to any further trouble or delay in obtaining the money I had advanc'd, as I charged no commission for my service. " O, sir," says he, " you must not think of persuading us that you are no gainer; we understand better those affairs, and know that every one concerned in supplying the army finds means, in the doing it, to fill his own pockets." I assur'd him that was not my case, and that I had not pocketed a farthing; but he appear'd clearly not to believe me; and, indeed, I have since learnt that immense fortunes are often made in such employments. As to my balance, I am not paid it to this day, of which more hereafter.

Our captain of the paquet had boasted much, before we sailed, of the swiftness of his ship ; unfortunately, when we came to sea, she proved the dullest of ninety-six sail, to his no small mortification. After many conjectures respecting the cause, when we were near another ship almost as dull as ours, which, however, gain'd upon us, the captain ordered all hands to come aft, and stand as near the ensign staff as possible. We were, passengers included, about forty persons. While we stood there, the ship mended her pace, and soon left her neighbour far behind, which prov'd clearly what our captain suspected, that she was loaded too much by the head. The casks of water, it seems, had been all plac'd forward; these he therefore order'd to be mov'd further after, on which the ship recover'd her character, and proved the best sailer in the fleet.

The captain said she had once gone at the rate of thirteen knots, which is accounted thirteen miles per hour. We had on board, as a passenger, Captain Kennedy, of the Navy, who contended that it was impossible, and that no ship ever sailed so fast, and that there must have been some error in the division of the log-line, or some mistake in heaving the log. A wager ensu'd between the two captains, to be decided when there should be sufficient wind. Kennedy thereupon examin'd rigorously the log-line, and, being satisfi'd with that, he determin'd to throw the log himself. Accordingly some days after, when the wind blew very fair and fresh, and the captain of the paquet, Lutwidge, said he believ'd she then went at the rate of thirteen knots, Kennedy made the experiment, and own'd his wager lost.

The above fact I give for the sake of the following observation. It has been remark'd, as an imperfection in the art of ship-building, that it can never be known, till she is tried, whether a new ship will or will not be a good sailer; for that the model of a good-sailing ship has been exactly followed in a new one, which has prov'd, on the contrary, remarkably dull. I apprehend that this may partly be occasion'd by the different opinions of seamen respecting the modes of lading, rigging, and sailing of a ship ; each has his system ; and the same vessel, laden by the judgment and orders of one captain, shall sail better or worse than when by the orders of another. Besides, it scarce ever happens that a ship is form'd, fitted for the sea, and sail'd by the same person. One man builds the hull, another rigs her, a third lades and sails her. No one of these has the advantage of knowing all the ideas and experience of the others, and, therefore, can not draw just conclusions from a combination of the whole.

Even in the simple operation of sailing when at sea, I have often observ'd different judgments in the officers who commanded the successive watches, the wind being the same. One would have the sails trimm'd sharper or flatter than another, so that they seem'd to have no certain rule to govern by. Yet I think a set of experiments might be instituted, first, to determine the most proper form of the hull for swift sailing ; next, the best dimensions and properest place for the masts ; then the form and quantity of sails, and their position, as the wind may be; and, lastly, the disposition of the lading. This is an age of experiments, and I think a set accurately made and combin'd would be of great use. I am persuaded, therefore, that ere long some ingenious philosopher will undertake it, to whom I wish success.

We were several times chas'd in our passage, but outsail'd every thing, and in thirty days had soundings. We had a good observation, and the captain judg'd himself so near our port, Falmouth, that, if we made a good run in the night, we might be off the mouth of that harbor in the morning, and by running in the night might escape the notice of the enemy's privateers, who often cruis'd near the entrance of the channel. Accordingly, all the sail was set that we could possibly make, and the wind being very fresh and fair, we went right before it, and made great way. The captain, after his observation, shap'd his course, as he thought, so as to pass wide of the Scilly Isles; but it seems there is sometimes a strong indraught setting up St. George's Channel, which deceives seamen and caused the loss of Sir Cloudesley Shovel's squadron. This indraught was probably the cause of what happened to us.

We had a watchman plac'd in the bow, to whom they often called, *"Look well out before there,"* and he as often answered, "Ay *ay* but perhaps had his eyes shut, and was half asleep at the time, they sometimes answering, as is said, mechanically; for he did not see a light just before us, which had been hid by the studding-sails from the man at the helm, and from the rest of the watch, but by an accidental yaw of the ship was discover'd, and occasion'd a great alarm, we being very near it, the light appearing to me as big as a cart-wheel. It was midnight, and our captain fast asleep; but Captain Kennedy, jumping upon deck, and seeing the danger, ordered the ship to wear round, all sails standing; an operation dangerous to the masts, but it carried us clear, and we escaped shipwreck, for we were running right upon the rocks on which the lighthouse was erected. This deliverance impressed me strongly with the utility of light-houses, and made me resolve to encourage the building more of them in America, if I should live to return there.

In the morning it was found by the soundings, etc., that we were near our port, but a thick fog hid the land from our sight. About nine o'clock the fog began to rise, and seem'd to be lifted up from the water like the curtain at a play-house, discovering underneath, the town of Falmouth, the vessels in its harbor, and the fields that surrounded it. This was a most pleasing spectacle to those who had been so long without any other prospects than the uniform view of a vacant ocean, and it gave us the more pleasure as we were now free from the anxieties which the state of war occasion'd.

I set out immediately, with my son, for London, and we only stopt a little by the way to view Stonehenge on Salisbury Plain, and Lord Pembroke's house and gardens, with his very curious antiquities at Wilton. We arrived in London on 27th of July, 1757.*

---

* Here terminates the Autobiography, as published by Wm. Temple Franklin and his successors. What follows, was written the last year of Dr. Franklin's life, and was never before printed in English.—B.

AS soon as I was settled in a lodging Mr.Charles had provided forme, I went to visit Dr. Fothergill, to whom I was strongly recommended, and whose counsel respecting my proceedings I was advis'd to obtain. He was against an immediate complaint to government, and thought the proprietaries should first be personally appli'd to, who might possibly be induc'd by the interposition and persuasion of some private friends, to accommodatematters amicably. I then waited on my old friend and correspondent, Mr. Peter Collinson, who told me that John Hanbury, the great Virginia merchant, had requested to informed when I should arrive,that he might carry me to Lord Granville's, who was then President of the Council and wished to see meas soon as possible. I agreed to go with him the next morning. Accordingly Mr. Hanbury for me and took me in his carriage to that nobleman's, who receiv'd me with great civility; and after some questions respecting the present state of affairs in America and discourse thereupon, he said to me : "You Americans have wrong ideas of the nature of your constitution; you contend that the king's instructions to his governors are not laws, and think yourselves at liberty to regard or disregard them at your own discretion. But those instructions are not like the pocket instructions given to a minister going abroad, for regulating his conduct in some trifling point of ceremony. They are first drawn up by judges learned in the laws; they are then considered, debated, and perhaps amended in Council, after which they are signed by the king. They are then, so far as they relate to you, the *law of the land* for the king is the LEGISLATOR OF THE COLONIES." I told his lordship this was new doctrine to me. I had always understood from our charters that our laws were to be made by our Assemblies, to be presented indeed to the king for his royal assent, but that being once given the king could not repeal or alter them. And as the Assemblies could not make permanent laws without his assent, so neither could he make a law for them without theirs. He assur'd me I was totally mistaken. I did not think so, however, and his lordship's conversation having a little alarm'd me as to what might be the sentiments of the court concerning us, I wrote it down as soon as I return'd to my lodgings.* I recollected that about 20 years before, a clause in a bill brought into Parliament by the ministry that had propos'd to make the king's instructions as laws in the colonies, but the clause was thrown out by the

---

* An account of this conversation with Granville is given in the following letter from Franklin to Mr. James Bowdoin:

" LONDON, 13 *January,* 1772.

" DEAR SIR : I should very readily have recommended your son to the care of my friend, Dr. Priestly, he had continued to superintend the academy at Warrington; but he has left that charge some time since, and is now pastor of a congregation at Leeds in Yorkshire. I am much obliged to you for introducing me to the acquaintance of Mr. Erving, who appears a very intelligent, sensible man. The governing of colonies by instruction has long been a favorite point with ministers here. About thirty years since, in a bill brought into Parliament relating to America, they inserted a clause to make the king's instructions laws the colonies, which, being opposed by the then agents, was thrown out.

"And I well remember a conversation with Lord Granville, soon after my arrival here, in which he expressed himself on that subject in the following terms. 'Your American Assemblies slight the king's instructions, pretending that they are not laws. The instructions sent over to your governors are not like the pocket instructions given to ambassadors, to be observed at their discretion, as circumstances may require. They are drawn up by grave men, learned in the laws and constitutions of the realm; they are brought into Council, thoroughly weighed, well considered, and amended if necessary, by the wisdom of that body, and, when received by the governors, they are the laws of the land; for the king is the legislator of the colonies.' I remember this the better, because, being a new doctrine to me, I put it down as soon as I returned to my lodgings. To be sure, if a governor thinks himself obliged to obey all instructions, whether consistent or inconsistent with the constitution, laws, and rights of the country he governs, and can proceed to govern in that train, there is an end of the constitution, and those rights are abolished. But I wonder that any honest gentleman can

Commons, for which we adored them as our friends and friends of liberty, till by their conduct towards us.1765 it seem'd that they had refus'd that point of sovereignty to the king only that they might reserve it for themselves.

After some days, Dr. Fothergill having spoken to the proprietaries, they agreed to a meeting with me at Mr. T. Penn's house in Spring Garden. The conversation at first consisted of mutual declarations of disposition to reasonable accommodations, but I suppose each party had its own ideas of what should be meant by *reasonable*. We then went into consideration of our several points of complaint, which I enumerated. The proprietaries justify'd their conduct as well as they could, and I to the Assembly's. We now appeared very wide, and so far from each other in our opinions as to discourage all hope of agreement. However, it was concluded that I should give them the heads of our complaints in writing, and they promis'd then to consider them.

---

think that there is honor in being a governor on such terms. And I think that the practice cannot possibly continue, especially if opposed with spirit by our Assemblies. At present no attention is paid by the American ministers to any agent here whose appointment is not ratified by the governor's assent; and, if this is persisted in, you can have none to serve you in a public character, that do not render themselves agree-

able to these ministers, and those otherwise appointed can only promote your interests by conversation as private gentlemen or by writing. Virginia had, as you observe, two agents, one for the Council, the other for the Assembly; but I think the latter only was considered as agent for the Province.

"He was appointed by an act, which was expired in the time of Lord Botetourt, and was not revived. The other, I apprehend, continues; but I am not well acquainted with the nature of his appointment. I only understand that he does not concern himself much with the general affairs of the colony."—*Sharks' Works of Franklin,* vol. vii. p. 549.—B.

I did so soon after, but they put the paper into the hands of their solicitor, Ferdinand John Paris, who managed for them all their law business in their great suit with the neighbouring proprietary of Maryland, Lord Baltimore, which had subsisted 70 years, and wrote for them all their papers and messages in their dispute with the Assembly. He was a proud, angry man, and as I had occasionally in the answers of the Assembly treated his papers with some severity, they being really weak in point of argument and haughty in expression, he had conceived a mortal enmity to me, which discovering itself whenever we met, I declin'd the proprietary's proposal that he and I should discuss the heads of complaint between our two selves, and refus'd treating with any one but them. They then by his advice put the paper into the hands of the Attorney and Solicitor-General for their opinion and counsel upon it, where it lay unanswered a year wanting eight days, during that time I made frequent demands of an answer from the proprietaries, but without obtaining any other than that they had not yet received the opinion of the Attorney and Solicitor-General. What it was that when they did receive it I never learnt, for they did not communicate it to me, but sent a long message to the Assembly drawn and signed by Paris, reciting my paper, complaining of its want of formality, as a rudeness on my part, and giving a flimsy justification of their conduct, adding that they should be willing to accommodate matters if the Assembly would send out *some person of candour* to treat with them for that purpose, intimating thereby that I was not such.

The want of formality or rudeness was, probably my not having address'd the paper to them with their assum'd titles of True and Absolute Proprietaries of the Province of Pennsylvania, which I omitted as not thinking it necessary in a paper, the intention of which was only to reduce to a certainty by writing, what in conversation I had delivered *viva vocc.*

But during this delay, the Assembly having prevailed with

Gov'r Denny to pass an act taxing the proprietary estate in common with the estates of the people, which was the grand point in dispute, they omitted answering the message.

When this act however came over, the proprietaries, counselled by Paris, determined to oppose its receiving the royal assent. Accordingly they petition'd the king in Council, and a hearing was appointed in which two lawyers were employ'd by them against the act, and two by me in support of it. They alledg'd that the act was intended to load the proprietary estate in order to spare those of the people, and that if it were suffer'd to continue in force, and the proprietaries who were in odium with the people, left to their mercy in proportioning the taxes, they would inevitably be ruined. We reply'd that the act had no such intention, and would have no such effect. That the assessors were honest and discreet men under an oath to assess fairly and equitably, and that any advantage each of them might expect in lessening his own tax by augmenting that of the proprietaries was too trifling to induce them to perjure themselves. This is the purport of what I remember as urged by both sides, except that we insisted strongly on the mischievous consequences that must attend a repeal, for that the money, £100,000, being printed and given to the king's use, expended in his service, and now spread among the people, the repeal would strike it dead in their hands to the ruin of many, and the total discouragement of future grants, and the selfishness of the proprietors in soliciting such a general catastrophe, merely from a groundless fear of their estate being taxed too highly, was insisted on in the strongest terms. On this, Lord Mansfield, one of the counsel rose, and beckoning me took me into the clerk's chamber, while the lawyers were pleading, and asked me if I was really of opinion that no injury would be done the proprietary estate in the execution of the act. I said certainly. "Then," says he, " you can have little objection to enter into an engagement to assure that point." I answer'd, " None at all." He then call'd in Paris, and after some discourse, his lordship's proposition was accepted on both sides; a paper to the purpose was drawn up by the Clerk of the Council, which I sign'd with Mr. Charles, who was also an Agent of the Province for their ordinary affairs, when Lord Mansfield returned to the Council Chamber, where finally the law was allowed to pass. Some changes were however recommended and we also engaged that they should be made by a subsequent law, but the Assembly did not think them necessary; for one year's tax having been levied by the act before the order of Council arrived, they appointed a committee to examine the proceedings of the assessors, and on this committee they put several particular friends of the proprietaries. After a full enquiry, they unanimously sign'd a report that they found the tax had been assess'd with perfect equity.

The Assembly looked into my entering into the first part of the engagement, as an essential service to the Province, since it secured the credit of the paper money then spread over all the country. They gave me their thanks in form when I return'd. But the proprietaries were enraged at Governor Denny for having pass'd the act, and turn'd him out with threats of suing him for breach of instructions which he had given bond to observe. He, however, having done it at the instance of the General, and for His Majesty's service, and having some powerful interest at court, despis'd the threats and they were never put in execution.*

---

* The following allusion to Gov'r Denny's removal occurs in a letter which Franklin wrote to his wife while the negotiations here described were progressing.–B.

" I see the governor's treatment of his wife makes all the ladies angry. If it is on account of the bad example, that will soon be removed. the Proprietors are privately looking out for another; being determined to discard him, and the place goes a-begging. One, to whom it was offered, sent a friend to make some inquiries of me. The Proprietors told him they had there a city-house and a country-house, which he might use rent free; that everything was so cheap he might live on five hundred pounds sterling a year, keep a genteel table, a coach, etc, and his income would be at least nine hundred pounds. If it fell short of that, the Proprietors would engage to make it up. For the truth of his being able to live genteelly and keep a coach for five hundred pounds a year, the Proprietors referred him to Mr. Hamilton, who, it seems, told him the same story; but, on inquiry of Mr. Morris, he had quite a different account, and knew not which to believe. The gentleman is one Mr. Graves, a lawyer of the Temple. He hesitated a good while, and I am now told has declined accepting it I wish that may not be true, for he has the character of being a very good sort of man: though while the instructions continue, it matters little who is our governor. It was to have been kept a secret from me, that the Proprietors were looking out for a new one; because they would not have Mr. Denny know any thing about it, till the appointment was actually made, and the gentleman ready to embark. So you may make a secret of it too, if you please, and oblige all your friends with it"—*Sparks' Edition of Franklin's Works,* vol. vii. p. 170

APPENDIX No. 1

Vie de Franklin, dcrite par lui-meme, suivie de ses CEuvres morales, politiques et litteraires, dont la plus grand partie n'avait pas encore etc publlee. Traduit de 1'Anglais, avec des notes, par J. Castera. *Eripuit coelo fulmen, sceptrumque tyrannis.* Paris, chez F. Buisson. Imp. Lib., rue Hautefeuille, No. 20. An VI. de la Republique (1799).

Preface of the Translator.

"DURING the last years that Benjamin Franklin passed in France, much was said in the circles he frequented of the Confessions of Jean Jacques Rousseau, the first part of which had just appeared. This work, of which one may say as much good as ill, and which is sometimes so attractive by the charms and sublimity of its style, sometimes so repulsive by the impropriety of its revelations of facts, induced some of the friends of Franklin to counsel him also to write the memoirs of his life. He consented to do so.

" These friends thought with reason that it would be curious to compare the history of a writer who seems to have used his brilliant imagination merely to render himself unhappy, with that of a philosopher who incessantly employed all the resources of his mind to assure his own happiness by contributing to the happiness of all mankind. In effect, how interesting it is to consider the different ways followed by these two men, both bom in the simple rank of artisans, both left to themselves from infancy and almost without teachers ! Each educated himself and attained great celebrity. But one indolently passed many years in obscure servitude, where a sensual woman retained him, while the other, relying entirely upon himself, labored constantly with his hands, lived with the strictest temperance, the severest economy, and at the same time supplied generally the needs, even the fancies of his friends.

. "Let not this comparison, so entirely to the advantage of Franklin, lead any one to suppose that I seek to depreciate Jean Jacques. No one more than I loves or admires the rare talent of this eloquent writer, but I have supposed his course, placed in contrast with Franklin's, might furnish a useful and grand lesson for the young.

"A part of the life of Franklin had already been translated into French, and in a sufficiently careful manner. Notwithstanding, I have dared to translate it anew.

" The English editor has added to what he had been able to procure of the MS. of Franklin, the continuation of his Life composed in Philadelphia. I have been fortunate enough to add to what this publisher has furnished me various pieces which he has not known, and a second fragment of the original Memoirs, but I have yet to regret not having had all these Memoirs, which go, it is said, to 1757. It is not known why Mr. Benjamin Franklin Bache,* who has them in his possession, and is now re siding in London, keeps them so long from the public. The works of a great man belong less to his heirs than to the human race.

"Perhaps the reader will not be indisposed to run his eye over a letter which the celebrated Dr. Price addressed to one of his friends upon the subject of Franklin's Memoirs.

"HACKNEY, 19th *June,* 1790."

---

*It was Wm. T. Franklin who is here referred to.

APPENDIX No. 2.

Letter from Dr. Franklin to M. le Veillard.

[From the Le Veillard Collection.]

" PHILADELPHIA, *April* 15 1787.

"DEAR FRIEND: I have received a number of letters from you, which gave me great pleasure, tho' I have not regularly answered. When you shall consider the situation of a man who had been many years absent from home, the multiplicity of private affairs he must consequently have to settle, the public business of a great government to be attended to, and this under the frequent teasing of a painful disease, you will probably make some charitable allowance for his delay in writing to his friends, and not charge it all as the effect of forgetfulness and want of affection.

" I now have all your letters of the last year before me, and shall go thro' them in order. That of March 25, announced a M. de la Villele, nephew of the late Madame de la Frete. as intending a voyage thither, but he has not yet appeared in these parts. If he arrives while I live, he will be paid every attention and civility in my power to show him.

" I thank you for the trouble you have taken in selling my forte piano and dividing the money as I desired.

"The Lodge of the Nine Sisters have done me too much honor in proposing the prize you mention.

" As to the little history I promis'd you, my purpose still continues of completing it, and I hoped to do it this summer, having built an addition to my house, in which I have plac'd my library, and where I can write without being disturb'd by the noise of the children, but the General Assembly having lately desired my assistance in a great convention to be held here in May next for amending the Federal Constitution, I begin to doubt whether I can make any progress in it till that business is over.

"Yours of the 23rd of May did not arrive here till the 5th of October, and this is not the only instance of the long time letters are delayed in your seaports. It is true that we had, as you mention, two parties in this State–one for preserving the Constitution as it is, and the other for adding an Upper House as a check to the Assembly. But having try'd it seven years, the strongest party was for continuing it, and since my arrival no obstruction has happened in public business, such as you had been informed of, by the seceding of one party from the Assembly. Having served one year as President of Council, I had not resolution enough to refuse serving another, and was again chosen in November last, without a single dissenting voice but my own. By our laws one cannot serve more than three years, but I think I shall decline the third.

" I am quite of your opinion that our independence is not quite complete till we have discharg'd our public debt. This State is not behindhand in its proportion, and those who are in arrear are actually employed in contriving means to discharge their respective balances, but they are not all equally diligent in the business, nor equally successful; the whole will, however, be paid, I am persuaded in a few years.

"The English have not yet delivered up the ports on our frontiers, agreeable to treaty ; the pretence is that our merchants have not paid their debts. I was a little provok'd when I first heard this, and I wrote some remarks upon it which I send you. They have been written near a year, but I have not yet published them, being unwilling to encourage any of our people who may be able to pay in their neglect of that duty. This paper, therefore, is only for your amusement and that of our excellent friend, the Duke de Rochefoucault.*

" You blame me for writing three pamphlets and neglecting to write the little history; you should consider they were written at sea, out of my own head ; the other could not so well be written there, for want of the documents that could only be had here.

---

* The following was written in the margin: " This omitted at present for want of time to copy it."

"As to my malady, concerning which you so kindly inquire, I have never had the least doubt of its being the stone. I am sensible that it is grown heavier ; but on the whole it does not give me more pain than when at Passy, and except in standing, walking or making water, I am very little incommoded by it. Sitting or lying in bed I am generally quite easy, God be thanked; and as I live temperately, drink no wine, and use daily the exercise of the dumb-bell, I flatter myself that the stone is kept from augmenting so much as it might otherwise do, and that I may still continue to find it tolerable. People who live long, who will drink of the cup of life to the very bottom, must expect to meet with some of the usual dregs, and when I reflect on the number of terrible maladies human nature is subject to, I think myself favored in having to my share only the stone and the gout.

"In yours of August 21st, you mention your having written the 21 st and 29th of June, which letters were in a paquet, with one from the Duke de Rochefoucault, two from M. and Mad. Brillon, etc. I have not been so happy as to receive these letters ; they never came to hand.

"You were right in conjecturing that I wrote the remarks on the *Thoughts concerning Executive Justice,* I have no copy of those remarks at hand, and forget how the saying was intro duced that it was better 1000 guilty persons should escape than one innocent suffer. Your criticisms thereon appear to be just, and I imagine you may have misapprehended my intention in mentioning it. I always thought, with you, that the prejudice in Europe which supposes a family dishonored by the punishment of one of its members, was very absurd, it being, on the contrary, my opinion that a rogue hanged out of a family does it more honor than ten that live in it.

"What you mention of our paper money, if you mean that of this State, Pensilvania, is not well understood. It was made before my arrival, and not being a legal tender can do no injustice to anybody, nor does any one here complain of it, tho' many are justly averse to an increase of the quantity at this time, there being a great deal of real money in the country, and one bank in good credit. I have myself purchased ten *actions* in it, which, at least, shows my good opinion of it.

"Besides the addition to my house, mentioned above, I have been building two new houses on my front, next the street They are of brick, and each 24 feet wide by 45 deep, and three stories high. The affairs in dealing with so many workmen and furnishers of materials, such as bricklayers, carpenters, stone-cutters, painters, glaziers, lime-burners, timber-merchants, copper-smiths, carters, laborers, etc., etc., have added not a little to the fatiguing business I have gone through in the last year, as mentioned above, and strengthen in some degree my apology for being so bad a correspondent.

" Mr. Brabanzon has requested me to send him some seeds in time to plant this spring, but his letter came in my hand too late. They will be got the ensuing autumn and sent, so as to be ready for planting next year.

"Temple and Benjamin will write to you. This letter goes by Mr. Paine, one of our principal writers at the Revolution, being the author of *Common Sense,* a pamphlet that had prodigious effects.

" He does not speak French, or I should recommend him to your civilities, as I do to those of our friend the good Duke.

" The last letter I have had the pleasure of receiving from you is that of Nov. 19, 1786. I cannot give you a better idea of my present happiness in my family than in telling you that my daughter has all the virtues of a certain good lady that you allow me to love; the same tender affections and intentions, ingenuity, industry, economy, etc. Embrace that good dame for me very warmly, and the amiable daughter. My best wishes attend the whole family, whom I shall never cease to love while I am.

"B. FRANKLIN."

APPENDIX No. 3.

Benjamin Franklin to M. le Veillard.

[From the Le Veillard Collection.]

"PHILADELPHIA, *Oct.* 24, 1788.

"MY DEAR FRIEND: I have lately received your two kind letters of June 18 and Aug. 6. I do not find that I ever received those you mention of the 15th Sept.

"I have been much afflicted the last summer with a long-continued fit of the gout, which I am not quite clear of, though much better; my other malady is not augmented. I have lately made great progress in the work you so urgently demand, and have come as far as my fiftieth year. Being now free from public business, as my term in the Presidentship is expired, and resolving to engage in no other public employment, I expect to have it finished in about two months, if illness or some unforeseen interruption does not come. I do not therefore send a part at this time, thinking it better to retain the whole till I can view it all together and make the proper corrections.

"I am much concerned to hear the broils in your country, but hope they will lead to its advantage. When this fermenta tion is over and the troubling parts subsided, the wine will be fine and good, and chear the hearts of those who drink of it

"Our affairs mend daily and are getting into good order very fast Never was any measure so thoroughly discussed as our proposed new constitution. Many objections were made to it in the public papers, and answers to these objections. Much party heat there was, and some violent personal abuse. I kept out of the dispute and wrote only one little paper on the occasion, which I enclose. You seem to me to be too apprehensive about our President's being perpetual. Neither he nor we have any such intention. What danger there may be of such an event, we are all aware of, and shall take care effectually to prevent it. The choice is from four years to four years, the appointments will be small; thus we may change our President if we don't like his conduct, and he will have less inducement to struggle for a new election. As to the two Chambers, I am of your opinion, that one alone would be better; but, my dear friend, nothing in human affairs and schemes is perfect, and perhaps that is the case of our opinions.

"It must have been a terrible tempest that devastated such an extent of country. I have sometimes thought it might be well to establish an office of insurance for farms against the damage that may occur to them from storms, light, insects, & etc. A small sum paid by a number would repair such losses and prevent much poverty and distress.

" Our adventurous merchants are much successful in the East India trade. Perhaps it would be better for us if we used none of the commodities of those countries, but since we do use them, it is an advantage that we have them cheaper than when they came through Britain. As to the other merchandise she formerly supplied us with, our demand is daily diminishing. Our people are more and more sensible of the mischievous consequences of drinking rum ; the leaders of several religious sects have warned their people against it, and the consumption has, this last year, been less by one-third. This will affect her islands. And the restraints she has laid on our trade have contributed to raise a spirit of industry in families, who now manufacture more than ever for themselves, that must lessen greatly the importation.

" Embrace for me *bien tendrement* your good dame and children. With sincere esteem and hearty attachment, I am ever, my dear friend,

"Yours, most effecttionately

"B. FRANKLIN.

" M. LE VEILLARD.

"*P. S.*–The wine is arriv'd, but it was not well secur'd or bottled. One of the casks had leak'd a great deal, and the case we have opened had two-thirds of the bottles empty or broken. Temple is in the country; he has receiv'd your letters, but does not know of this opportunity."

APPENDIX No. 4.

Wm. T. Franklin to M. le Veillard.

[From the Le Veillard Collection.]

"PHILADELPHIA 17 *Nov.,* 1788.

"La demidre lettre que j'ai recue de vous, mon cher ami, est dattee le 6 Aout. Vous ne m'accusez pas la reception de la mienne du mois de Fevrier,* et je crains qu'elle ne soit restee N. York avec plusieurs autres que j'ai ecrites en meme terms. Vous savez sans doute que les Pacquetbots sont interrompus depuis quelque terms, ce qui est cause j'imagine que je n'ai pas encore reeju la glace pour ma machine electrique que vous m'anonates au mois de Fevrier dernier. Voulez vous bien mon ami, vous informer* si elle est encore partie du Havre, et si elle y reste encore, donnez des ordres pour qu'on me 1'envoye par le premier batiment marchand ou outre qui part pour Philadelphie ou N. York; et qu'on mecris une lettre d'avis en meme terns. Actuellement que nous sommes sur les commissions, permittez que je vous donnent encore quelques unes; mais a cette condition que si elle vous cause trop d'embarras vous ne les executerez pas. Vous savez que j'ai une partie de la petite Bibliotheque des Theatres; cette ouvrage me plait, et je voudrai 1'avoir complet J'ai les treize volumes du I[r] annee, 1784, et les No- 1, 2, 3, 4, 5, 6, 7, 9, 10, du 2[de] annee 1785. Il me manque en consequence le No. 8 du 2de annee, et tous les Nos. qui on parru depuis le No. 10. Tachez je vous prie de mes les procurer; je dois les avoir aux prix des souscripteurs. Je ne sais si je n'ai pas souscrit pour la 2[de] annee? Voici encore ce que je desirerai avoir, Memoire sur les moyens

---

* Je me trompe, en relisant votre lettre je vois que vous l'avez recu.

* It will be perceived by the orthography of his letters, which I have deemed it my duty to follow strictly, that Wm. Temple Franklin did not profit to the utmost, by his opportunities of learning French during his eight years' residence with his grandfather at Passy.

de construire des planchers en bois avec plus de solidite et d'economie que 1'on n'a fait jusqu'k present pour le Sieur Panseron; chez l'auteur, Rue des Macons I'4e2de. Histoire japonoise de Tangai et de Neardane, p- Crebillon fils. 3me- Une pinte des plus beaux marrons de Lyons—pour planter. Tout cela peut etre mise dans une petite boiette, et si elle est bien distinctement addressee, elle me parviendra sans difficult; mais il sera toujours prudent que je recoive une lettre d'avis par la meme occasion. Mon ayeul n'a regu que les 5 premiers volumes du Dicte. d'Agrice- de l'Abbe Rozier, il desireroit avoir la suite; ainsi que la Bibliotheque Physyco Economique, depuis l'an 1785—et ce qui k paru depuis la derni&re envoye que vous ou M. Grand lui a fait des Memoires des Chinois. Pour ce qui regarde mes commissions les 69's que vous avez a moi seront, peutetre assez, si non vous vous addresserez M. Grand, ainsi que pour ce que vous debourserez pour mon ayeul. Nous avons regu le vin de Cahusac qui est fort bon; mais il faut que celle dans les caisses ait ete. mis en bouteille dans un terns da favorable attendu que, un tiers des bouteilles etait casses ou vides, les bouchons etant partis. Celui en futaille a un peu perdue en quantity mais rien en comparaison de celui en bouteille. Le vin est en general bien gout ici, mais il faut du terns pour changer le gout de nos buveurs de Madre, et de Bordeaux. Je me suis inform de plusieurs personnes au sujet de M. Bourgoin, dont vous desirez avoir des nouvelles; mais jusqu'k present je n'ai pu savoir s'il est arrive en Amrique. Nous avous Philadelphie plusieurs Francois, entre autres un M. de Ferriere qui connait tout le monde & Passy, et je me rapelle de 1'avoir vu chez M. Filled, mais je crois qu'il portait alors un autre nom. la k la croix de St Louis, et on dit qu'il & a etc prevot de Marechaux de France. Cest un homme d'environs 40 k 45 ans, d'une figure agrable, et il me parait ce qu'on ap- pelle en France bonne enfant. Dbnnez moi un peu son His- toire—il parle de s' tablir aux environsde Philadelphie et d'y faire venir sa femme de Paris. 11 est arrive en Amerique avec M. de St. Try et M. Brissot de Warville. Notre nouveau Gouvernement va toujours son train—plusieurs Etats ont leurs

Senateurs, le peuple doivent elir leur Representatives dans peu; c'est au mois de Mars prochain qu'ils doivent s'assembler. Il n'y & qu'une voix pour le President General, 1'ilustre Washington al' e gard du Vice President les avis sont partags entre les General Knox, Messieurs Hancock, Adams, etc. Mon ayeul ayant servi ses trois ans, comme President de cet Etat, ou elu sa place le General Mifflin. Mon ayeul s'appelle actuelment un *free man,* et je crois qu'il serait difficile de l'engager changer cet etat. Il parait on ne peut pas plus content de jouir de la liberty et du repos. Il est maintenant occup ecrire la suite de sa vie que vous avez desirez avec tant d'empressement Sa santé se retablit tous les jours. Adieu, mon ami. Rapellez moi au souvenir de tous nos amis communs, et dites mille choses tendre pour moi k toute votre famille. J'creis M. votre fils.

W. T. F.

"M. Le Veillard."

APPENDIX No. 5.

Benjamin Franklin to M. le Veillard.

[From the Le Veillard Collection.]

"Philadelphia, *Sept.* 5,1789.

"Dear Friend: I have had notice of sundry books sent out by you, but none of them are come to hand except the *Dictionnaire d'Agriculture,* by 1'Abbd Rogier. My grandson also complains of not receiving a package or case sent by you to him, he knows not by what conveyance, nor where to enquire for it.

"It is long since I have had the pleasure of hearing from you, the last letter I have received being dated the 21st of February, but when I have no new letter from you, I console myself by reading over some of the old ones, as I have lately done those of the 1st April, '88, and the 10th of Oct and 27th Nov., '88. Every time I read what you write, I receive fresh pleasure. I have already answered those last-mentioned letters, and now have before me that of the 21st of February only. I am sorry …y friend Morris failed in the attention he ought to hav…wn you, but I hope you will excuse it when you …hat an American transported from the tranquil villages …untry and set down in the tourbillon of such a great Paris must necessarily be for some days half out of his .

…hope you have perfectly recovered of your fall at Madam Helvetius's, and that you now enjoy perfect health; as to mine, I can give you no good account. I have a long time been afflicted with almost constant and grievous pain, to combat which I have been obliged to have recourse to opium, which indeed has afforded me some ease from time to time, but then it has taken away my appetite and so impeded my digestion that I am become totally emaciated, and little remains of me but a skeleton covered with a skin. In this situation I have not been able to continue my Memoirs, and now I suppose I shall never finish them. Benjamin has made a copy of what is done for you, which shall be sent by the first safe opportunity. I make no remarks to you concerning your public affairs, being too remote to form just opinions concerning them; indeed, I wonder that you, who are at the same distance from us, make so very few mistakes in your judgment of our affairs. At present we think them in a good way, the Congress are employed in amending some of their faults supposed to be in our constitution, and it is expected that in a few weeks the machine will be in orderly motion. The piece of M. Target, which you mention as having sent me, yet not come into my hand. I am sorry to hear of the scarcity which has afflicted your country. We have had here a most plentiful harvest of all the productions of the earth without exception, and I suppose some supplies will be sent to you from hence, tho' the term during which the importation was admitted was too short, considering the distance.

" My family join in every affectionate sentiment respecting you

"Your sincere friend,

"B. FRANKLIN."

APPENDIX No. 6.

Wm. Temple Franklin to M. le Veillard.

(From the Le Veillard Collection.]

"PHILADELPHIE, 22 *Mai,* 179.

"Vous avez deja & appris, mon cher ami, la perte que vous et moi, et tout le monde a essuez dans la mort de ce bon et aimable papa. Quoique nous l'attendions depuis longtemps, elle ne nous a pas moins choquee lorsqu'élle est arrivée. Il vous aimait bien tendrement, ainsi que toute votre famille, et je ne doute pas que vous ne partagerez mes justes douleurs. Je comptais vous écrire les details de la mort par M. de Chaumont, mais 1'occupation qu'elle me donne pour l'arrangement de ses affaires et surtout de ses papiers, m'en ont empeche, et m'empeche meme k present de rdpondre & vos dernferes lettres, ainsi qu' a celle que Mlle, votre fille a bien voulu mécrire, en m'envoyant de son ouvrage. J'ai etc. on ne peut pas plus touche de cette marque de sa con- descendance et de son amitie, et je vous prie de lui en témoigner ma reconnaissance en attendant que j'ai 1'honneur de lui £crire, qui sera certainement par la premiere occasion pour France. Tout paresseux que je suis pour £crire, sa bonté m'éveillera. Cette lettre vous arrivera par la voie d'Angleterre. J'ai cru devoir profiter de cette occasion pour vous apprendre que mon ayeul, entre d'autres legs, m'a laissé *toutes ses papiers et manu- scrits,* avec la permission d'en tirer tout le profit qui sera en mon pouvoir. En consequence, je vous prie trfcs instament, mon cher ami, de ne pas montrer a qui que ce soit, cette partie de sa vie qu'il vous a envoyée il y h quelque terms, attendu que quelqu'un pourrait en tirer copie, et la publier, ce qui nuirait infiniment & la publication que je compte faire, aussitat qu'il sera possible, de sa vie entiére, et de ses autres ouvrages. Comme j'ai 1'original ici de la partie que vous avez, il ne sera pas néces- saire de me 1'envoyer, mais je vous prie toutefois de la mettre sous envellope, bien cachet ée, et a mon addresse, pour qu'en cas d'accident, elle ne passe pas en d'autres mains. Si, cependant, elle est nécessaire pour assister celui qui doit faire son aloge 1'Academie, vous pouvez la preter pour cela, avec stipulation qu'on n'en prendra pas copie, et d'autres precautions qui vous paraitront nécessaires. On n'a pas encore nommé aux emplois en Europe; il est possible que j'en aurai un, ce qui me mettrait & meme d'assister la publication des ouvrages de mon ayeul; mais quand meme on ne pense pas & moi, il est trés probable que je me résous de faire le voyage d'Europe, attendu que je suis bien persuade d'en tirer plus de bénéfice de la publication en le faisant en Angleterre ou en France que dans ce pays-ci.

"Adieu pour cette fois, dans deux ou trois semaines j'espére pouvoir vous £crire directement, ainsi qu'k mes autres amis, et *amies,* en France.

"Aimez-moi, mon cher ami; j'ai plus que jamais besoin de votre amitié.

"W. T. FRANKLIN."

APPENDIX No. 7.

Preface to Memoirs of the Life and Writings of Benjamin Franklin, by Wm. Temple Franklin. Edition of 1817.

"An apology for presenting to the republic of letters the authentic memorials of Benjamin Franklin, illustrative of his life and times, written almost entirely with his own hands, would be at once superfluous and disrespectful. If any observation be at all requisite in the shape of explanations, it must be in answer to the inquiry, why such interesting documents have been so long withheld from public view? To this the editor has no hesitation in replying, that were he conscious of having neglected a solemn trust, by disobeying a positive injunction ; or could he be convinced that the world has sustained any real injury by the delay of the publication, he certainly should take shame to himself for not having sooner committed to the press what at an earlier period would have been much more to his pecuniary advantage ; but aware as he is, of the deference due to the general feeling of admiration for the illustrious dead, he is not less sensible that there are *times* and *seasons* when prudence imposes the restriction of silence in the gratification even of the most laudable curiosity. It was the lot of this distinguished character, above most men, to move, in the prominent parts of his active life, within a sphere agitated to no ordinary degree of heat by the inflammatory passions of political fury; and he had scarcely seated himself in the shade of repose from the turmoil of public employment, when another revolution burst forth with far more tremendous violence, during the progress of which his name was adduced by anarchists as a sanction for their practices, and his authority quoted by dreamy theorists in support of their visionary projects.

"Whether, therefore, the publication of his Memoirs and other papers, amidst such a scene of perturbation, would have been conducive to the desirable ends of peace, may be a matter of question ; but, at all events, the sober and inquisitive part of mankind can have no cause to regret the suspension of what might have suffered from the perverted talents of designing partisans and infuriated zealots. It may fairly be observed, that the writings of Dr. Franklin are calculated to serve a far more important purpose than that of ministering to the views of party and keeping alive national divisions, which, however necessitated by circumstances, ought to cease with the occasion, and yield to the spirit of philanthropy. Even amidst the din of war and the contention of faction, it was the constant aim of this excellent man to promote a conciliatory disposition, and to correct the acerbity of controversy. Though no one could feel more sensibly for the wrongs of his country, or have more enlarged idea on the subject of general liberty, his powerful efforts to redress the one and extend the other, were always connected with the paramount object of social improvement, in the recommendation of those habits which tend more effectually to unite men together in the bonds of amity. Happening, however, to live himself in a turbulent period, and called upon to take a leading part in those scenes which produced a new empire in the Western World, much of his latter Memoirs and correspondence will be to exhibit his undisguised thoughts upon the public men and occurrences of the day. These sketches, anecdotes, and reflections will now be read by men of opposite sentiments, without awakening painful recollections or rekindling the dying embers of animosity, while the historian and the moralist may learn from them the secret springs of public events, and the folly of being carried away by political prejudice.

"While, therefore, some contracted minds in different countries may be querulously disposed to censure the delay that has taken place in the publication of these posthumous papers, it is presumed that the more considerate and liberal on either side of the Atlantic will approve of the motives which have operated for the procrastination, even though the period has so far exceeded the *nonum premarum annum* assigned by Horace, the oldest and best of critics, for the appearance of a finished performance.

"The editor, in offering this justificatory plea to the public, and taking credit for having exercised so much discretion as to keep these relics in his private custody till the return of halcyon days and a brightened horizon, when their true value might be best appreciated, feels that he has discharged his duty in that manner which the venerable writer himself would have prescribed, could he have anticipated the disorders which have ravaged the most polished and enlightened states since his removal from this scene of pride and weakness, where nations as well as individuals have their periods of infancy and decrepitude, of moral vigor and wild derangement.-

"Shortly after the death of Dr. Franklin, there were not wanting the usual train of *literary speculators* to exercise their industry in collecting his avowed productions, together with those which public rumor ascribed to his pen. These miscellanies were printed in various forms, both in England and America, greatly to the advantage of the publishers ; nor did the possessor of the originals avail himself of the general avidity and the celebrity of his ancestor, to deprive those persons of the profits which they continued to reap from repeated editions of papers that have cost them nothing. When, however, they had reason to apprehend that the genuine Memoirs and other works of Franklin, as written and corrected by himself, would be brought forward in a manner suitable to their importance and the dignified rank of the author in the political and literary world, invidious reports were sent abroad, and circulated with uncommon diligence; asserting that all the literary remains of Dr. Franklin had been purchased at an enormous rate by the British ministry, who *(mirabile dictu)* it seems were more afraid of this arsenal of paper than of the power of France, with all her numerous resources and auxiliaries. This convenient tale, absurd as it was, found reporters both in Europe and in the United States, who bruited it about with so much art as to make many who were unacquainted with the legatee of the manuscripts, believe it to be true, and to lament feelingly, that such inestimable productions should be suppressed, and lost for ever, through the cupidity of the person to whom they were bequeathed. Provoking as the story was, the party whom it most affected, and whose interests it was designed to injure, felt too much of the *conscia mens recti* to do otherwise than treat the ridiculous invention with contempt, from a persuasion that the refutation of an improbable falsehood is beneath the dignity of truth. He, therefore, endured the opprobrium without complaint, and even suffered it to be repeated without being goaded into an explanation; contented to wait for the time when he might best fulfill his duty and shame his-calumniators. That period has at length arrived, and the world will now see whether an enlightened government could be weak enough to be frightened by the posthumous works of a philosopher ; or whether a man of integrity, bred under Franklin, bearing his name, and entrusted with his confidence, could be bribed into an act of treachery to his memory.

" Of the present collection it remains to be observed, that the only portion which has hitherto appeared in any form, is the first fasciculus of the Memoirs of Dr. Franklin, extending from his birth to the year 1757, forming one hundred and seventy-five pages only of the present volume. But even what has formerly been printed of this part, can scarcely lay claim to *originality,* since the English edition is no more than a translation from the French, which of itself is a professed version of a transcription ; so that the metamorphoses of this interesting piece of biography may be said to resemble the fate of Milton's epic poem, which a French Abb£ paraphrased into inflated prose, and which an English writer, ignorant of its origin, turned back again under the double disguise into its native tongue.

"Admitting, however, that the small portion of the Memoir given to the world, is substantially correct in the materials of the narrative, the present publication of it *must be infinitely more estimable by being printed literally from the original autograph.*

"It is much to be regretted, that Dr. Frankin was not enabled, by his numerous avocations and the infirmities of old age, to complete the narrative of his life in his own inimitable manner. That he intended to have done this is certain, from his correspondence, as well as from the parts in continuation of the Memoir which are now for the first time communicated to the world. But the convulsed state of things during the American Revolution, the lively concern which he had in that event, and his multiplied public engagements after contributing to the establishment of the independence of his country, prevented him from indulging his own inclinations, and complying with the earnest desire of his numerous friends."

APPENDIX No. 8.

Preface to " Correspondence Inedit e, etc. de B. Franklin" By M. Charles Malo.

[Translation.]

"In publishing in France a complete Correspondence of Dr. Franklin, I have intended to afford the public an opportunity of enjoying the only part of the works of this celebrated man which has remained unknown to us up tó this time. This

Correspondence has the inappreciable advantage of being neither altered nor abridged. France, England, America, there play a part so important that I should reproach myself if I had suppressed the smallest passage of it. Franklin will be found there in this Correspondence complete and characteristic, with all that freedom of speech so piquant and so noble which he indulged toward all the courts of Europe.

"Two or three journals have announced a *Select Correspondence* of Franklin. It is my duty to enlighten the public on this fraudulent speculation of M. Temple (Franklin). Desirous of prejudicing the interests of French booksellers, and at the same time desperate at having been so unfortunately anticipated by the appearance of a *Complete Correspondence*^ this gentleman had no other resource but to make a *Selected Correspondence;* but he has not foreseen that in reducing to one-half the work which I publish today in two octavo volumes, he would really give only an abridgment of it, an extract; that his boasted *Selection* will be but an insignificant piece of claptrap, a thing of shreds and patches. When, in fact, will the formidable scissors stop of a foreigner who is directed by considerations of self-love, and animated by local passions? In purchasing 'the Abridged

Correspondence' of M. Temple (Franklin), one will still not have Franklin. But let us be just. If M. Temple (Franklin) cuts up and pitilessly lacerates a Correspondence as yet entirely unpublished, and which was absolutely unknown in France, in revenge, and by an equally reasonable calculation, he is about to reproduce for the fourth time, that is to say to satiety, the [4] Memoirs of the Life of Franklin,' printed at Paris, for the first time, in 1791 (one volume in 8vo., by Buisson); for the second time, in the year II. (one volume in I2no., Rue Therese); and for the third time, in 1800 (two volumes in 8vo., by Buisson), from the English edition of Dundee.

" I owe this confidence to my readers, especially to that public which M. Temple (Franklin) appeals to, that it may be duly instructed as to the merit of the editions of which this person wishes to give France the benefit "Since the month of January, and by many French bookpublishers, with a competition much more formidable than the '*Extracts of Correspondence]* which M. Temple (Franklin) announces to-day, and to satisfy also the impatient subscribers of this *Complete Correspondence^* the literary gentleman charged with it has judged proper to confide to two literary men, equally known and esteemed, MM. Cohen and Breton, the translation of a certain number of sheets of the second volume.

"The style of Franklin became, as he advanced in years, less clear and less vigorous; that of his correspondents also was frequently diffuse and confused. In imposing upon himself the rule never to depart from the original in any respect, the translator has necessarily encountered numberless difficulties, and has seen himself forced to reproduce thousands of abstract ideas. By the aid of a convenient *selection* he might easily have been able to avoid the one, and substitute his own ideas for the others; but the glory of belittling a great man, of *abridging* Franklin, was reserved for one of his descendants. Ought we to inherit from one we have assassinated ?"

APPENDIX No. 9.

Extract from letter of Dr. Franklin to Benjamin Vaughan, dated Nov. 2, 1789.

*"You request advice from me respecting your conduct, and desire me to tell you their faults. As to your conduct, I know nothing that looks like a fault, except yr. declining to act in any public station, although you are qualified to do much public good in many you must have had it in your power to occupy. In respect to yr. writings, your language seems to me to be good and pure, and your sentiments to be generally just; but your style or composition wants perspicuity, and this I think owing principally to a neglect of method. What I would therefore recommend to you is, that before you sit down to write on any subject you would spend some days in considering it, putting down at the same time, in short hints, every thought which occurs to you as proper to make a part

of yr. intended piece. When you have thus obtained a collection of the thoughts, examine them carefully with this view, to find which of them is properest to be presented first to the mind of the reader, that he being possessed of that, may be better disposed to receive what you intend for the second; and thus I would have you put a figure before each thought to mark its future place in your composition. For so every preceding composition preparing the mind for that which is to follow, and the reader often anticipating it, he proceeds with ease and pleasure and approbation, as seeming continually to meet with his own thoughts. In this mode you have a better chance for a perfect production; because the mind attending first to the sentiments alone, next to the method alone, each part is likely to be better performed, and I think, too, in less time.

*You see I give my counsel rather bluntly, without attempting to soften my manner of finding fault by any apology, which would give some people great offence ; but in the present situation of affairs between us, *when I am soliciting the advantage of your criticism upon a work of mine,* it is, perhaps, my interest that you should be a little offended in order to produce a greater degree of wholesome severity. *I think with you that if my Memoirs are to be published, an edition of them should be printed in England for that country, as well as here for this, and I shall gladly leave it to your friendly management."*

---

* Sparks' Works of Franklin, vol x. p. 397.